Living Languages: An Integrated Approach to Teaching Foreign Languages in Primary Schools

Living Languages is simply bursting with practical and original ideas aimed at teachers and trainee teachers of foreign languages in primary schools. Written by a team of experienced linguists, this book will inspire and motivate the foreign language classroom and the teachers who work within it.

Living Languages comprises eight chapters and is structured around the integrated classroom, merging language learning with different aspects of the wider curriculum, such as multimedia, performance, celebrations and festivals, creativity and alternative approaches to teaching languages. A DVD is also included with the book, containing additional teaching materials and the associated films and audio recordings which make this a fully-developed and effective teaching resource.

Over fifty real-life case studies and projects are presented, all of which have been tried and tested in the classroom, with several having won recent educational awards. Ideas and activities outlined in this unique resource include:

- **Languages across the curriculum** helping to cement cross-curricular links and embed new languages in different contexts, linking subjects such as history, science, PE and mathematics with French, German and Spanish;
- Arts and crafts projects in **Languages, making and doing,** including making books, creating beach huts and cooking biscuits;
- **Languages, celebrations and festivals projects** including the German Christmas market, Spanish Day of the Dead, celebrating Mardi Gras and the European Day of Languages among many others;
- **Continuing Professional Development** to inspire primary teachers to continue their individual professional development. The chapter contains concrete examples of others' experiences in this area and includes details of support organisations and practical opportunities.

Each project is explored from the teachers' perspective with practical tips, lesson plans and reflections woven throughout the text, such as what to budget, how to organise the pre-event period, how to evaluate the activity and whom to contact for further advice in each case. Activities and examples throughout are given in three languages – French, German and Spanish.

Catherine Watts is currently Director of the Routes into Languages South consortium and is Principal Lecturer in English Language and German with the Faculty of Arts as well as contributing to the EdD, PGCE and MA in Education at the University of Brighton, UK.

Clare Forder is the Programme Manager for the regional Routes into Languages South consortium at the University of Brighton and has had sustained contact with teachers and pupils in the secondary sector over the past few years.

Hilary Phillips has been a Lead Teacher for Primary Languages in Brighton and Hove since 2003 and has co-presented workshops at many national conferences. She is currently teaching French in Key Stage Two at a primary school in Brighton and Hove.

Living Languages: An Integrated Approach to Teaching Foreign Languages in Primary Schools

Edited by Catherine Watts

Catherine Watts, Clare Forder and Hilary Phillips

Routledge
Taylor & Francis Group

LONDON AND NEW YORK

First published 2013
by Routledge
2 Park Square, Milton Park, Abingdon, Oxon OX14 4RN

Simultaneously published in the USA and Canada
by Routledge
711 Third Avenue, New York, NY 10017

Routledge is an imprint of the Taylor & Francis Group, an informa business

British Library Cataloguing in Publication Data
A catalogue record for this book is available from the British Library

Library of Congress Cataloging in Publication Data

Living languages : an integrated approach to teaching foreign languages in primary schools / [edited by] Catherine Watts, Clare Forder and Hilary Phillips.
p. cm.
ISBN 978-0-415-67562-8 -- ISBN 978-0-415-67563-5 (pbk.) -- ISBN 978-0-203-80939-6 (ebook) 1. Language and languages--Study and teaching (Primary) 2. Language and languages--Study and teaching (Primary)--Audio-visual aids. 3. Project method in teaching. 4. Interdisciplinary approach in education. I. Watts, Catherine. II. Forder, Clare. III. Phillips, Hilary.
P53.67.L57 2012
372.65'044--dc23
2012008881

ISBN: 978-0-415-67562-8 (hbk)
ISBN: 978-0-415-67563-5 (pbk)
ISBN: 978-0-203-80939-6 (ebk)

Typeset in Bembo
by Fish Books Ltd., London

Printed and bound in Great Britain by the MPG Books Group

Contents

To our families and friends
CW, CF, HP

Contributors

Catherine Watts is a Principal Lecturer at The University of Brighton (School of Humanities) where she has worked for nearly thirty years. Catherine teaches German and English and works with the PGCE teacher trainees in modern languages. In 2002 she was awarded her doctorate by King's College, University of London in the field of foreign languages in education. She led the research team for Brighton and Hove City Council's MFL Primary Pathfinder project in 2002/3 and since 2007 has directed the Routes into Languages regional consortium in the South.

Clare Forder is based at the University of Brighton and works as a project manager for the Routes into Languages regional consortium in the South, part of the national Routes into Languages initiative. Over the last five years she has planned, designed and delivered small- and large-scale activities for students studying languages at secondary school and college. She was part of a seven-country research project into early language learning in Europe and is currently studying for a Professional Doctorate in Education where her research field is languages education in England.

Hilary Phillips started her teaching career as a secondary school French specialist for 13 years and then retrained to be a Primary classroom teacher. Hilary has been a Lead Teacher for Primary Languages in Brighton and Hove since 2003 and has co-presented workshops at many national conferences with her inspirational colleagues. She is currently teaching French in Key Stage Two at St Andrew's Primary School in Brighton and Hove.

Acknowledgements

The authors and publishers would like to thank the following for helping us to organise each project contained in this book. Our thanks are due to a great many people and we have tried to make this list as comprehensive as possible. We hope we have not left anyone out!

The students and staff at St Andrew's Primary School, Hove, East Sussex.

Monika Lind, the Burkart family, Anja Merkel, Olivier Boulocher, Luz Del Carmen Broadbridge, María Emmerson and María C. Cooke for their translation assistance.

Jessica Langford, Oscar Stringer, Mike Horton and Alex Chown for their help and technical support for the Animation project.

Nicola Goodland, Claire Ross and Alex Chown for much of the artwork.

Daryl Bailey for writing Part VIII based around workshops delivered with Hilary Phillips.

Katja Neubauer and UK–German Connection for *Die Zaubermaus*.

UK–German Connection and The German Embassy for their Advent calendars.

Anne Lee and Dan Smith (Deputy Head Teacher) at St John's Church of England Primary School, Grove Green, Maidstone, Kent, for the Healthy Lunches project.

Christie Cavallo, class teacher and International Links Subject Leader at Southwater Infant Academy, Southwater, West Sussex, for help with the eTwinning project.

Tanya Riordan for the design of the Drawing in Spanish project and Maggi McEwan and Bob Gould for their assistance with the same.

The National Centre for Languages (CILT), part of CfBT Education Trust, for their help with the European Day of Languages project.

Tamsin Day for her help with the cookery materials.

List of abbreviations

PE	=	Physical Education
FL	=	Foreign Language
FLA	=	Foreign Language Assistant
IT	=	Information Technology
CPD	=	Continuing Professional Development
PGCE	=	Post Graduate Certificate in Education
PSHE	=	Personal, Social, Health and Economic Education
CLIL	=	Content and Language Integrated Learning
MFL	=	Modern Foreign Languages
CILT	=	National Centre for Languages, part of CfBT Educational Trust
ICT	=	Information Communications Technology
INSET	=	In-service Training

Preface

This book is aimed at teachers of foreign languages (students, novice and experienced) in the primary sector (Key Stage Two). It is set against a backdrop of change and uncertainty at the time of writing, with expectations that foreign languages will become a compulsory component of the primary curriculum ebbing and flowing under the rule of different governments. With much work having been done since 2002, if not earlier, to enable primary schools to offer foreign languages across the Key Stage Two curriculum on a compulsory basis, and with much time and money having been invested in the process, this book offers a refreshing and practical approach to help sustain the momentum whilst the situation stabilises and becomes less fragile. The book could also be easily adapted for use with Key Stage One students should the need arise.

Early language learning is the foundation for all later language learning and there is much evidence to suggest that the earlier we begin, the more effective the learning is (Speak to the Future, 2011). Across the rest of Europe this is widely recognised, with many more contact hours per week being offered to primary-aged students than in the UK on a compulsory basis. Students in primary schools enjoy learning foreign languages, understand their importance and have a developing awareness of, and interest in, other cultures. It is therefore vital to harness this enthusiasm effectively.

Living Languages: an integrated approach to teaching foreign languages in primary schools is simply bursting with fresh and creative ideas to help you bring your language lessons to life. All of the projects stem from classroom practice and present small thematic chunks of new language in a motivating way which fits with the broad Key Stage Two curriculum. The authors have over sixty years of classroom practice between them and have designed the projects in this book to demand minimum expenditure, thus making them easily replicable and extremely 'doable'!

Whether you want to focus on literacy and language, thereby enabling students to develop a clearer understanding of how their own language works in the process, or whether you wish to make wider links outside the classroom, to name just two Part themes, this is the book for you! It presents over fifty small-scale projects in French, German or Spanish (or sometimes all three, or two in combination), each designed to fit into a forty-minute teaching slot, which is the most common way to teach languages in primary schools (TES, 2011). The projects are easy to replicate, manage and translate into other languages to suit your own practice. Examples are very practical, with the additional DVD materials frequently offering picture galleries of finished work, extension activities/translations and useful websites to help you explore the projects further. We hope you enjoy using them!

Viel Spass!   **¡que lo pase bien!**   **Amusez-vous bien!**

PART

1

Languages across the curriculum

Introduction

The nine projects presented in this first part straddle the curriculum, helping to cement cross-curricular links and embed new language in different contexts. Projects in this part combine, for example, history and mathematics with French, biology and science with German, and Physical Education with Spanish and French too. Ideas for filling short breaks using French throughout the day are also included, as is an exciting project which combines art with Spanish. An example of Content Language Integrated Learning (CLIL), where a subject is taught entirely in the foreign language, also features in this part, as the frozen continent of Antarctica is explored in Spanish and French.

Thus a wealth of ideas for cross-curricular innovation and design are presented here with many examples of different creative activities that can be carried out with your class. These may include a short play (Florence Nightingale) for example, making a mermaid's purse (Life cycles) or creating a work of art (Drawing in Spanish), to mention just a few. All are fun, all are manageable and all will bring languages to life in your lessons!

Project 1   Fun with parachutes

Project outline

Requirements: large space, such as hall or playground
Event time: minimum of 20 minutes as part of a lesson. It is ideal for relieving stress at busy times of the school year, for example before or after SATS, or as a run up to Christmas plays. Use outdoor space in the summer when possible
Language used: French

Introduction

How can you inject an element of lively fun and enjoyment into lessons while children practise language learning skills? One very successful method is to use a parachute to play games, ideally in a large space indoors or outdoors. Just the sight of the parachute with its colourful canopy and its strange and sometimes unpredictable movement adds drama to the lesson, but the added bonuses of these games are the Personal, Social, Health and Economic education (PSHE) emphasis on co-operation and team spirit and the opportunity to keep fit at the same time. Students will be using oracy skills and language learning strategies to support their active learning. Students throughout Key Stage Two enjoy these activities and quickly learn the preliminary rules of safety and suitable behaviour.

Organisation

Most primary schools have a parachute in a Physical Education (PE) cupboard or Reception Class or in use for Nurture groups. To use with a whole class you need a parachute at least six metres wide (easily available from educational supplies catalogues). From the start, teach the students to unroll and wrap up the parachute in a co-operative and sensible way, so that they begin and end the lesson in an orderly manner, rather than snatching at the handles and running wild! It is helpful to be very firm about the level of behaviour you expect from the first lesson, as students react with great excitement to the prospect of running about under or over or with the parachute. Key phrases are *Déroulez le parachute* and *Roulez le parachute* (Unravel and roll up the parachute).

Plan the order of your games carefully, so that you have the most active games in the middle of the lesson, and ensure that you start and end with quieter activities, so that you can return to the classroom with an energised but calmer class.

Students don't necessarily need to wear their PE kit for these games, unless you choose lots of ideas involving rolling on the floor, etc. If they are in PE kit, you can involve students who have forgotten their kit or aren't doing PE that day to hold up picture or text cards for you; call out some instructions; give out team points or praise others in the foreign language.

Starter games

Un, deux, trois champignon!

You need a way to signal the starting position of a new activity (usually with everyone crouching down holding the parachute, ready to use it), and this simple game fits the bill. Start with the parachute on the ground with everyone crouching down, holding the edge. Count together: *one, two, three, mushroom.* As you say *mushroom*, everybody stands and raises the parachute high in the air and keeps it there.

Vocabulary

un, deux, trois, champignon!

When you've practised a few times, tantalise the students by delaying saying *champignon* and instead saying the names of fruit or vegetables (or any food) which begin with the same sound: for example, *chou, chou-fleur, chocolat* (*cabbage, cauliflower, chocolate*). They soon learn to concentrate on responding to the correct word and enjoy the trick you play.

La Fusée!

As an alternative, you could start as before, crouching and holding the parachute, and then you count backwards, with the students repeating after you, as though a rocket is about to launch. Raise the parachute on *Lift off!*

Vocabulary

La fusée: rocket

dix, neuf, huit, sept, six, cinq, quatre, trois, deux, un, zéro! Décollage!

La Roue

This is a quiet activity to get used to moving in unison. Hold the parachute with one hand and then the other as you walk or run around in a circle in one direction and then the other or jump up and down and see how the parachute reacts.

Vocabulary

la roue:	the wheel
prenez le parachute:	hold the parachute
…avec la main gauche:	with your left hand
…avec la main droite:	with your right hand
marchez vers la droite/vers la gauche:	walk to the right/to the left
courez:	run
sautez deux fois, trois fois:	jump twice, three times
arrêtez:	stop

Passez vite!

This one is a good exercise in working together. Students soon realize that if they all pull together, the parachute will go further.

Everyone holds the parachute firmly in both hands (don't use the handles, as this is about speed) and then counts together up to ten as they pass the parachute around very quickly in one direction. When they reach number ten, work out how far the parachute has gone around the circle of students. Can you see how far it went? Repeat the process and see if you can get it back to the starting place in a total of three counts of ten. Is it easier in the opposite direction? (**Note**: it's easier to recognise where you began once the parachute is rather worn and has a few loose ends or holes!)

Vocabulary

passez vite:	pass quickly
… vers la gauche/vers la droite:	to the left/to the right

Les yeux, le nez

Everyone takes a step backwards to start this one so that the parachute is flat and tight at waist level. Assuming you have taught a few body parts, call out the name of one, and everyone raises the parachute to that part of their face or body. After a few goes, try calling out a body part at the top of the body, for example *eyes* and the next one at the lower part of the body, for example *feet*. It's harder than you think to move the parachute quickly.

Vocabulary

la tête:	head
les yeux:	eyes
le nez:	nose
la bouche:	mouth
le cou:	neck
l'estomac:	stomach
les genoux:	knees
les pieds:	feet

Lentement, vite

You'll be surprised by the 'tug' of the parachute as it's raised in the air. Hold tight so that it isn't pulled out of students' hands.

All stand, holding the parachute which is lying on the floor. Then you call, they repeat and move the parachute different ways: *up in the air, down below, slowly up, slowly down, fast up, fast down*. Keep them waiting before you call the *fast up* and *fast down*, as these will be their favourites.

Vocabulary

lentement:	slowly
vite:	fast
en haut:	up
en bas:	down

> ### Think ahead
>
> It helps to have another adult to help you to keep the parachute aloft in the following games. Take positions on opposite sides of the parachute, so that you can each support one half of the canopy when all the children run at the same time. This can be a good teaching opportunity to spread the word about using a parachute effectively. Show everyone that playing games in a structured way is more fun and more valuable.

Main activities

Salade de fruits

This familiar game is given a new lease of life under the parachute. You can use any new vocabulary, for example food/body parts/colours/animal names, etc. Give each student in rotation one of four nouns to remember, for example *lemons, oranges, apples, strawberries*. Raise the parachute, keep it up in the air as much as possible while you call out a fruit, so that all the students with that noun have to run under the parachute and change places with each other. When you call *fruit salad* everybody has to change places before the parachute falls to the ground.

Vocabulary

salade de fruits:	fruit salad
les citrons:	lemons
les oranges:	oranges
les pommes:	apples
les fraises:	strawberries

This also works well with whole phrases: e.g. weather expressions – *It's hot/cold*.

Vocabulary

il fait chaud/froid:	it's hot/cold
il pleut:	it's raining
il neige:	it's snowing

Les Animaux

This starts like the previous game, but involves more moving about and saying words in a group. Give each student the name of one of four animals to remember, for example, *rabbit, bird, spider, snake*. Call out a name – for example *snake* – and all the snake students run clockwise round the outside of the circle. When they reach their original place, they run under the parachute into the middle of the space, raise their arms in the air and call out their animal name, then run back to their place. Try two or more groups running and calling together.

Vocabulary

les lapins:	rabbits
les oiseaux:	birds
les araignées:	spiders
les serpents:	snakes

Silent statements

This game involves changing places silently under the parachute when a phrase is spoken by the teacher. Raise the parachute, and then everyone takes a step forward under the canopy and pulls the parachute down behind their head so that the whole group is enclosed in a cocoon-like space. Call out a statement and the students for whom the statement is true change places under the parachute. Start with simple statements suitable for your class such as *change places if you have blue eyes/like apples/love chocolate/hate snakes/are nine years old*, etc.

Useful tip
A favourite alternative to standing in the cocoon shape under the parachute in the last game is to move under the parachute in the same way, but then **to sit on the**

ground with the parachute under your bottom. This creates a magical space where you can whisper statements or sing a little language song, although it's almost impossible to move about. Students love creating this hidden space and it looks intriguing if you do it on the ground in the playground in the summer. Younger students walk round the shape, not quite knowing if it's human or animal. **But take note:** it gets hot inside the cocoon, and more air to breathe will be needed after a few minutes, so keep it for a reward or incentive.

Vocabulary

Changez des places si …:	Change places if …
… vous avez les yeux bleus:	you have blue eyes
… vous aimez les pommes:	you like apples
… vous aimez le chocolat:	you like chocolate
… vous détestez les serpents:	you hate snakes

You could extend these sentences with two options: for example, if you have blue eyes **and brown hair**/if you like strawberries **but don't like apples**

Vocabulary

si vous avez les yeux bleus et les cheveux bruns;

si vous aimez les fraises mais vous détestez les pommes

Les Couleurs

This time students work co-operatively to move an object over the surface of the parachute. All step back a little to make a tight, flat surface with the parachute. Roll the parachute in at the circumference to reduce its size and keep it about waist height. Throw a soft ball or bean bag onto the surface. Call out the name of one of the colours of the canopy so that children have to work together to move the ball or bag onto that section of the parachute. Thus students move the ball *towards the blue … green … red … yellow*, etc.

Vocabulary

vers le bleu, vert, rouge, jaune: towards the blue, green, red, yellow

Le Serpent

Make a tight, flat surface on the parachute as in the previous game. Throw a skipping rope onto the surface and call out instructions to make it move like a snake to a colour or jump in a section for example *make it slither towards the blue* or *make it jump once/twice*.

Look in your PE cupboard to see what equipment you could use on the surface of the parachute to encourage the students to move objects to the left/right/to the blue, etc.

Vocabulary

faites glisser le serpent vers le bleu.

faites sauter le serpent une fois/deux fois.

Cache–cache

This is a friendly choosing and singing game which you may have to play many times so that everyone has a turn, or you could keep it for birthday treats. Everybody stands holding the parachute at waist height. Choose two people (usually a boy and a girl to avoid arguments) **to sit** under the middle of the parachute. Everyone else walks around in a circle holding the parachute and singing a little song to the tune of *Frère Jacques*. When one of the two students hears their name sung, he/she puts his/her hand through the hole in the middle of the parachute and waves appropriately. Sing for one student and then the other. The song goes:

Where is Maddie? × 2 (Substitute the name of the girl)

There she is! × 2 (All point to the waving hand. Use *there **he** is* for the boys)

Hello Maddie! × 2

Goodbye! × 2

Here is the song in French

Où est Maddie? × 2

La voici! × 2 (For a boy, substitute *le voici*)

Bonjour Maddie! × 2

Au Revoir! × 2

Vocabulary

cache-cache: hide and seek

Où habites–tu?

It is possible to have an activity with a student lying on the parachute and everyone else carrying the parachute around, but you need to establish good behaviour in the group first and think carefully about the child you choose and the class you are working with. Check risk assessments at school and choose a sensible and small person to begin with! This is a singing game to practise language about where you live. Everyone stands holding the parachute at about knee height. One student sits or lies in the centre of the parachute. Everyone moves round slowly in a circle carrying the parachute and sings *Where do you live?* to the tune of *Nice One, Cyril*. At the end of the verse, they stand still and the child in the centre responds with *I live in Brighton* (substitute place name), etc.; everybody then responds with a verse of *He/she lives in Brighton*, etc.

Vocabulary

Où habites-tu?: Where do you live?

1st Verse of song

Students: *Où habites-tu?* × 3

Student replies: *J'habite à Brighton*

2nd verse of song

Students: *Il habite à Brighton* × 3 *(il* for a boy/*elle* for a girl)

Student: *J'habite à Brighton*

Les requins

This is a noisy, fun game but a great opportunity to learn vocabulary for an emergency. The parachute is spread out over the surface of the floor, and everyone sits around the perimeter with their feet underneath the parachute. It looks strange but gets even stranger! One student is chosen to go under the parachute with their hand held up to make a shark-fin shape in the parachute and moves around as invisibly as possible. When the 'fin' is noticed by a student, they point to it and shout a warning *Look out!* The shark chooses a student victim and touches their feet, trying to pull them under the parachute. They shout *Help!* before going under the parachute and becoming either a second shark or a replacement shark (depending on how many sharks you want to have under the canopy and the excitement level in your class)

Vocabulary

les requins: sharks

Attention!:   Look out!

Au secours!:   Help!

La chasse au trésor

This is a treasure-hunt game which can be played as a competitive game for two teams. Fill two pillowcases or bags with a selection of objects which the students must be familiar with from language lessons. Each bag must have a version of the same object, so that the two teams can each find their own object. Examples include: balls; teddies; Father Christmas toys; oranges; socks; hats, etc. Allocate two teams and members of the teams who will take it in turns to retrieve objects. Place each bag under the parachute near a team.

   Call out the instructions to:

- look for something navy blue/light blue/dark blue (could be a scarf, paper, etc);
- look for something to play badminton/table tennis (could be a shuttlecock/tennis bat);
- something for your hand/neck/head/hair (a glove/scarf/comb);
- something for the garden/kitchen (a packet of seeds, a wooden spoon);
- something for Christmas/Easter (a Father Christmas toy, Easter chick toy).

Vocabulary

Cherchez quelque chose de ...

... bleu marine: navy blue;

... bleu clair: light blue;

... bleu foncé: dark blue.

Cherchez quelque chose pour ...

... jouer au badminton/au ping-pong: play badminton/table tennis;

... la main/le cou/les cheveux: your hand/neck/hair;

... le jardin/la cuisine: the garden/kitchen;

... Noël/Pâques: Christmas/Easter.

The two students run under the parachute, rummage through the pillowcases and try to be the first to find the correct object. Meanwhile the other students shake/agitate the parachute to make it harder for those underneath. They could also sing a song, to the tune of *Frère Jacques*, until the winner emerges.

Vocabulary

Secouez/agitez le parachute: shake the parachute

Song: who has won: qui a gagné? (sing to the tune of *Frère Jacques*)

Qui a gagné? × 2

Maddie ou Ben? × 2 (Substitute children's names)

Qui a gagné? × 2

Ah c'est Ben × 2

La Tempête

This game helps you to tell a short story and practise weather expressions at the same time. It is the most requested parachute game of them all and never fails to bring some fun to the lesson.

Raise the parachute and then settle it at waist level, keeping it tight and smooth. Begin the story by saying that the parachute today is the sea, and that one of two soft toys (hold them up) is going on a journey by boat. Let the students decide which animal is going. Say goodbye to the one not chosen. Choose a sensible student to throw the chosen toy onto the parachute and everyone calls *bon voyage* to him. Make it clear that the sea is calm and that the weather is fine, sunny, clear, etc. Students keep the parachute absolutely still at this stage or rocking very gently. Gradually introduce worse weather statements – for example, it's raining, a bit windy, a lot of wind, bad weather and finally a storm – while the students shake the parachute gradually more violently until the toy leaps in the air and is tossed about! Keep it going for some fun and then, when you've had enough, reverse the statements and bring the toy back to land. You could end with *Poor Teddy! He's sea-sick*.

Vocabulary

Qui va dans le bateau? Nounours ou le tigre? (depending on your choice of toy). *Bon voyage!*: Who's going in the boat? Teddy or the tiger? Good journey!

La mer est calme; …:	The sea is calm; …
… il fait beau: …:	it's fine;
… il fait chaud: …:	it's warm;
… il y a du soleil: …:	it's sunny;
… il y a un peu de vent: …:	there's a bit of wind;
… il y a plus de vent: …:	there's more wind;
… il y a beaucoup de vent: …:	there's a lot of wind;
… il fait mauvais: …:	the weather's bad;
… il y a une tempête/un orage:	there's a tempest/storm.
Pauvre Nounours. Il a le mal de mer!:	Poor Teddy. He's sea-sick!

Some quiet games to finish the session

Joyeux anniversaire

This is a treat for a birthday student. The student chooses a couple of friends and they all lie down on the floor close together. Everyone else walks slowly in a circle around them holding the parachute very low over the birthday group's faces while singing *Joyeux anniversaire* four times. You could use the same format, with the parachute being softly raised and lowered over their faces. Another alternative is for the group to wrap themelves lightly in the parachute (being careful not to suffocate themselves!) while the song goes on around them and then they untangle themselves. The last version has the idea that they are presents wrapped up for the birthday person.

An alternative for a birthday is for the student to lie down in the centre of the parachute while everyone carefully picks up the parachute and gently rocks him or her to and fro whilst singing the birthday song in French.

Doucement!

This is a refreshing way to end an exhausting session. Ask a third of the class to lie on the floor, setting themselves out like the spokes of a wheel, heads in the centre. The others raise and lower the parachute high and low so that it nearly touches the children on the floor, with no sound except for a whisper of *softly! doucement!* Decide together on the number of times you will lower the parachute – for example, five times is probably enough – then swap the students for another third, and then the final third, until everyone is cool and calm.

Fun with parachutes: additional DVD materials

1.   Picture Gallery
2.   Key words and phrases in Spanish and German

Project 2   Florence Nightingale

Project Outline

Requirements: classroom space, hall
Event time: 40-minute sessions; songs; role play as part of an assembly
Language used: French

Introduction

It makes sense to look for a cross-curricular theme when planning a primary language unit, as we all know the heavy demands on time of the broad primary curriculum. Humanities subjects have often been the source of creative links to language work. Looking at the topic of Florence Nightingale or Victorians, ideas for adding song, movement and active learning are easy to find. Think back to simple games we all played in groups as children. How can they be adapted to provide an inclusive activity for learning a language and getting children moving and communicating?

Playground games are a good starting point, as they involve large groups of children, have a familiar format and yet have an element of 'choosing'. The following ideas have been tried and tested in Key Stage Two classrooms (Years Three to Six – ages eight to eleven) and fit into the regular pattern of lessons, or can be used to showcase language learning as part of an assembly. Additional materials on the accompanying DVD for this project include students' drawings for the picture gallery and the English script of the accompanying play for Years Three and Four (ages eight and nine).

Organisation

Donnez-moi la lampe, Florence/Give me the lamp, Florence

This choosing game, played in a circle, is an inclusive way to reinforce vocabulary learned in earlier lessons and is a good PSHE (Personal, Social, Health and Economic Education) exercise to encourage working together. To create a circle game or dance, you need simple repetitive phrases which students can pick up easily, a word or two to add at each new stage and straightforward movements, backwards and forwards or to the right and left, for all the students to perform together. One student is selected to be in the middle, others are chosen to join him or her, and everyone joins in the singing and moving about.

For Florence Nightingale, consider which items might be essential to the wounded soldiers that Florence and the nurses might provide, for example, a lamp, water, bread, a letter, soap, a towel, a book. It seems sensible to teach students vocabulary which is adaptable and useful in many contexts, so consider which words will have a broader remit: for example, for everyday use. Students could make lanterns in class in the familiar way with crepe paper slit down the middle, a tongue of flame/light in the centre and a simple handle to carry them. Or you could look at the lanterns made in the St Martin's Day celebrations (Project 7 in Part III). Other simple props are easy to make or find in the primary classroom, for example, red crêpe paper sash for a nurse, strips of cloth for bandages, handwritten envelopes addressed to Scutari Hospital, simple book covers made by the class.

There are a variety of ways to organize this circle game:

1. All students are nurses, each carrying a lantern, and they should move around in a big circle. One is selected to be a soldier in the middle. S/he puts a sling around an arm and lies on the floor/sits on a chair. All students parade around singing until another is chosen to be the nurse giving the first object. S/he joins the student in the middle, all put thumbs up while they sing *Ça va mieux!* (that's better) and all parade again until the next student is chosen to give the next object and so on.

2. Students are in a circle with just the props in the centre. The student chosen to be the soldier chooses the next prop, holds it up and also chooses a friend to be the next nurse. The students call out the word and sing together. The next time, the nurse chooses both the prop and an extra nurse, and so on.

3. Students are in two concentric circles but are facing a partner. The outer circle students are all nurses, the inner circle are the soldiers, all dressed accordingly with lamp or bandage. As they sing together, the outer circle moves clockwise while the inner group moves anti-clockwise. When each verse ends, they face a new partner each time, and the nurse gives or mimes giving the new object.

Florence circle song to the tune of *Polly put the kettle on*

1. *Donnez-moi la lampe, Florence, Donnez-moi la lampe, Florence, Donnez-moi la lampe, Florence, Ça va mieux!* (thumbs up)

2. *Donnez-moi du pain, Florence* × 3   *Ça va mieux!*

3. *Donnez-moi de l'eau, Florence* × 3   *Ça va mieux!*

4. *Donnez-moi la lettre, Florence* × 3   *Ça va mieux!*

5. (Other verses can ask for *une pomme, un livre, du lait, du savon*, etc)

6. *Donnez-moi la main, Florence* × 3   *Dormez bien!*

Useful tip

Create an atmosphere of night-time in the hospital ward as you perform the song, by shutting the blinds, turning off the lights and just lighting the room by a candle safely in a proper lantern (check risk assessment or use battery-operated candles!). At the end of the song, the students sing 'Dormez bien' (sleep well), sit down where they are, and the candle is blown out. Pre-arrange with the students that you will all whisper counting up to 20 or 30 in French before the candle is blown out. If you have a sensible class, they could snore for a few minutes, or select a chosen group to snore on behalf of the class!

Pauvre Soldat! Poor Soldier

Familiar songs can be a good piggyback for practising new language. In the Florence Nightingale topic, an obvious theme is the soldiers' injured body parts and questions or statements about which part is hurting. Using a repeated question or statement, children can adapt their song according to which part of the body is injured. This is a part-song to get a conversation going:

■ Practise humming the tune of London's Burning;

■ Select half the class to be **soldiers** and the other half to be **nurses**;

■ Sing the song which follows according to a pre-arranged list of injured parts of the body. Nurses point to the soldiers and soldiers hug or touch their injured body parts as they sing;

■ For the first few times, the soldiers just repeat one part of the body but, once they have got the idea, challenge them to change to two different ones, for example: *J'ai mal au bras; J'ai mal au dos*;

■ When the class is comfortable with the routine, choose someone to stand at the front, point without warning to a body part (which the students definitely know) and the rest of the class have to sing that body part;

■ Each group could make up their own version, practise it and present to the rest of the class;

■ Each group could practise improvising with a student pointing unexpectedly to a body part. Find a winning table which is more accurate or quicker than the other groups.

Pauvre Soldat to the tune of *London's burning*

1. Nurses' group: *Pauvre soldat, pauvre soldat. Íl a mal, il a mal!*

2. Soldiers' group: *J'ai mal au bras, j'ai mal au bras*

3. All: *Pauvre soldat, pauvre soldat!*

4. Other possibilities: *J'ai mal au dos, j'ai mal au cou, j'ai mal au pied, j'ai mal au
    ventre, j'ai mal à l'oeil*

Using the classroom to enhance language learning

Key Stage One classrooms (Years One and Two – ages four and five) and many Key Stage Two classrooms (ages six to eleven) have areas set up as shops, caves, castles, etc. Think about an interactive area which encompasses your primary language too. Props can be labelled in dual languages, speech bubbles placed on the wall to prompt conversation, and examples of songs you have used could be laminated and displayed prominently.

In your Book Corner any language classbooks you and the students have created could be available (see also Projects 1 and 7 in Part II, as well as Part VI for inspiration). As we all know, students love to see their own work or photo or even hear their own voice reproduced to enjoy with a friend in free time, wet playtime or Golden Time. If you have followed the Home Reading Scheme (see Project 2 in Part VII), provide a DVD, a DVD player and a copy of the talking books you have made, for the children to listen to in a cosy place with a friend.

Florence Nightingale Classroom Display

L'Hôpital de Scutari

Make a Red Cross as a wall poster and place a label on the wall for the hospital name. The table needs to be covered with white cloths as sheets and cushions for pillows. Teddy is in bed with bandages on his body. A basket can be available full of bandages, pots for medicine, plastic thermometers, water bottles, letters from home. You will also need nurses' headbands with the Red Cross on them and white shirts or simple white aprons for students to wear. A basket of simple plastic food – labelled, for example, bread, apple, banana – will also be useful.

Vocabulary

Red Cross:	*La Croix Rouge*
Hospital:	*L'hôpital*
Nurse:	*L'infirmière*
Teddy:	*Nounours*
Bandage:	*Les pansements*
Medicine:	*Les médicaments*
Water:	*De l'eau*
Letter:	*Une lettre*
Here is…:	*Voici…*
Crimean War:	*La Guerre de Crimée*

Wall Display

- No entry sign (when you want the hospital to be off limits): *Défense d'entrer*
- List of illnesses: for example, *J'ai mal au bras*, etc.
- Possible things to offer a patient: *De l'eau, une pomme, une lettre, du pain*
- List of soldiers' names: *Liste de soldats* (with list of French boys' and girls' names found on the Internet)
- List of nurses' names : *Liste d'infirmières* (as above: names from Internet)
- Words to *Pauvre Soldat* song
- List of what Teddy likes: *Nounours aime les pommes, les bananes, de l'eau*, etc.
- Prompts for children (as follows)

Prompts for children

Comment ça va?	How are you?
Comment tu t'appelles?	What is your name?
Tu voudrais?	Would you like?
Je voudrais...	I would like...
J'ai mal à la tête	I've got a headache
J'ai faim	I'm hungry
J'ai soif	I'm thirsty
Pauvre Nounours!	Poor Teddy!
Ça va mieux!	That's better!
Merci beaucoup!	Thank you very much!
Dors bien / Dormez bien	Sleep well (to one person/more than one)
Bonne nuit!	Good night!

A short play for Years Three or Four: La Petite Florence

Notes

An English version of this playscript is included in the accompanying DVD to this project.

You need props as for the classroom display of a hospital presented previously.

Characters

Florence:	dressed in long skirt, white pinafore with red cross and headband with red cross.
Second nurse:	dressed like Florence.
Two soldiers:	looking ragged with bandages around head, leg and torn clothes.
Other children:	as nurses or soldiers lying down or standing or sitting in the circle or clustered in pairs of nurse/soldier.

Florence (to audience): *Bonjour. Je m'appelle Florence Nightingale. Je suis infirmière.*

(approaches **first soldier**) *Comment tu t'appelles?*

First soldier:	*Je m'appelle Jean.*
Florence:	*Quel âge as-tu?*
First soldier:	*J'ai vingt ans*
Florence:	*Comment ça va?*
First soldier:	*J'ai mal à la tête* (clutches head).
Florence:	*Pauvre soldat!* (stays by his side, stroking his head).

Second nurse (to audience): *Je m'appelle Alice. Je suis infirmière.*

(Goes to **second soldier**): *Comment tu t'appelles?*

Second soldier:	*Je m'appelle Jacques.*
Second nurse:	*Quel âge as-tu?*
Second soldier:	*J'ai dix-huit ans.*
Second nurse:	*Comment ça va?*
Second soldier:	*J'ai mal à la jambe* (clutches leg).
Second nurse:	*Pauvre soldat!*
Florence:	*Voici l'hôpital* (points to hospital). *Tout est sale* (points to dirty places and holds nose in disgust). *Nettoyez!*
	(Lots of nurses clean up with brooms, brushes, cloths.)

Florence (comes back and points again): *Nettoyez!* (all scurry to clean up).

First soldier (calling out with thirst): *J'ai soif, j'ai soif!*

Florence:	*Voici de l'eau* (gives him some water).

Second soldier (calling out with hunger): *J'ai faim, j'ai faim!*

Second nurse:	*Voici du pain* (gives him some bread).

Florence (inspects all round room and nods): *Oui, ça va mieux!*

(Speaks to **first soldier**): *Ça va mieux?*

First soldier:	*Oui, ça va mieux!*

Second nurse speaks to **second soldier**: *Ça va mieux?*

Second soldier:	*Oui, ça va mieux!*
Florence:	*Voici ma lampe* (holds it up all around the hospital. Soldiers look up and smile and raise arms in air).
All together:	*Oui la lampe. Bonne nuit! Tout va mieux!*

Florence Nightingale additional DVD materials

1. Picture Gallery
2. English version of the play script

Project 3   Antarctica

Content and Language Integrated Learning

This project presents a geography topic (the continent of Antarctica) through the medium of a foreign language (Spanish). This method of combining a foreign language with a specific and unrelated topic is often referred to as Content and Language Integrated Learning or CLIL. CLIL is a modern term for an old method which is known by numerous different names, such as immersion (*Språkbad*, Sweden), multilingual education (Latvia) or integrated curriculum (Spain). For Do Coyle, one of the pre-eminent authorities on CLIL in the UK context,

> Content and Language Integrated Learning (CLIL) is a dual-focused, educational approach in which an **additional language** is used for the learning and teaching of both content *and* language. That is, in the teaching and learning process, there is a focus not only on content, and not only on language. Each is interwoven, even if the emphasis is greater on one or the other at a given time.
>
> (Coyle *et al.* 2010: 1)

CLIL is a relatively new method in UK language teaching. A small but dedicated number of secondary schools influenced by the Canadian immersion movement introduced major European languages, such as French, German and Spanish, as the medium of instruction from the 1970s and 1980s onwards. The number of schools, both primary and secondary, offering bilingual instruction in some core subjects, such as History and Geography, increased in the 1990s, and especially since the turn of the millennium (see Coyle *et al.* 2009, Coyle *et al.* 2010 for case studies and information on how to set up CLIL).

CLIL can help stimulate a real interest in language learning because of its focus on using language for a purpose and on authentic, real-life topics. The approach fosters independent learning, develops skills across a range of subjects and enriches the curriculum by focusing on four important dimensions – the four Cs: content, cognition, communication, culture. There are a number of clear benefits of CLIL. It is different from traditional learning; it is time-efficient, because both subject content and language are learned together; it can foster communication and intercultural understanding and development; it refreshes classroom practice and provides teachers with the opportunity to be creative in interpreting the curriculum (see Coyle *et al.*, 2009).

Key characteristics, such as choosing appropriate content and fostering cultural understanding, can support curriculum designers and teachers in developing CLIL in their school contexts (Coyle *et al.*, 2009: 14–15). CLIL can be implemented in various ways, depending on the context of a specific school and the requirements of the curriculum. CLIL can comprise anything from a sequence of two to three lessons to more sustained modules over a term or school year. Finding the balance between content and language, and defining appropriate outcomes for both subject and language development, is a key factor in successful CLIL implementation. The project presented here is

aimed at supporting those teachers who are taking their first steps with CLIL. It explores the continent of Antarctica through Spanish (with the same project being presented in French in the additional DVD materials).

Introduction

> ### Project outline
>
> **Requirements**: a normal school classroom with PowerPoint facilities.
> **Event time:** one 40-minute lesson.
> **Languages targeted:** Spanish and French.

This project in its initial stages sought to introduce a new model of collaboration in CLIL (content and language integrated learning) by bringing together:

- 'novice' teachers who wish to introduce CLIL into their classrooms;
- 'expert' practitioners of CLIL to act as a model;
- native speaker teachers of the target language from Aston University to offer support with language and materials. The project in its early stages by was led by staff from Aston University who worked with the novice teachers and native speakers to achieve the following aims.

For learners
The long-term aims were to:

- make the learning of languages motivating and relevant;
- give opportunities to use languages in a meaningful way right from the start;
- encourage learners to make connections across subject areas;
- become more independent.

For teachers
Through introducing CLIL into their classrooms teachers can:

- discover innovative and exciting ways of developing pedagogic practice, contributing to their Continuing Professional Development (CPD);
- develop teamwork and collaboration across subject areas;
- develop the curriculum in line with the needs of their learners.

For schools/colleges
The introduction of CLIL in schools can:

- provide team-working opportunities for teachers in order to promote CPD;
- develop innovative opportunities for curriculum delivery;
- stimulate increased interest in foreign languages.

The project presented here was thus designed to meet several needs. It is simple but nevertheless effective and introduces the notion of CLIL in a gentle but motivating way to both teachers and learners. Language learning is embedded in the exploration of the continent Antarctica and the project presented here in Spanish is designed to cover one lesson of 40 minutes. Suggestions for homework possibilities are also included. *Taking steps towards CLIL* was developed under the Links into Languages national initiative (see useful websites on the accompanying DVD for further details).

The activities presented are designed to stimulate an interest in the topic of Antarctica as well as present language items. The materials are presented in five main sections: vocabulary; geography; images of Antarctica; landscape and the environment; follow-on. Students can be encouraged to write up a small project on the topic in the target language with appropriate images (these can be found easily on Google images) after the lesson for homework.

Accompanying DVD materials include a list of useful websites which are relevant to the project, whilst excerpts from the film *The March of the Penguins* and the documentary *The Frozen Planet* support the whole beautifully.

Section 1 *vocabulario*

Make a glossary to use during the lesson by matching up the words. Copy the English words next to the correct Spanish one. Three are done for you.

Antártida	....	**penguins**
ártico	....	sun
nieve	**snow**	ice
ballena	....	polar
hielo	....	mountain
pingüino	**penguins**	north
continente	....	fish
polar	....	Antarctica
sol	....	birds
noche	....	**snow**
montaña	....	night
norte	....	temperatures
foca	....	**summer**
sur	....	whale
pájaros	....	winter
peces	....	continent
temperaturas	....	seal
invierno	....	arctic
verano	**summer**	south

Answers

la Antártida	Antarctica	*ártico*	arctic	*nieve*	snow
pingüino	penguins	*continente*	continent	*polar*	polar
noche	night	*montaña*	mountain	*norte*	north
pájaros	birds	*peces*	fish	*foca*	seal
invierno	winter	*hielo*	ice	*sol*	sun
verano	summer	*ballena*	whale	*sur*	south
temperaturas	temperatures				

Section 2 *Nuestro mundo*

Aim: for students to learn the names of the seven continents in Spanish and to present the seven continents, and in particular the continent of Antarctica, visually.

Ask: *¿cuántos continentes hay en el mundo?*

Nombra los continentes

Aquí tienes un mapa de nuestro mundo con los continentes

Conceal the name of one continent and ask students if they can say its name in Spanish.

Ask: *¿Qué continente falta?* Then do the same with the remaining six continents.

Section 3 *¡Vamos a explorar!*

Aim: to introduce the continent of Antarctica in a visual way and to revise key vocabulary presented in Section 1.

Say: *Vamos de viaje …*

… ¿qué continente vamos a visitar? Mira las imágenes

Section 4 *El paisaje antartico*

Aim: to discover some key facts about Antarctica and its environment.

1. *Aquí tienes la Antártida/el Polo Sur*

Las montañas están cubiertas de nieve y de hielo.

Las temperaturas siempre son negativas. La temperatura media es de -57 grados.

En verano en la Antártida hay 24 horas de sol. En invierno en la Antártida hay 24 horas de noche.

2. *Aquí tienes los icebergs*

El hielo flota en el mar. Un 90% del hielo del mundo está situado en la Antártida.

La mayoría de un iceberg está debajo del agua.

3. Aquí tienes los animales de la Antártida

Las ballenas y las focas viven en la Antártida.

4. Aquí tienes los pingüinos. Ellos también viven en la Antártida

¡En el Polo Norte no hay pingüinos!

Los pingüino padres comen los peces y luego se los dan a sus bebés

Los pingüinos y los emperadores viven en la Antártida

4. La gente

Roald Amundsen fue el primer hombre que llegó al Polo Sur

¡Tuvo que ponerse ropa térmica a causa del frío!

Section 5 Follow-on

Students may wish to write a short and simple project using the language and information learned in this session. Alternatively, they could design a poster in groups (*Un poster de la Antártida*), which they illustrate themselves or with downloaded images. The task and the worksheet that follow are designed to help students organize their thoughts in Spanish, based on the lesson they have just received, by recapping the language and facts they have learnt.

Actividad 1

Los siete continentes
Which of the following are continents? Circle the correct ones.

Francia	*Asia*	*Inglaterra*	*Europa*
África	*El Polo Norte*	*Canadá*	*Australasia*
La Antártida	*China*	*América del Sur*	*India*
América del Norte			

Answers
Asia, Europa, África, La Antártida, América del Sur, América del Norte y La Australasia son continentes. Hay siete en nuestro mundo.

Actividad 2

Which of these is NOT true about *la Antártida*?

- *El Polo Sur es la región más fría de nuestro planeta*
- *Los leones viven en la Antártida*
- *Las temperaturas siempre son negativas*
- *Las temperaturas siempre son positivas*
- *La Antártida es pequeña como Inglaterra*
- *El continente de La Antártida es grande como América del Norte y Europa juntos*
- *Los pingüinos viven en el Polo Sur*
- *Hay 24 horas de sol en verano y 24 horas de noche en invierno*

Answers
These sentences are NOT true:

- *Los leones viven en la Antártida.*
- *Las temperaturas siempre son positivas.*
- *La Antártida es pequeña como Inglaterra.*

Actividad 3

Choose five Antarctic facts that you have learnt this lesson and make an illustrated poster together about *la Antártida.*

Here are the facts that have been presented during this session.

1. *Las montañas están cubiertas de nieve y de hielo.*
2. *Las temperaturas siempre son negativas.*
3. *La temperatura media es de -57 grados.*
4. *En verano en la Antártida hay 24 horas de sol.*
5. *En invierno en la Antártida hay 24 horas de noche.*
6. *Las ballenas y las focas viven en la Antártida.*
7. *¡En el Polo Norte no hay pingüinos!*
8. *Los pingüino padres comen los peces y luego se los dan a sus bebés.*
9. *Los pingüinos y los emperadores viven en la Antártida.*
10. *Roald Amundsen fue el primer hombre que llegó al Polo Sur*
11. *¡Tuvo que ponerse ropa térmica a causa del frío !*
12. *La Antártida está situada en el Polo Sur.*
13. *El hielo flota en el mar.*
14. *Un 90% del hielo del mundo está situado en la Antártida.*
15. *La mayoría de un iceberg está debajo del agua.*

Antarctica: additional DVD materials

1. *Antartica* translated into French
2. Useful websites

Project 4   Wilhelm Röntgen

Project outline

Requirements: normal classroom, A4-sized thin cardboard, scissors, butterfly pins, hanging thread
Event time: 40 minutes
Language targeted: German

Introduction

This project introduces students to the German physicist Wilhelm Conrad Röntgen and combines German with science most effectively through the topics of X-rays and body parts. Students learn the parts of the body by building a skeleton and the language learned is consolidated by means of two games. A picture gallery with a completed skeleton is included in the accompanying DVD for this project, as well as some useful websites to support the ideas presented.

Background

Wilhelm Conrad Röntgen was a German physicist who lived from 1845 to 1923. In 1895 he discovered what we now call X-rays. He was awarded the first Nobel Prize for Physics in 1901. Ask your class to think for a moment about what an X-ray is and why X-rays are so useful to us today. Here are some prompts you could use to stimulate a mini-discussion.

Who uses X-rays a lot, for example? (Doctors and dentists).

Why are X-rays so useful? (They are useful especially in medicine because they are special photographs of the hard parts inside our bodies, like our skeletons. This helps doctors to see what, if anything, is wrong).

Has any one in your class ever had an X-ray? Why?

Perhaps your students know someone who has had one. Why?

Perhaps someone even has an X-ray photograph they could bring into school to show everyone what one looks like. This could be displayed (with permission), together with the skeletons the class will make later perhaps.

Is there anything dangerous about X-rays? (think about dentists perhaps who always escape to the other side of the room when they take an X-ray).

Activity 1: Your body

Ask the class to see if they can work out what the German body parts are called in English. Some of them are pretty close and often students are very good at making the connections. In fact, only *der Kopf* (the head) is significantly different to its English counterpart. Afterwards you can check the students' answers as a class activity by asking individuals to name the parts in English from the German. It is a good idea to learn the gender of the nouns in German from the start, which is why they are included in the exercise. Two useful words in addition are: *der Knochen* (bone) and *das Gelenk* (joint).

Instructions to your students: Here are some of the parts of your body in German from your head to your waist. You could see them all on an X-ray if you had one taken. What do you think they are in English?

der Kopf	*die Schulter*	*der Arm*
der Ell(en)bogen	*das Handgelenk*	*die Hand*
der Finger	*der Daumen*	*die Brust*

Did you know?

If you want to wish someone good luck in English you can say 'Break a leg!' Germans say *Hals- und Beinbruch!* (Neck and leg break!), but it means the same thing! And instead of crossing your fingers, in German you 'press your thumb' for good luck: *Daumen drücken!*

Answers

der Kopf:	head
die Schulter:	shoulder
der Arm:	arm
der Ell(en)bogen:	elbow
das Handgelenk:	wrist
die Hand:	hand
der Finger:	finger
der Daumen:	thumb
die Brust:	chest

Only selected parts of the body are listed here, as overload is off-putting, but you could extend this vocabulary later by looking at the list of useful websites on the accompanying DVD to this project for extra parts of the body in German.

Instructions: Can you match these body parts from your waist to your toes to the correct place on the skeleton? Draw a line from the word to the right bone.

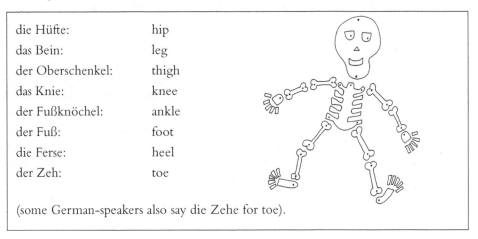

die Hüfte:	hip
das Bein:	leg
der Oberschenkel:	thigh
das Knie:	knee
der Fußknöchel:	ankle
der Fuß:	foot
die Ferse:	heel
der Zeh:	toe

(some German-speakers also say die Zehe for toe).

Activity 2: Simon says …

In order to practise the body parts in German, play a game of 'Simon says ….' or in this case 'Simon sagt...'. One person is Simon (the teacher first to demonstrate). Say the sentence with a word from either list above such as "*Simon sagt berühre deine Zehen*" (touch your toes). The students should touch the correct part of the body. However, if Simon does not start the sentence with "Simon says …" and the students still move to touch the body part mentioned, they are out. So there are two ways to be out. First, if students touch the wrong body part and second, if they make a move and Simon has not started the sentence with "Simon says ..". Students should sit down if they are out and the winner is the person left standing.

Activity 3: Building the skeleton

A completed skeleton is included in the additional DVD materials for this project.

1.   Enlarge the picture of the skeleton in Activity 1 to A3 and photocopy it for each person in your class onto thin, white cardboard. It is best to use cardboard to stop the skeleton curling up at the edges once completed.

2.   Cut around the outline of the shapes. The feet and hands can be kept as one section each, i.e. do not cut out each finger or toe.

3.   Using a hole punch, make a small hole on each spot.

4.   Connect the bones using butterfly pins at the spots.

5.   Finally hang the skeleton up with a loop of thread in the top hole on the head and display in your classroom along with the body part words in German and a picture of Wilhelm Röntgen.

Activity 4: Language revision

Encourage your students to point to the correct body part on the skeleton as you say the word in German. After the words have all been used by you once, each student can have a go at saying the word in German and asking someone else in the class to point out the bone on the skeleton. If the answer is correct, the 'speaker' sits down, the 'pointer' becomes the speaker and a new student is picked to do the pointing.

Wilhelm Röntgen additional DVD materials

1.   Completed skeleton

2.   Useful websites

Project 5   Making languages count

Project Outline

Requirements: standard Maths equipment, for example, number fans, 100 square
Event time: five minutes of a lesson, any spare few minutes of the day
Language used: French

Introduction

Students do not always recognize the relevance of a language and are surprised to find that they can perform Maths tasks in another language. These easy Maths games could be used at the beginning of a language lesson or as a quick filler at any time of the school day. Although they are not substitutes for the usual oral and mental starter activities which begin Maths lessons, they are good for developing two skills at the same time and reveal to English children's amazement that children all over the world study similar Mathematical questions. The activities in this project can easily be translated into other languages. Numbers one to 24 are included in German in the first project in Part III (*It's*

Christmas!), whilst numbers from one to 30 in Spanish are presented on the additional DVD materials which accompany this project.

Organisation

Use all the normal Maths equipment to help. These games assume knowledge of numbers up to 30.

- **Number fans:** use them for a language too! You say the number, they show the fan. In pairs, one student says a French number, the pair shows its double (*le double*).
- **100 square:** cover up a number with a post-it. Students say what's missing.
- **Counting:** you count aloud, stop and students guess the missing number. You can work on quite high numbers for this, as they soon work out the sequence.
- *Changez* **game:** starting with zero, each student in turn calls out a number in order around the class. At intervals, the teacher calls out *Changez* and students have to count in reverse.
- *Jetez vite!:* decide in advance if you are going to count in twos or threes, etc. Throw a beanbag/soft toy from person to person at random across the circle or class, and each has to say the next number in that times table. Don't go higher than ten times, as the numbers get too difficult.
- **Double dice game:** everyone is in a circle. Two big foam dice are thrown to others at random. The first receiver has to work out the tens number in the language and the second receiver has to add the other number, for example, first person: *trente*; second person: *six*. Everyone then choruses: *trente-six*.
- **Multiple twist game:** decide in advance on a multiple you are going to look out for: for example, multiples of four. Count round the room or circle as quickly as possible. When you get to a multiple of the chosen number, the student gets up, spins around fast and then sits down again. Carry on around the group until you run out of number knowledge.
- **Action Numbers:** students choose a partner and decide who is partner number one and who is partner number two. They count up to ten quickly with partner one starting and partner two saying the next number. Before they start they have to agree on an action each time a certain number is reached, for example, when they say one, they clap their hands; if six, they bend their knees; if eight, they jump up high. Once they reach ten, they start again but increase speed. Restrict the special action numbers to two or three at first. When they get the idea, challenge them to do the same up to 20 and make the actions more complex.
- *Pair/Impair:* put the words *pair, impair* on the board and see if anyone can guess their meaning. If not, explain that all French numbers are either *pair or impair*. Point out that **im** is a prefix in French and English, for example, possible/impossible. What could it mean? Work out that they are *even* and *odd*. Recap on recognizing even/odd numbers. Look at a 100 square, point to any number, and they call out *pair* or *impair*.
- **Digit flips:** have a team game where a volunteer from each team says the number made when someone turns over the digits to make a two-digit number. If you don't have a digit flip, use two sets of cards of numbers up to nine. Remember to keep your

totals low if your children only know up to about 30. This is a good incentive for students to want to learn higher multiples of ten.

Learning higher multiples of ten

Teach the word *le multiple* and recap on what it means. Stick number cards on the board for 30, 40, 50, 60 with word cards for those numbers, but **keep them separate**. Can students work out matching pairs? Use initial sounds to help match up *six/soixante; cinq/cinquante*, etc. Show remaining cards/ numbers for 70, 80, and 90, 100. Can they work out the system and match words and numbers? For example, 70= 60 + 10; 80 = four × 20; 90 = four × 20 +10.

How could they recognize *cent/100?* List all the words beginning with *cent*: for example, century. In pairs, students work out the in-between numbers, for example, 82, 74, all the 90s.

Vocabulary

dix = ten;	vingt = 20;	trente = 30;
quarante = 40;	cinquante = 50;	soixante = 60;
soixante-dix = 70;	quatre-vingts = 80;	quatre-vingt-dix = 90;
cent 100;	quatre-vingt-onze = 91;	quatre-vingt-douze = 92 etc

Maths games for running around

Fruit salad with numbers

All in a circle.

- Give each student a number up to ten (beginners). Call out number, swap places.
- Give out consecutive numbers, for example, one to 32, 50 to 82. Swap places if you are a multiple of five, ten or two. Swap places if you are odd, even.
- Call out a multiplication question which fits the numbers in the circle: for example, *deux fois six*. The student with the answer runs round the outside of the circle back to their place.

Vocabulary

Fois: times

- **Ladders:** students sit on the floor in pairs with their legs stretched out towards a partner, making the rungs of a ladder down the middle of a hall. Give each pair a number that you would like them to practise, such as multiples of ten or teen numbers. If you have a confident and able class, call out a multiplication question which fits their numbers. Each pair runs down the ladder, up round the outside and back to their place when their number is called.
- **Number cards:** put numbers up on the walls around the room. Call out a number, students run to it, or face it if it's too much of a crush. Call *pair*, and they have to run to an even number; call *un multiple de cinq* and they have to run to a multiple of five, etc. Call out a simple calculation, and they run to the answer.

Vocabulary

Plus:	plus/add
Moins:	less/take away

Team games

Deux équipes

1. Stick or write the same numbers up on both sides of the board. Put the class in two teams. You call out a number; a student from each team has to race to hit their number.

2. Use word cards and separate number cards. Students have to find a matching pair.

3. Call out a calculation. Students have to find the answer.

Star game

1. Have cards of different colours with numbers on reverse (for example, between ten and 20 or multiples of ten). Stick them on the board.

2. Make two teams. Teams take it in turns for a student to say the French colour and guess the number on the back (give them a clue about the kinds of numbers involved).

3. Award two points for correct answer; one for only the colour; some random cards with points awarded for no number.

Pontoon or Vingt-et-un

1. Students play in pairs with one die between them and a whiteboard and pen.

2. Taking turns to throw the die, they keep adding the next number to their score in French or else stick (*je reste*).

3. The aim is to be the first to get to 21 **exactly**. The winner calls out *J'ai gagné!* The loser calls out *J'ai perdu!* Both call out *Ça ne fait rien!*

Vocabulary

J'ai gagné:	I won
J'ai perdu:	I lost
Ça ne fait rien!:	It doesn't matter!
Vingt et un:	21
C'est trop!:	It's too much!
Je reste:	I'm sticking

Making languages count: additional DVD materials

1. Numbers from 1 to 30 in Spanish

Project 6   Playing games

Project Outline

Requirements: hall or playground spaces
Event time: warm-up times in PE lessons or ten minutes of language lesson
Language used: Spanish and French

Introduction

Physical Education (PE) lessons offer a great opportunity for truly active learning experiences. You can reinforce language skills and knowledge through the context of PE, and your pupils will have fun, get fit and improve their language work at the same time. These games require no special equipment other than the occasional ball or hoop, so could be played in any space. They could form part of a conventional PE lesson or just be saved for language lessons.

Additional materials for this project include photographs to be used as a template for display and instructions for the games in French.

Organisation

Warm-up games

Starting the lesson

Ask the pupils to find a space and be silent.

Vocabulary

buscar un sitio:	find a space
Silencio / callaros:	be quiet

Moving around the PE space

Warm up for PE by calling out instructions in quick succession to walk, run, jump, and turn on the spot.

Vocabulary

andar:	walk
correr:	run
saltar:	jump
torcer a la derecha:	urn to the right
torcer a la izquierda:	turn to the left
parar:	stop

Numbers game warm up

Pupils walk, run or jump around the space. Call out a number – pupils have to find enough partners to quickly stand together or sit together in a group of that number. Then walk or run again and repeat with a different number each time. Invite a child to call out the numbers.

Vocabulary

andar, correr, saltar: (as above)

poneros en grupos de … tres, cuatro, cinco, etc.

Body parts warm up

Pupils walk, run or jump around the PE space. When you call out *touch ankles*, students have to quickly find a partner or partners and hold their ankle against that of their partner until you instruct them to move again. Repeat with moving around the hall in different ways and calling out different body parts.

Vocabulary

andar, correr, saltar: (as above – with body parts for example)

tocaros los codos: touch elbows

las rodillas: knees

los tobillos: ankles

Compass points / Colours game

Display flashcards of compass points – students could stand holding them or place them on the wall or floor, or else simply tell the students where North is so that they have to work out other directions for themselves. Students run around the space; call out a compass point so that students have to move to that point quickly. Keep the students moving briskly from one point to the next. Alternatively, place sheets of coloured card/sugar paper on the walls and play with colour names.

Vocabulary

correr hacia:	run towards
el norte:	the North
el sur:	the South
el este:	the East
el oeste:	the West
el noreste:	the North-east
el noroeste:	the North-west
el sureste:	the South-east
el suroeste:	the South-west
rojo:	red
azul:	blue
amarillo:	yellow
verde:	green
naranja:	orange
rosa:	pink

Pirates game

Teach each instruction and action separately first. Then call out the instructions in quick succession so that children have to listen and respond quickly.

Vocabulary and Actions

Los Piratas:	The pirates
Viene el capitán:	Captain's coming (stand straight and salute)
Subir la cuerda:	Climb the rigging (mime climbing a rope ladder)
Limpiar el suelo:	Scrub the deck (on knees, mime scrubbing the floor)
Hombre al agua:	Man overboard (sit down and mime rowing)
Vienen los tiburones:	Sharks coming (lie down and put both legs in the air)
Se acerca una tormenta:	Storm brewing (huddle together)
Al ataque:	Attack (on one knee as if to fire a canon)
A proa:	To the bow of the ship (you need to define which is the front)
A popa:	To the stern (run to the back)

Top Tips

Take photos of your own pupils doing the actions (a photographic consent form model is presented in Appendix One) and make flashcards to put on the wall. Students who have forgotten their PE kit or are not doing PE could still join in by:

- calling out instructions in Spanish;
- holding up cards for you;
- giving team points or saying praise words in Spanish.

Arm stretch exercise

Students follow instructions given below:

Vocabulary

Arriba, abajo:	Put both arms out in front, raise up and lower
Repetir:	Repeat
Lento, lento:	Raise arms slowly and lower slowly
Rápido, rápido:	Raise arms quickly and lower quickly
¡parar!:	Put one arm out with hand in a stop signal
Otra vez …:	And again …(Repeat the sequence)

Hoops game

Space a series of large hoops out on the floor and follow instructions to:

Vocabulary

andar, correr, saltar: (as before)

coger el aro con … pick up the hoop with …

… *la mano derecha*: …your right hand

… *la mano izquierda*: …your left hand

saltar adentro del aro: jump inside the hoop

saltar afuera del aro: jump outside the hoop

Fruit salad (changing places game)

Sit or stand in a circle. Give each student one of four nouns to remember: for example, lemon, banana, cherry, strawberry. Call out a fruit; all students with that noun have to run across the circle and change places with each other. When you call *fruit salad*, everybody has to change places.

Vocabulary

macedonia:	fruit salad
limones:	lemons
plátanos:	bananas
cerezas:	cherries
fresas:	strawberries

Playing games: additional DVD materials

1. Picture gallery
2. French vocabulary for games

Project 7   Drawing in Spanish

routes into
LANGUAGES

Project outline

Requirements: see 'Organisation' section
Event time: 25 minutes for a basic session (can be extended with further activities)
Languages targeted: Spanish

Introduction

Drawing in Spanish is a fun activity that encourages students to combine their artistic skills with their knowledge of Spanish. The example presented here has been adapted from a larger-scale project for secondary school students and their parents devised by tutors and Post-Graduate Certificate in Education (PGCE) trainees at the University of

Portsmouth as part of the Routes into Languages initiative in the South. It is straight-forward in its approach but does require some prior organisation, all of which is outlined below.

The idea of using the medium of art/drawing to teach a foreign language is a simple one which yields positive end results. Students must use the target language effectively to create their piece of artwork. At the same time, concentrating on producing their drawings allows them to absorb new vocabulary often without realising they are doing so. Depending on how you choose to deliver this activity (see below) students will also receive cultural input which helps to cement their interest in the target language.

The model explained here uses pictures by the Colombian artist Fernando Botero, but other Spanish-speaking artists could be chosen. Similarly, this project can be adapted for other languages by choosing artists from other countries.

Organisation

As mentioned above, this activity requires a certain degree of prior planning and organi-sation in order to run smoothly in the classroom. However, it is not complicated, and materials prepared can be used again. The steps below explain how to run a basic 25-minute session but, depending on your available time, you may wish to extend the activity for a longer period or run a series of short sessions. Extension materials can be found on the accompanying DVD along with a list of useful websites.

Requirements

You will need the following:

flipchart stand with flipchart paper;

oil pastels (enough for the group);

coloured pens or pencils;

A3 plain white paper;

4 × envelopes;

sticky-tack;

name labels;

4 × sheets of A4 coloured card;

5 × sheets of A5 white card;

2 board pens.

Preparation

To prepare for the basic 25-minute activity you will need to:

1.   Go to http://www.fernandobotero.com/art.shtml, where you can find examples of Fernando Botero's paintings. Select four of the pictures (not the *Mona Lisa*, as this will be used as an example) and print them and the *Mona Lisa* out (ideally in colour, but black and white will also be sufficient).

2. For each picture you have printed out (not the *Mona Lisa*) write eight to ten different adjectives describing it and put them in an envelope, so that you have four sets of words (one set of words per picture).

3. Write or print out the following words on separate pieces of paper or card which are to be displayed around the classroom during the activity: *grueso/a; oscuro/a; insulto; humor; es; tiene; feo/a; bonito/a; brillante; gordo/a; acción; figura; más; menos; en comparacíon con.* Note that these words describe the works of Fernando Botero, so if you choose a different artist, you will need to use different words. These words can also be amended, depending on the target language ability of your group.

4. Prepare name cards for each table. Here we have chosen names of Spanish-speaking cities to keep with the theme of the activity: Barcelona, Buenos Aires, Sevilla, Santiago, Bogotá. More cities can be added, depending on the size of your group.

Starter activity (5–10 minutes)

Display Fernando Botero's *Mona Lisa* picture on the flipchart so everyone can see. Using the words displayed in the room, ask each table of students to write four sentences to describe the painting. Students should be able to justify their choice of words in Spanish where possible. Give an example to get the activity started.

After five or six minutes the groups should stop what they are doing and listen to each table read out their four descriptions. Ask each group whether they agree or disagree with each other. Following this read out the objective and outcome of the activity:

Objective: by the end of the lesson you will have created your own piece of art based on the style of Fernando Botero, using Spanish.

Outcome: you will be able to compare and contrast the piece of art you have created with that of Fernando Botero, as well as describe it, in Spanish.

Art activity (15–20 minutes)

Tell the class that each table will be working together as a group for the next activity. Give each group one of the envelopes containing the eight to ten words prepared beforehand. These words describe one of the paintings by the chosen artist that you initially selected (each table should have words describing a different picture) and should be used to help the group recreate the corresponding painting. The groups should use the oil pastels and pencils to draw their version of the painting. Allow approximately 10–15 minutes for this part.

Once all the paintings have been recreated, ask each group to display their picture for the whole room to see. Then give out your print-outs of the corresponding paintings, so that people can compare their work to that of the original.

The activity ends by giving students five minutes to think of four brief sentences in Spanish to describe the differences and similarities between their painting and that of the artist. The words displayed in the room can be used for this, and groups can also refer to dictionaries. If appropriate, the groups could also try to express an opinion about either their work or that of the artist. Go round each group to hear what they have to say.

Reflections

This activity is a great way of engaging students with the target language whilst asking them to produce something tangible. Working in groups allows those with a higher command of the target language to help those with lower abilities and, by the same token, encourages those who are less confident to speak up and try out their language skills. Focusing on an artist from a Spanish-speaking country also lends a sound cultural element to the session and could be extended further to include links to other curriculum areas, such as history and geography.

Drawing in Spanish: additional DVD materials

1. Extension activities × 2
2. Useful websites

Project 8   Short break fillers

Project outline

Requirements: any classroom space; students sitting one behind the other for massage lessons; prior instruction about performing peer-to-peer massage
Event time: five or ten minutes in any day, anywhere
Language used: French

Introduction

One of the joys of being a class teacher in a primary school is having incidental slots of time between lessons, or just before lunchtime or home time, when you can be creative with your time and get to know your class better. Each teacher uses this time differently; these little breaks are ideal for language learning and create a welcoming atmosphere in the class.

Note: make sure that you follow the health and safety rules for peer-to peer-massage if your school has not been involved in training by professionals.

Organisation

Massage

One recent development in primary schools has been the use of peer-to-peer massage sessions where students and adults have received training sessions about how to give and receive simple massage strokes to the back and shoulders while a carefully structured story is recited. There are several conditions governing massage technique: students give and receive massage only with other students; each student has the right to refuse to give or receive massage; feedback is given at the end of the session to the giver; students learn about touching each other safely and respectfully. The story recited is related to different kinds of finger strokes and can be adapted to fit many themes across the curriculum, for example, Christmas, Fireworks, Henry VIII, Weather, Seaside (students particularly enjoy making up a series of lines and action to fit Henry and the fate of his wives!).

A language-based story works well with this concept and can be put up on the whiteboard with suitable illustrations to identify the strokes involved, for example, long, smooth finger runs, dotting with finger tips, edge of hand firm pressing. The following examples can be read aloud by the whole class and used as a template for other topics.

The accompanying DVD materials for this project include a picture gallery and some traditional rhymes to use and adapt for massage purposes.

Massage topics

1. *Noël* (**Christmas**)

    Dans la grande maison: in the big house
    (Firm shapes with finger tips to draw the house the whole width of the back)

    Voici l'arbre de Noël: here's the Christmas tree
    (Flat hands making cloud shapes to cover the shape of the tree)

    Voici les branches très longues: here are the very long branches
    (Long strokes with each hand in turn firmly sweeping down the length of each branch)

    Les étoiles brillent: the stars shine
    (Gentle dotty pressing to make stars on the end of each branch)

    Voici les guirlandes de Noël: here's the Christmas tinsel
    (Sweep both hands gently over the branches to make the tinsel effect)

    En haut de l'arbre voici l'ange de Noël: at the top of the tree here's the Christmas angel
    (Finger tip shaping for the angel)

    Et dans le jardin il neige doucement: and in the garden it's snowing softly
    (Both hands dotting all around the back for snow)

2. *Une journée d'été* (**A summer's day**)

    Le soleil brille: the sun is shining
    (Both hands with palms flat on the back moving out in all directions like sun rays)

    Il fait chaud: it's hot
    (Quick sweeps of each hand as if to wipe your brow in the heat)

    Un garçon nage dans la mer: a boy is swimming in the sea
    (Both hands on back making firm breast stroke swimming movements alternating with shorter up and down movements as if kicking with feet)

    Tout est calme: everything is calm
    (Press hard with whole hand slowly, then the other very calmly)

    Un requin arrive sous les vagues: a shark approaches under the waves
    (Hand sideways on alternately making sharp jagged movements to show swimming shark)

Il attaque: it attacks
(Fists tap all over back)

Au secours!!!: Help!!!
(Both hands flat on back, rush from top to bottom of back)

La mer est calme: the sea is calm
(Soft swimming motions all over back with flat palms)

Brain breaks

These have long been part of the primary school toolbox, ideal for reviving flagging concentration and injecting a lively element between more formal lessons. Add a language for variety once a week.

Vocabulary

Claquez les doigts … en haut/en bas/à droite/à gauche/doucement/fort.
Click your fingers … high/low/to the right/to the left/softly/loudly.

Dessinez … un carré/un rectangle/un cercle/un octogone/un triangle … dans l'espace … avec la main gauche/la main droite/les deux mains.
Draw … a square/a rectangle/a circle/an octagon/a triangle in the air … with your left hand/right hand/both hands together.

Haussez les épaules … en avant/en arrière/en haut/en bas.
Shrug your shoulders … forwards/ backwards/ up high/ low down.

Dessinez en trois D … un cube/ un cylindre/ une sphère … dans l'espace.
Draw in Three D … a cube/ a cylinder/a sphere … in the air.

Ecrivez votre nom dans l'espace avec le doigt/ avec la main/ avec les deux mains.
Write your name in the air with your finger/ with your hand/ with both hands.

Essayez de vous chatouiller!
Try to tickle yourself!

Short break fillers: additional DVD material

1. Picture gallery
2. Traditional rhymes for massage

Project 9   Life cycles

Project outline

Requirements: normal classroom, the following stationery items to make a mermaid's purse: A4-sized white paper; scissors; coloured crayons; glitter; drawing paper; shredded paper or small pieces of tissue paper; a pencil or knitting needle; googly eyes
Event time: 40 minutes class time and 30 minutes preparation time
Language used: German

Introduction

Most primary-school classrooms seem to have a tank full of tadpoles in the Spring term – and perhaps yours is no exception! This project combines science with German and explores the life cycles of two creatures: the frog and the lesser-spotted dogfish. Whilst the latter is perhaps less well-known than the frog, its egg cases (or mermaids' purses) are often washed up on our beaches, particularly after storms at sea. Examples of mermaids' purses, both fresh and dried, are contained in the accompanying DVD materials to this project as well as a short story entitled *Adam and the embryo*, which is about a boy who finds a mermaid's purse on the beach and takes it home. In *Life cycles* students can even make their own mermaids' purses (each one with a secret message inside) and take them home too.

The Frog

Some information about frogs and their life cycle follows both in English (first) and then in German. The German text could be cut up and displayed as discrete sentences next to their English translations around the life-cycle picture on your classroom wall. The sentences in the text are kept short to allow this. Alternatively, you could just use the following key vocabulary to support your lesson and introduce a German angle in a very simple way.

Key Vocabulary

Der Frosch:	frog
Der Froschlaich:	frog spawn
Das Fröschlein:	froglet
Die Kaulquappe:	tadpole

The Frog

Frogs are amphibians. They have moist, slimy skin. They always live near water, as they need water to breed in. All frogs can swim. Some can climb trees. Some can even glide from tree to tree – and some are poisonous. The poison from just one golden tree-frog, for example, could kill up to 1,500 people! Tree frogs are good at camouflage too. They can change colour very quickly if they need to hide themselves from enemies or their prey.

Frogs go back to the water when it is time to breed. The female frog lays her eggs in or near a pond or stream. She lays up to 20,000 eggs in a large mass. This mass of eggs is called 'frogspawn'. You might find some in a pond from February onwards if you are lucky.

Frogspawn hatches into tadpoles in the water. The tadpole grows legs and arms and gradually loses its tail. It is now a froglet. Finally the young frog hops out of the water onto land.

Frogs have long back legs. These help the frogs to swim well. When you swim breast-stroke, you are swimming in the same way as a frog. Frogs use their long back legs for jumping on land too. The kind of frog you might find in your garden can jump about 60 centimetres! That's a long way for a frog!

Der Frosch

Frösche sind Amphibien. Sie haben eine feuchte, schleimige Haut. Sie wohnen immer in Wassernähe, weil sie es brauchen, um darin ihre Eier zu laichen. Alle Frösche können schwimmen. Einige können auf Bäume klettern. Einige können auch von Baum zu Baum gleiten – und einige sind giftig. Zum Beispiel kann das Gift von nur einem goldenen Baumfrosch bis zum 1.500 Menschen töten! Baumfrösche können sich auch sehr gut tarnen. Sie können ihre Farbe sehr schnell wechseln, falls sie sich vor Feinden oder ihrer Beute verstecken müssen.

Frösche gehen ins Wasser zurück, wenn es Zeit ist, sich fortzupflanzen. Das Weibchen legt ihre Eier in oder in der Nähe eines Teiches oder Baches ab. Sie legt bis zu 20,000 Eier, die einen großen Klumpen bilden. Dieser Klumpen heißt 'Froschlaich'. Wenn Du Glück hast, kannst. Du vielleicht ab Februar Froschlaich in einem Teich finden.

Aus dem Froschlaich schlüpfen im Wasser Kaulquappen. Die Kaulquappen bilden Beine und Arme aus und verlieren allmählich ihren Schwanz. Es ist jetzt ein Fröschlein. Endlich hüpft das Fröschlein aus dem Wasser aufs Land.

Frösche haben lange Hinterbeine. Diese helfen dem Frosch beim Schwimmen. Beim Brustschwimmen schwimmst Du genauso wie ein Frosch. Frösche benutzen ihre Hinterbeine auch, um aufs Land zu springen. Die Froschart aus Deinem Garten kann ungefähr 60 Zentimeter springen. Das ist weit für einen Frosch!

The life cycle of a frog

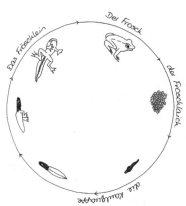

Something interesting

German also say they 'have a frog' when their voices are not clear, but their frogs go in their necks (*der Hals*) and not in their throats! So they say: *ich habe einen Frosch im Hals*!

Something else interesting!

Sei kein Frosch! (literally 'Don't be a frog') translates into English as 'Don't be a spoilsport'!

The Lesser-spotted Dogfish

You might not have heard of a lesser-spotted dogfish (some people call them 'catfish'), but you might have heard of a shark! Lesser-spotted dogfish belong to the shark

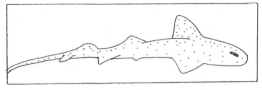

family, as do rays. There are about 375 species of shark, and you probably know some of them, such as the goblin shark, the hammerhead shark and the great white shark.

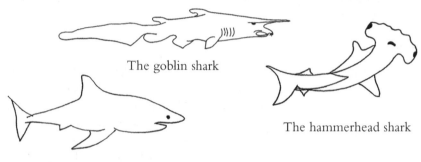

The goblin shark

The hammerhead shark

The great white shark

Most sharks are not dangerous! Only about three people a year are killed by a shark (not nearly as many as are run over and killed by cars, for example). Sharks are older than dinosaurs. They have been around for over 400 million years. You can sometimes find fossilized shark teeth buried on beaches if you are very lucky and looking in the right place at the right time (low tide).

The shark family lays interesting egg cases and sometimes these are washed up on the beach. You can often find these cases if you go beachcombing along the strandline (the point of the highest tide on the beach, where interesting objects are left behind when the tide goes out).

Some people call these egg cases 'mermaids' purses', as they imagine that mermaids use them as little bags for keeping precious things in. The most common egg cases you can find are those belonging to the lesser-spotted dogfish which look like the picture below.

These egg cases are light brown, rectangular in shape and about as long as your little finger. If you hold one up to the light, it gleams golden-amber. At both ends there are curly tendrils. The mother uses these to tie the egg cases firmly onto seaweed to stop them floating away. The baby lesser-spotted dogfish lives inside the egg case for about nine months – just like humans do. Then it breaks out of the case and swims away. It will grow to be about 90 centimetres long which is almost as long as your arm!

Rays also lay egg cases which you may find washed up on the beach. Rays' egg cases are bigger and blacker and they have points, rather then tendrils, at each corner. You can see the difference between the two types from the following photographs.

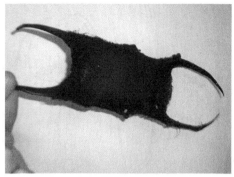

*A mixed collection of egg cases from rays
(the black ones) and the lesser-spotted
dogfish (the lighter, smaller ones)*

The egg case of a ray

In the additional DVD to this project there is a short story called *Adam and the embryo* which you could read to your class. It is about a boy who found a mermaid's purse on a beach and took it home with him.

How to make a mermaid's purse

Making a mermaid's purse with your class is good fun and relatively simple.

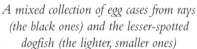

Shopping list

A4-sized white paper; scissors; coloured crayons; glitter; drawing paper; shredded paper or small pieces of tissue paper; a pencil or knitting needle; googly eyes.

Instructions

1. Photocopy the two templates for the front (A) and back (B) of the mermaid's purse enough times so that each student in the class has a complete mermaid's purse.
2. Ask your class to colour their purses on both sides. They can choose to colour them in any way they like. Some students like to make their mermaid's purses look like real ones and colour them brown/black. Glitter makes these ones look brighter. Other children like colouring hearts or flowers or stripes and they should be encouraged to do so. There is a photograph of finished paper mermaid's purses on the DVD accompanying this project to inspire you!
3. Students should bring their coloured mermaid's purses to the gluing table to have three sides only glued into position: i.e. sides and base are glued together. The top edge should be left open so that the stuffing can be inserted.
4. Whilst they are waiting for the glue to dry, students can draw a small embryo to put inside their mermaid's purse. They do not have to draw an embryo. They could write a message in German perhaps or a draw small picture or even a secret wish. It is amazing what students will draw to put inside their purses given a free rein!

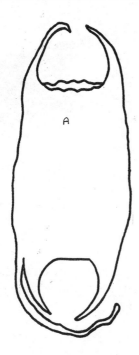
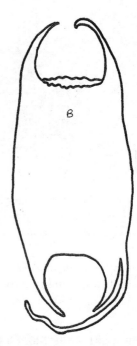

5. Students should then stick a pair of googly eyes on the front of their mermaid's purses.

6. The purses should then be stuffed with shredded paper or small pieces of tissue paper to make the purse 3D (you don't need much stuffing to give that effect). The school office will usually greet anyone looking for shredded paper with open arms!

7. Poke the stuffing down inside the mermaid's purse with a pencil or a knitting needle. Seal the top with glue.

8. Students should now go to the glitter table to add the finishing touches to their work. The finished mermaid's purses can be displayed around the science area in your classroom or strung up on a 'washing line' across the room. They make an unusual and colourful display!

Reflections

Making mermaid's purses with around thirty students can be quite messy! Students can use their normal tables for the colouring and writing/drawing their secret messages, but it is a good idea to have three extra tables, with each one supervised by an adult (parents are quite willing to come in for an afternoon to help). One table can be the glitter table, with a glitter tray to catch the spillage and the remaining two for the gluing. Strong glue is recommended, rather than PVA glue (which takes a comparatively long time to dry).

Life cycles: additional DVD materials

1. Picture gallery – real and paper mermaids' purses

2. Short story: Adam and the embryo

3. Useful weblinks

2

Languages, making and doing

Introduction

This part is all about making and doing and combining the same with language learning. Seven exciting, crafty projects are presented here, all stemming from classroom practice, and each one sure to inspire you and your students. Whether you want to cook biscuits, animate static objects, make simple books or build a beach hut with your class, all you need is presented in this part – and much more besides. The ideas are original, simple, practical and, above all, fun – enabling you to add that magical creative dimension to your language lessons.

Project 1   Creating imaginative, simple books

Project outline

Requirements: Card; scissors; binding for class book: for example, spiral binder or treasury tags
Event time: 45 minutes of a lesson
Language used: French/Spanish/German

Introduction

Making simple books with primary students is an inspiring way to use language creatively. These individual projects are an ideal way to provide opportunities for communication in a language or a class display, or to keep on the class bookshelves for story time. Students could take them home to tell stories with their families and teach them the little conversations.

Organisation

Materials such as A4 card, scissors and glue are available in every primary classroom. Make sure you try out the ideas in advance and have a template ready to show the class what the end product should resemble (see picture gallery for this project on the accompanying DVD). This first example consists of a page contributed by each student, divided into an upper and lower half. When each page is complete, a whole book can be put together and the pages cut across the middle to make a mismatching book.

How to make a half-and-half-page habitats book

1. Each child has a piece of A4 card of any colour.

2. Halfway down the page, lightly draw a line across the page to divide it into two sections.

3. In the top half, ask the children to draw an animal to fill up the space, colour it in a lively way and label it in the target language: to say, for example, *un éléphant habite…/un elefante vive…/ein Elefant lebt …*

4. In the bottom half, draw the habitat of the animal, colour it and label in the target language, for example, *dans le jungle/en la jungla/in dem Dschungel.*

5. Encourage the children to draw different animals from each other; even birds or fish, as long as they know the target language for them (a small class dictionary might help here, and you will need some suggestions up your sleeve too!). Try to get 30 different species from the class! Similarly, try to accumulate different habitats, for example: *dans le désert/en el desierto/in der Wüste; à la ferme/en la granja/auf dem Bauernhof; dans l'air/en el aire/in der Luft; dans la mer/en el mar/im Meer; dans la forêt/en el bosque/im Wald; dans la maison/en la casa/zu Hause; dans le zoo/en el zoo/im Zoo; dans un arbre/en el árbol/in einem Baum; sous la terre/debajo del suelo/unter der Erde; dans un nid/en un nido/in einem Nest.*

6. Gather together all the finished card pages and assemble in a mixed order, so that you have a jumble of different animals rather than all the fish together.

7. Make a front cover for example (Where do you live?) *Où habites-tu? Dónde vives? Wo lebst du?* with a good animal picture from a child. You may also want to add a strong piece of plain card at the end to keep the book firmly in place.

8. If you have access to a spiral binder, use it to put the book together. If not, make four holes down the left side of the pages with a strong hole punch and attach all the pages and covers with treasury tags.

9. With a strong pair of scissors, carefully cut along the midway lines of each page EXCEPT FOR THE FRONT AND BACK COVERS, to separate each page into its two halves.

10. You should now have a half-and-half funny book of matches and mismatches of animals and their habitats.

11. Open the book at any animal and then turn the lower sections to find a 'wrong' habitat.

12. Choose a couple of children to find random animals and habitats every day and read them aloud.

Alternatives

Try other themes for a half-and-half book. Here are some suggestions.

1. Animal word and its food: *un lapin mange …/un conejo come …/ein Kaninchen isst …/un singe mange…/un mono come …/ein Affe isst …; … l'herbe/la hierba/das Gras; …des bananes/los plátanos/die Bananen.*

2. Rooms of the house and something you would do there: *dans la cuisine …/en la cocina …/in der Küche…/dans la chambre…/en el dormitorio…/in dem Schlafzimmer…/… je dors/duermo/ich schlafe/ je mange mon petit déjeuner/como mi desayuno/ich esse mein Frühstück.*

3. I like to eat something with something else: *j'aime manger les frites…/me gusta comer patatas fritas…/ich esse gern die Pommes…/j'aime manger des spaghettis…/ me gusta comer espaguetis…/ich esse gern die Spaghetti…/… avec du sel/con **sal**/ mit Salz/avec du fromage/con queso/mit Käse.*

4. I go somewhere by some transport: *je vais à l'école…/voy a la escuela…/ich fahre in die Schule…/je vais aux magasins…/voy a las tiendas…/ich fahre zu den Geschäften…/… par le train/en tren/mit dem Zug/à vélo/en bicicleta/mit dem Rad.*

Note: In German the destination comes last in a proper sentence. For example: *Ich fahre mit dem Zug in die Schule.*

Creating imaginative, simple books: additional DVD materials

1. Picture gallery

Project 2   At the seaside

Project outline

Requirements: normal classroom, A4-sized thin cardboard, scissors, coloured crayons, glitter, drawing paper; time to prepare the beach hut pieces
Event time: 40 minutes
Language used: French/Spanish/German

Introduction

This is a useful project which appeals to everyone, particularly when the summer draws nearer! Through the identification of key vocabulary connected to the theme of the seaside, your students can learn and practise new words and create short sentences to describe what they can do on the beach. This new language is then revisited as students make and decorate their own little beach huts and place various items inside before closing the door behind them.

On the beach/Am Strand

Ask students to look at the beach scene in the first picture and label what they can see using the words in German that follow. A translation of this vocabulary in both French and Spanish is presented in the accompanying DVD to this project. Although it may seem daunting to ask students to try to match up words in an unfamiliar language to pictures without an English translation, they are often very good at it and can see connections between the two languages quite easily. Check the answers with the class before moving on to the language extension task.

Instructions to students

Look at the picture of the seaside scene and the words in German below. Each word is the name of something in the picture. Can you guess what it is? Draw a line from the word to the picture when you are sure you know the meaning. Try to use your imaginations to see if you can make a sensible guess. Some of the words do sound and look similar – but others are not similar at all.

die Krabbe	*das Meer*	*die Muschel*
der Sand	*die Jacht*	*die Sonne*
das Fähnchen	*die Sonnencreme*	*der Gummiring*
der Strandball	*die Badehose*	*die Möwe*
das Eis	*die Sonnenbrille*	*das Netz*
der Badeanzug	*der Seestern*	*die Sandburg*
das Haifischei	*der Liegestuhl*	*das Strandhäuschen*
das Strandlaken	*der Hut*	*das Buch*

Talk about the picture with your class. You could enlarge it and display it on the wall with the words in German around the edge. You could ask students to make their own pictures and colour them in using perhaps twelve of the German words presented.

Answers

die Krabbe:	crab	*das Meer*:	sea
der Sand:	sand	*die Jacht*:	yacht
das Fähnchen:	flag	*die Sonnencreme*:	sun cream
der Strandball:	beach ball	*die Badehose*:	trunks
das Eis:	ice-cream	*die Sonnenbrille*:	sunglasses
der Seestern:	star fish	*die Sandburg*:	sand castle
das Haifischei:	mermaids' purse	*der Liegestuhl*:	deck chair
das Strandlaken:	beach towel	*der Gummiring*:	rubber ring
der Badeanzug:	swimming costume	*das Strandhäuschen*:	beach hut
die Muschel:	shell	*die Sonne*:	sun
das Buch:	book	*die Möwe*:	seagull
das Netz:	net	*der Hut*:	hat
die Welle:	wave		

Extension Task

What can you do on the beach? *Was **kann** man am Strand **machen***? Using the format that follows, see if you can talk your students through seven things they can do when they go to the beach. Keep the sentences simple. Point out that the second verb goes to the end of the sentence. You might like to display the verbs beforehand.

Verbs to use

schwimmen	*essen*	*lesen*	*fischen*	*suchen*
bauen	*spielen*			

Was kann man am Strand machen? Here are seven suggestions:

1. *Man **kann** im Meer **schwimmen***: You can swim in the sea.
2. *Man **kann** ein Eis **essen***: You can eat an ice-cream.
3. *Man **kann** ein Buch **lesen***: You can read a book.
4. *Man **kann** nach Krabben **fischen***: You can fish for crabs.
5. *Man **kann** nach Muscheln **suchen***: You can look for shells.
6. *Man **kann** eine Sandburg **bauen***: You can build a sand castle.
7. *Man **kann** mit den Wellen **spielen***: You can play with the waves.

Making your beach hut

In the first picture there is a beach hut – *ein Strandhäuschen*. Beach huts are very much part of British seaside life, and students are often fascinated by them and by what people keep inside them. Germany only has one coastline, in the north, and there the beach users have large canopied chairs made of wicker (*der Strandkorb*, which literally means a 'beach basket') which you can buy or hire.

Ask your class to imagine they have a beach hut, perhaps rented for the summer season. What colour would it be on the outside? And on the inside? What would they keep inside? Tell them that they are each going to make a beach hut and that, as they are making it, they should think about some things they can keep inside which they can name in German.

Instructions

1. Copy the template for the roof and the template for the body of the hut onto thin, white cardboard – one for each member of the class. White cardboard is easier to colour and decorate.

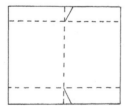
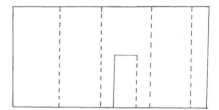

2. Make the roof templates up into proper roofs before you give one to each of your students. This is done by scoring along the dotted edge and cutting along the solid lines. Fold the roof along the middle line. Fold the side lines as well. Then cut the half-triangle and glue firmly to the inside of the roof to make a V-shape. You will also need to score along the dotted lines of the beach hut body and cut one side and the top of the door as well to make it easier for the students later.

3. Each student should receive from you one roof template and one hut template. Tell them to put the roofs to one side for the moment.

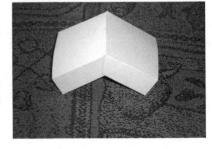

4. Students should decorate their huts on the outside according to taste! The door should be a different colour to the rest of the hut.

5.	Above the door there should be a number – any number. If students are going to decorate their doors with a sticker (see, for example, the picture gallery for this project on the accompanying DVD) now is the time to do it, before the hut is folded up.

6.	Students should now work on the inside of the hut. They should draw small pictures of some of the things they would keep inside it. They should be able to say what they have put inside it in German at the end of the session, so they will need to think about the vocabulary they have just learned. They should also bear in mind that most beach huts do not have electricity, so televisions and video are not really appropriate!

7.	Now the body of the huts can be glued together and put to one side.

8.	Students should put some glue on their roofs and sprinkle them with glitter to give a frosted appearance.

9.	When the roof is dry, the roof can be glued around the edge and stuck onto the top of the hut.

10.	Leave all the huts to dry for a while and then add them to your classroom display.

Reflections

Making beach huts with around thirty students can be quite messy! Students can use their normal tables for the colouring, but it is a good idea to have three extra tables with each one supervised by an adult (parents are quite willing to come in for an afternoon to help). One table can be the glitter table with a glitter tray to catch the spillage and the remaining two for the gluing. Strong glue is recommended rather than PVA glue which takes a comparatively long time to dry.

Linked activity

If your class are enthusiastic about making things to do with the seaside, they could also make a mermaid's purse. These interesting egg cases are often washed up on the beach, especially after storms. In the last project in Part I (*Life cycles*) there is a presentation about how to make one, which can also be followed by a short story about a boy who found a mermaid's purse and took it home (*Adam and the embryo*).

At the seaside: additional DVD materials

1.	Seaside vocabulary in French
2.	Seaside vocabulary in Spanish
3.	Picture gallery – winter, summer and Hallowe'en huts on display
4.	Useful weblinks

Project 3   In the kitchen

Project outline

Requirements: normal classroom, ingredients as described, access to an oven
Event time: 40 minutes
Language used: French and German

Introduction

What a lovely lesson – you learn some new words in French and then eat what you have made! Most children are excited by the idea of cooking in school time, and, if you have access to an oven, these biscuits are simple to make and very tasty! Here is a recipe in French (and English) for some chocolate-chip cookies – which are bound to be popular with your class! The additional DVD materials for this project contain a recipe in German (and English) for some German Christmas biscuits, which are also fun to make. The additional DVD materials for this project contain some lovely websites too, where French and German recipes abound!

Cookies au chocolat

Voici une recette de biscuits américains traditionnels. La recette est rapide et facile. Tu peux varier en y ajoutant 120g de noix pilées.

Here is a recipe for traditional American biscuits. The recipe is quick and simple. You can vary it by adding 120g of crushed nuts.

Il te faut (pour 18 biscuits environ):	To make around 18 biscuits you need :
120g de beurre ramolli	120g of softened butter
70g de sucre en poudre	70g of sugar
0.5 de cuillère à café de bicarbonate de soude	0.5 teaspoons of bicarbonate of soda
0.5 de cuillère à café d'essence de vanille	0.5 teaspoons of vanilla essence
0.25 de cuillère à café de sel	0.25 teaspoons of salt
180g de pépites de chocolat	180g of chocolate chips
140g de farine	140g of flour
1 oeuf	1 egg
70g de sucre roux	70g of brown sugar

This is a good opportunity to introduce some basic kitchen equipment to your class. All of these items can be demonstrated as you work through the recipe. You could enlarge and laminate the list of vocabulary items to display with pictures around the cookery area in your classroom, along with the 'golden rules' which follow.

a plate:	*une assiette*
a spoon:	*une cuillère*
a knife:	*un couteau*
a fork:	*une fourchette*
a cup:	*une tasse*
a measuring jug:	*un verre gradué*
a packet:	*un paquet*
a set of scales:	*la balance*
the oven:	*le four*
baking sheet:	*la plaque à four*
oven glove:	*un gant de cuisine*
bowl:	*la jatte*
wire rack:	*une grille*
an apron:	*un tablier*

La recette pour faire environ 18 biscuits.

Il faut:

1. ***préchauffer*** *le four à 190° C (thermostat 5).*
   Preheat the oven to 190° C (gas mark 5).

2. ***battre*** *les deux sortes de sucre avec le beurre jusqu' à obtenir une crème.*
   Cream the two kinds of sugar with the butter

3. ***casser*** *l'oeuf dans la jatte et battre le tout.*
   Break the egg into the bowl and mix everything together

4. ***ajouter*** *à cette crème l'essence de vanille.*
   Add the vanilla essence to the mixture.

5. ***incorporer*** *petit à petit la farine, le bicarbonate de soude et le sel. Bien mélanger le tout.*
   Gradually add the flour, the bicarbonate of soda and the salt. Mix everything together well.

6. ***verser*** *les pépites de chocolat et mélanger-les en tournant pour bien les répartir dans la pâte à biscuit.*
   Add the chocolate chips and mix them in by turning the mixture over in order to spread them evenly thoughout the biscuit mixture.

7. ***beurrer*** *les plaques à four et déposer des cuillerées de ce mélange, en petits tas bien espacés.*
   Grease the baking sheets and put spoonfuls of the mixture onto them in small piles, well spaced out.

8. ***mettre*** *au four 10 à 12 minutes. Quand les cookies sont bien brunis et dorés, faire refroidir sur une grille. Les biscuits doivent être croquants à l'extérieur et moelleux à l'intérieur.*
   Put them in the oven for ten to twelve minutes. When the cookies are nicely golden-brown, leave them to cool on a wire rack. The biscuits should be crunchy on the outside and soft in the middle.

Bon appetit!

Some golden rules

Cooking is fun but there are a few golden rules it is wise to think about! Here they are in French which you could display in the cooking area of your classroom. An English translation is offered underneath.

Les règles d'or!

La cuisine, c'est drôle, mais attention aux casseroles brûlantes et aux couteaux! Tu dois absolument connaître et respecter quelques règles élémentaires. Applique-les chaque fois que tu fais la cuisine.

Attention!

N'entreprends rien s'il n'y a personne pour t'aider. Fais-toi aider par un adulte si tu dois utiliser un couteau pointu ou mettre quelque chose au four. Et n'hésite jamais à demander un conseil.

1. *Avant toute chose, lave-toi les mains et mets un tablier pour ne pas te tacher. Pense aussi à retrousser tes manches.*

2. *Rassemble les ingrédients. Pèse tous les aliments secs et mesure les liquides à l'aide du verre gradué.*

3. *Vérifie sur la recette que tu as tous les ingrédients et tous les ustensiles sous la main et que tu sais comment procéder.*

4. *Attention aux couteaux! Tiens-les toujours la pointe en bas et sers-toi d'une planche à découper.*

5. *Lorsque tu utilises la cuisinière, place toujours les casseroles avec le manche sur le côté. Cela t'évitera de les renverser.*

6. *Pour tourner tes sauces, utilise une cuillère en bois et tiens fermement le manche de la casserole.*

7. *Si tu dois manier des plats chauds ou faire quelque chose de difficile, demande de l'aide à un adulte.*

8. *Enfile un gant de cuisine avant d'empoigner des casseroles chaudes ou de mettre un plat au four.*

9. *Ne pose pas les plats chauds directement sur la table, mais sur une planche en bois ou un dessous-de-plat.*

10. *Sèche-toi bien les mains avant de brancher ou de débrancher le mixer ou un autre appareil électrique.*

11. *Garde toujours une éponge à portée de main. Si tu renverses quelque chose, répare tout de suite les dégâts.*

12. *Lave tes ustensiles au fur et à mesure. Lorsque tu as terminé, range-les et laisse la cuisine en ordre.*

Golden rules!

Cooking is fun but you need to be careful about hot saucepans and knives! You really need to know and respect some basic rules. Follow them each time you are in the kitchen.

Be careful!

Never do anything unless someone is there to help you. Ask an adult each time you see it in an instruction. Let an adult help you each time you need to use a pointed knife or put something in the oven. And never hesitate to ask for advice.

1.	Before anything else, wash your hands and put an apron on to prevent stains. Think about rolling back your sleeves too.

2.	Collect up your ingredients. Weigh all dry foods and measure liquids using a measuring glass.

3.	Check with the recipe that you have all the ingredients and all the utensils to hand and that you know what to do.

4.	Be careful with knives! Always hold them with the point downwards and use a chopping board.

5.	When you use the cooker, always put saucepans with their handles facing to one side. That will stop them being tipped over.

6.	Use a wooden spoon to stir sauces, and hold the handle of the saucepan firmly.

7.	If you need to handle hot dishes or do something difficult, ask an adult for help.

8.	Use an oven glove when handling saucepans or putting something in the oven.

9.	Don't put hot dishes straight onto the table, but use a wooden board or a place mat.

10.	Dry your hands well before switching a mixer on or off or using another type of electrical appliance.

11.	Always keep a cloth within arm's reach. If you spill anything, quickly wipe up the mess.

12.	Wash your utensils as you go along. When you have finished, tidy them away and leave the kitchen in good order.

In the kitchen: additional DVD materials

1.	Recipe in German for *Spritzgebäck* or piped biscuits

2.	Golden rules in German for the kitchen

3.	Useful websites

Project 4   Animation

Project Outline

Requirements: preparation time; animation software (you can do some really great animation without fancy expensive equipment or software); webcam.
Event time: this is best run as an ongoing activity or as an after-school/lunch club as one second of film on screen can take up to 25 frames.
Languages used: any language, but German is used in two examples on the DVD.

Introduction

Animation brings to life inanimate objects, be they cartoons, stick people, plasticine models, Fimo® figures, pine cones, silhouettes, rocks, twists of coloured wool – anything you like! You do not have to be good at art, and essentially all you need is imagination/inspiration for the ideas, patience to create and film the frames paper, a webcam and some software which does not need to be expensive. Making animations is hugely popular with many primary students and offers many possibilities for telling stories, explaining events, entertainment and communication – with much potential for foreign language use. As Oscar Stringer, professional animator says: "There is a degree of magic and mystery surrounding any form of animation, and I constantly see the same amazed reaction when children watch the first ten seconds of an animation they have made. This sense of amazement comes from the realisation that their models have been brought to life. They are really alive and have a character quite of their own! This magic really empowers students of all ages and abilities." Oscar's website details are included in the list of useful websites on the accompanying DVD.

Software

These software details and animation tips have been written by professional animator Jessica Langford. We are most grateful to her for letting us reproduce them here. Jessica's website details are included in the list of useful websites on the accompanying DVD to this project.

Many animation studios use programmes like Stop Motion Pro, or Dragon Stop Motion, but you can do some really great animation without fancy expensive equipment or software.

Have a look at ZU3d at www.zu3d.com. It's animation software for Windows PCs, designed for young people and schools to use.

A couple of other websites offer free downloads See for example SAM animation www.samanimation.com and Helium Frog www.heliumfrog.com.

The Animation for Education website (see useful websites on the accompanying DVD materials) is also well worth a visit as it provides information on webcams and software aimed at schools.

Animation tips

1. You can animate just about anything! You don't have to be brilliant at art. You can animate objects, plasticine characters, cardboard cut-outs, drawings, silhouettes, even yourselves! It's imagination and ideas that count.

2. There's a lot to think about when you make an animation film, so it's good to work with a friend.

3. Keep your ideas simple to start with, maybe animating just one or two characters in the first instance.

4. Prepare carefully. This saves time and unnecessary work later on.

5. Plan out your storyline and make a list of the main actions in each scene. It's very useful to draw up a simple storyboard. Divide an A4 sheet into 6 'boxes' and number them one to six. You may need several sheets for your film. A storyboard is a visual script showing the main actions and camera angles scene by scene. You can write notes about the sound track below each drawing. A storyboard helps everyone working on the film to see what the film will look like.

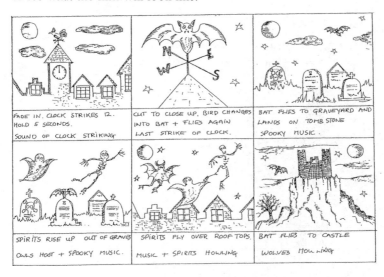
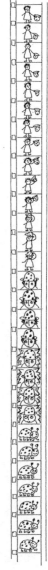

6. If you're working with a friend, make a character each. Take turns animating and operating the camera. This allows one person to concentrate on animating and the other to keep an eye on operating the camera and animation timings. Be patient! Animation is a very slow process.

7. Use different camera shots, close-ups and cut-aways to help tell your story and add drama. If you can add sound, save yourself work. For example, you don't need to animate a door opening. If the audience can hear it, they will imagine it themselves.

W.S. / Wide Shot   M.S. / Mid Shot   C.U. / Close Up.

8. Animation timings are always a surprise! One second of film on the screen is 25 frames. The amount you move your character depends on what kind of character it is. The slower the character's movement, the bigger the calibration. For example, if a snail has to move 30 centimetres across the scene and you want it to take five seconds on the screen, that's 125 frames. You can film two frames per animated movement, so you would need to animate (move) the snail 62 times! Divide the 30 centimetres into 62 calibrations so you know how much you need to move the snail each time. If it's a bee buzzing across the same space in two seconds, divide 30 centimetres into 25 calibrations. Move the character (make sure your hand is not in the frame!), take two frames and then move your character again. Your character must be **absolutely still** when you film it, so make sure the table, background art work, camera and tripod are firmly fixed and nothing wobbles!

TIMING AND MOVEMENT :-

1 SECOND = 24 FRAMES = 12 MOVEMENTS,
FILM 2 FRAMES AFTER EACH MOVEMENT.

ARM MOVES UP
IN ONE SECOND =
12 MOVES.

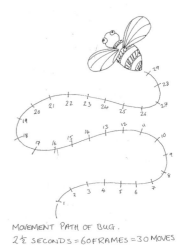

MOVEMENT PATH OF BUG.
2½ SECONDS = 60 FRAMES = 30 MOVES

4 SECONDS = 96 FRAMES = 48 MOVEMENT

9.   Most important rule – Enjoy!

On the DVD accompanying this project there are, first of all, two examples of short animations made by Alex in Year Five (aged 9) with soundtracks in German. Next there is a link to another film called *Hedgerow Tales*. This charming film was made by students at Buchlyvie Primary School in Stirlingshire, Scotland, and Winton Animation. It is just over five minutes long (which adds up to many thousands of frames – 7,200 in fact!) and is an excellent example of what can be done with everyday objects on your nature table/in your school's wildlife garden, combined with a soundtrack which is full of magical sound effects made by the students themselves: their own voices; rustling leaves; tapping stones; splashing water. The main story is about a group of creatures sitting around a campfire and telling each other stories. The teasel hedgehogs curling up in their burrow are simply delightful, as is the fish moving across the pond! A list of useful websites, which will lead you to software information as well as contacts for further information, is also included in the additional DVD materials.

Animation: additional DVD materials

1.   Two animations in German
2.   Examples of animated films × 3
3.   Selected stills from *Hedgerow Tales*
4.   Useful websites

Project 5   Creating word games

Project outline

Requirements: preparation time; paper; dictionary
Event time: 20 minutes for each activity
Languages used: German and Spanish

Introduction

Primary students tend to love games of all sorts whether physical (see, for example, *Fun with parachutes* in Part I) or involving words and new language. This project demonstrates how you can make simple word games that you can then set as an in-class task when some quiet time is needed, or give to students to do at home, perhaps as a whole-family activity. There are many websites which will help you to devise your own word searches and crosswords (see useful websites in the additional DVD materials for this project), but the word games presented here do not assume computer access, allowing you to be creative on a train perhaps, or when travelling away from your desk. There are occasions when you do have some spare thinking space and you could fill your thoughts with different areas of vocabulary that you would like to practise with your students through a variety of games. All you need is a piece of paper and a pencil to get started!

Word searches

The key to devising all word games lies in the planning. A word search is usually popular, and students are often familiar with what they have to do through magazines, comics and newspapers in their mother tongue.

Step One

To make a simple word search which will help your students revise specific areas of vocabulary, you first need to decide on a topic. If we take the topic 'fruit' as an example and work in Spanish, then you need to find a long word for a piece of fruit. This will be the word which defines the outline of your word search. A good example in Spanish of a long word in this vocabulary area is the word for an apricot: *el albaricoque*.

   You only need the noun and not the gender. Adding the gender could be a follow-on task for students once they have completed the word search.

Step Two

Albaricoque has eleven letters. Thus your word search will be eleven by eleven squares wide and long. Place your word in a line vertically, horizontally or diagonally. Word searches are normally written in capitals and your students will be used to this format.

Decision time!

1. You need to decide from the outset whether you will write some of the vocabulary items backwards as well as forwards. There are no rules here, but you need to take into account the abilities of your students.

2. You will also need to decide whether you are going to offer clues in writing – i.e., you provide the English translation of the words needed – or whether you are going to offer pictures of the items needed. In the 'Spanish fruit' example which follows, pictures have been drawn for the missing items and the words provided as well. Again there are no rules, but you obviously need to consider the abilities of your individual students. Pictures and writing are the easiest combination.

Step Three

Once your word is placed in the word square, which in this case is eleven squares by eleven, you need to add some other topic-related items which cross the original word on the grid. Here are examples of the next four words to be added.

```
M
A L B A R I C O Q U E
N                 V
Z                 A
A                 S
N A R A N J A S
A
S

L I M O N E S
```

Step Four

Now add in some more topic-related words until you are happy that you have sufficient vocabulary in the word search. Our 'fruit' example now has eight items in it and looks like this:

```
M         P
A L B A R I C O Q U E
N         Ñ       V
Z         A       A
A         S       S A
N A R A N J A S       Í
A                 D
S O N A T Á L P       N
                  A
L I M Ó N E S         S
```

Step Five

Complete the whole grid by filling in the empty spaces with random letters. Don't forget about the letters with accents as these can make the task more difficult if you put some in!

```
M W C S T P E D Ñ A S
A L B A R I C O Q U E
N C E Y O Ñ C I E V E
Z F F P T A V S T A B
A T B S A S B P A S A
N A R A N J A S C G Í
A F G Q A C B A U E D
S O N A T Á L P P L N
O R M N L P C A G E A
L I M Ó N E S Ñ E K S
```

Step Six

Now add your clues, and your word search is finished!

Eight pieces of fruit written in Spanish are hidden in this word search. Can you find them? Draw a circle around each word when you do find it. Here are the words in English and a picture of each one to help you!

Words

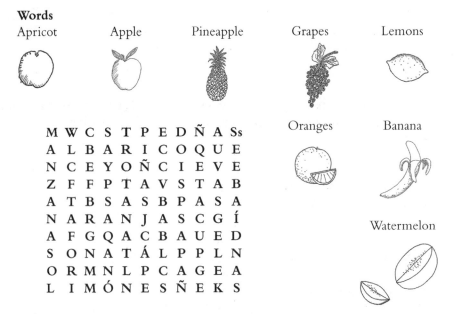

Apricot   Apple   Pineapple   Grapes   Lemons

```
M W C S T P E D Ñ A Ss
A L B A R I C O Q U E
N C E Y O Ñ C I E V E
Z F F P T A V S T A B
A T B S A S B P A S A
N A R A N J A S C G Í
A F G Q A C B A U E D
S O N A T Á L P P L N
O R M N L P C A G E A
L I M Ó N E S Ñ E K S
```

Oranges   Banana

Watermelon

An example of a word search which was made in the same way is included in German in the additional DVD materials for this project. The topic of this German one is 'Christmas presents'.

Crosswords

Simple crosswords are also fun to make and not particularly difficult either. Taking the same topic as before, but this time using German, the longest word in German for the eight fruit items is the word for watermelon (*die Wassermelone*), which has twelve letters. This word will be the spine of your crossword and will be placed vertically. The other words for the items of fruit simple cross it and each other where they can.

W
A
S
S
E
R
M
E
L
O
N
E

As the German words are arguably closer to the English translations, only the pictures are provided as clues this time. You will need to draw squares and add the numbers for each clue, but essentially your crossword is ready to use!

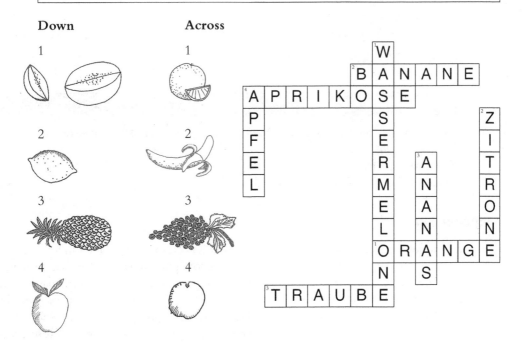

Down   **Across**

1   1

2   2

3   3

4   4

Building words

A favourite activity is to take a long word in the foreign language and make as many other words out of it as you can. It is surprising just how many words can be found in this way – and they do not necessarily have to be topic-related. For example, from the German word *Wassermelone* used above you can get all of the following words (and probably a few more!). This is an enjoyable way to while away that train journey!

Wasser	*Melone*	*was*	*er*	*man*
Essen	*Wesen*	*malen*	*so*	*wer*
Arme	*wen*	*wo*	*wem*	*Meer*
Samen	*losen*	*lesen*	*lerne*	*los*
Mal	*See*	*armlos*	*als*	*lassen*
leeren	*leer*	*Oma*		

Creating word games: additional DVD materials

1.   Word search in German: Christmas presents
2.   Useful websites

Project 6   Making cards

Project outline

Requirements: normal classroom, A4-sized white paper or thin cardboard, colouring pencils/felt-pens, glue, scissors
Event time: 30 minutes
Language targeted: French, German and Spanish

Introduction

Everyone likes to receive a greetings card, and it is both motivating and fun for students to be able to make them and send them in a foreign language! There are so many occasions when sending a card is appropriate: for example all the usual holidays – but also don't forget about World Hello Day and the European Day of Languages (both in Part III), as well as birthdays and other family days. This project explains how to create a few simple designs and then add a greeting in German, French or Spanish! A basic pop-up strip is presented first, which is followed by two examples of cards for different occasions made by folding triangles. A picture gallery with the completed versions of the cards demonstrated is included in the accompanying DVD for this project as well as some useful websites.

The pop-up strip

Instructions for your students.

1. Take two pieces of A4-sized paper or thin white cardboard. Fold each piece in half and put one piece aside.

2. In the middle of the folded edge of one of the pieces of paper, mark two crosses one centimetre apart.

3. Starting at the crosses draw two parallel lines out towards the middle of the paper but only 2.5 centimetres long.

4. Cut along the lines starting from the folded edge.

5. Fold the cut strip back and then fold it forwards again.

6. Open your card and hold it like a tent. Push the strip through to the other side of your card. Close the card and press firmly. Open it up again to see the little pop-up strip.

7. Draw a person or an animal or anything you like on another piece of paper and cut it out. Your figure can be a little bit wider and taller than the strip you have made.

8. Put some glue on your strip and stick your figure onto it. Make sure the bottom edge of your figure is on the same line as the bottom edge of the strip, otherwise the card will not open and close properly.

9. Now take the piece of card or paper you put to one side. This is now the outside of your card. Glue your card with the strip to the paper. When you open your card, the little figure you cut out will pop up.

10. Finally you need to decorate the front and inside of your card.

You can make a whole range of cards for various occasions by making different designs for the central pop-up piece. Here are some examples with appropriate greetings in French, German and Spanish:

Get well soon

Gute Besserung! (German)

Remets-toi vite! (French)

¡Que te mejores pronto! (Spanish)

Happy Birthday

Herzlichen Glückwunsch zum Geburtstag! (German)

Bon anniversaire! (French)

¡Feliz cumpleaños! (Spanish)

Good luck

Bonne chance! (French)

¡Buena suerte! (Spanish)

Viel Glück! (German)

Triangle-based pop-ups

Instructions for your students: the Valentine's card

1. Take two pieces of A4-sized paper or thin white cardboard. Fold each piece in half and put one piece aside.

2. Position the remaining piece of paper with the folded edge on your left. Fold the top corner downwards to make a triangle.

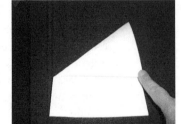

3. Fold back the triangle. Draw the top part of half a heart from the folded edge out to the triangle fold.

4.   Cut the top part of the heart but stop at the triangle fold line. Pull the heart out towards you. Press the fold lines to make the heart point forwards.

5.   Colour the heart and add some glitter too, if you like.

6.   Glue the outside of the card with the heart in it to the other piece of paper you laid to one side. Be careful not to put glue in the area of the pop-up heart.

7.   Now you need to decorate the front of your card and send it to someone you love.

I love you

Ich liebe dich! (German)

Je t'aime! (French)

¡Te amo! (Spanish)

Instructions for your students: the Easter card

1.   Follow instructions 1 and 2 for the Valentine's card.

2.   Fold back the triangle. Draw the top part of half a heart from the folded edge out to the triangle fold but smaller and lower down compared to the large heart you made for the Valentine's card.

3.   Cut the top part of the heart but stop at the triangle fold line. Pull the heart out towards you. Press the fold lines to make the heart point forwards. This is your flower vase.

4.   Colour the vase any colour you like and add some glitter too perhaps.

5.   Draw, colour and cut out some flowers, stems and leaves to put in the vase.

6.   Glue the flowers to the stems and the leaves to the stems.

7.   Glue the stems to the inside of the heart-shaped vase, making sure that the card will still fold in the middle. You could add a strip of blue paper in the background to make the sky.

8.   Glue the outside of the card with the heart in it to the other piece of paper you laid to one side. Be careful not to put glue in the area of the pop-up heart.

9.   Now you need to decorate the front of your card and send it to someone for Easter or perhaps for Mothers' or Fathers' Day.

Happy Easter

¡Felices Pascuas! (Spanish)

Frohe Ostern! (German)

Joyeuses Pâques! (French)

Instructions for your students: the Christmas card

1.   Take two pieces of A4-sized paper or thin white cardboard. Fold each piece in half and put one piece aside.

2.   Position the remaining piece of paper with the folded edge on your left. This time, fold the bottom corner upwards to make a triangle.

3.   Fold the triangle back and draw a curved line from the folded edge to the triangle fold.

4.   Cut along this curved line and stop when you reach the triangle fold mark.

5.   Open out the card and pull the shape towards you. If you press along the fold lines, your pop-up section will point towards you. This is going to be the dress of an angel, so you need to draw a face at the top of the triangle shape.

6.   Draw a halo and hair above the face, and add some hands and wings.

7.   Colour the angel's dress, and decorate the angel however you like.

8.   Finally, decorate the rest of your card.

Happy Christmas

Frohe Weihnachten! (German)

¡Feliz Navidad! (Spanish)

Joyeux Noël! (French)

For other greetings and useful phrases in different languages, the omniglot on-line dictionary can be very useful (see list of useful websites for this project on the accompanying DVD).

Making cards: additional DVD materials

1.   Picture gallery of completed cards

2.   Useful websites

Project 7   Language displays for the classroom

Project outline

Requirements: A4 card, scissors, glue, classroom equipment
Event time: half an hour for each item
Languages used: French and Spanish

Introduction

Displays are a crucial part of the primary classroom, showcasing excellent work done by each student and acting as a platform to teach vocabulary, ask questions and recap on lessons. Displays should be easy to create and assemble with written questions posed about the work shown. All these ideas have been tried and tested in classrooms and fit in with popular topics.

Organisation

Body topics

The face

On A4 white paper, each student draws their face shape, adding eyes, nose, etc., up to and including their neck, hopefully adding a big smile. They label the parts of the face in the language used, colour in the face realistically and mount on brightly coloured card. Hang the faces from the ceiling or a hoop or other structure so that they move in the breeze and add written questions about words used. Label the display *Bonjour, c'est moi! ¡Hola! Soy Yo.* An example of this display is included in the additional DVD materials for this project.

French		Spanish	
le nez:	nose	*la nariz*:	nose
la bouche:	mouth	*la boca*:	mouth
les yeux:	eyes	*los ojos*:	eyes
la tête:	head	*la cabeza*:	head
les cheveux:	hair	*el pelo*:	hair
les oreilles:	ears	*las orejas*:	ears
le cou:	neck	*el cuello*:	neck
les dents:	teeth	*los dientes*:	teeth

The body

You could use this idea in a similar way for the whole body.

Title: *Mon corps!/¡Mi cuerpo!*

French

la main:	hand
les doigts:	fingers
la jambe:	leg
le bras:	arm
l'estomac:	stomach
le coude:	elbow
le pied:	foot

Spanish

la mano:	hand
los dedos:	fingers
la rodilla:	leg
el brazo:	arm
el estómago:	stomach
el codo:	elbow
el pie:	foot

The skeleton

You could also label a skeleton picture (such as the one in Part I, Project 4, about Wilhelm Röntgen, who discovered X-rays) with its bones labelled.

Title: *Bones! Skeleton!/Les os! un squelette!/Los huesos! Un esqueleto!*

French		**Spanish**	
le dos:	back	*la espalda*:	back
les hanches:	hips	*las caderas*:	hips
others as above			

A monster

Make a monster picture with parts of the monster's body labelled as before. Two examples are included in the picture gallery for this project on the accompanying DVD.

Title: *Mon monstre/Mi monstruo.*

A poster

Make a large display of a child's body and label the parts in both languages, perhaps to celebrate European Day of Languages (see also Part III Project 3). Ask a child to lie down on the ground on large paper, draw round their body and ask children to colour the child in suitable clothes. Make multilingual labels as above.

Myself

Use a photograph of each child or a picture of their face and add a speech bubble with statements or a spidergram of sentences around it. Compile all the statements a child might know at an early stage of learning: for example, hello and goodbye; greetings for different parts of the day; name; age; family members; the town where they live, etc.

Title: *Bonjour!/¡Hola!*

French

bonjour:	hello/good morning/good day
bonsoir:	good evening
bonne nuit:	good night
au revoir:	goodbye
comment ça va?:	How are you?
je m'appelle …:	My name is …
j'ai … ans:	I am … years old
j'ai un père, une mère, un frère, une soeur:	I've got a father, mother, brother, sister
j'habite à Londres:	I live in London.

Spanish

hola, buenos días:	Good day
buenas noches:	Goodnight
adiós:	Goodbye
hasta la vista:	Good bye
cómo estás:	How are you?
yo me llamo …:	my name is …
tengo …. años:	I'm …. years old
tengo un padre, una madre, un hermano, una hermana:	I've got a father, mother, brother, sister
vivo en Londres:	I live in London

My Shield

Use the shape of a school shield, with its different sections, for each child to say four important things about themselves. It could be one family statement (for example, how many brothers or sisters), one statement about where they live (for example, house or flat), two statements about likes and dislikes (for example, I like playing tennis). Draw a picture of each statement with a sentence for each either inside the shield or near the rim.

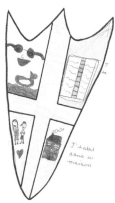

Title: *Mon bouclier/Mi escudo.*

French

Mon bouclier:	my shield
J'ai un frère/une soeur/deux soeurs:	I've got one brother/one sister/ two sisters
Je suis fille unique/fils unique:	I'm an only daughter/son
J'habite dans un appartement/une maison:	I live in a flat/house
J'aime/Je n'aime pas:	I like/ I don't like
faire du sport:	doing sport
écouter de la musique:	listening to music.

Spanish

Mi escudo:	my shield
tengo un hermano/una hermana/ dos hermanas:	I've got one brother/ one sister/two sisters
soy hijo único/hija única:	I'm an only son/daughter.
vivo en una casa/un apartamento:	I live in a house/flat
me gusta/no me gusta:	I like/I don't like
el deporte:	sport
escuchar música:	listening to music.

Colours

Each child draws a fish or bird or butterfly and colours it in just one or two colours. Label the colours, hang the pictures to float from the ceiling or make sea/sky background and scatter them over it. Butterflies work well, because you could make each side a different colour and attach them down the middle to make a 3D effect.

Title: *Les couleurs/Los colores*

French		Spanish	
le poisson:	fish	*el pez*:	fish
un oiseau:	bird	*el pájaro*:	bird
le papillon:	butterfly	*la mariposa*:	butterfly
rouge:	red	*rojo*:	red
bleu:	blue	*azul*:	blue
jaune:	yellow	*amarillo*:	yellow
vert:	green	*verde*:	green
rose:	pink	*rosa*:	pink
brun:	brown	*marrón*:	brown
orange:	orange	*naranja*:	orange
blanc:	white	*blanco*:	white

Balloons on a string

Each student draws four or more balloons as if tied together on a string, colours each balloon a different colour and labels the colours. Fasten the collection to a hoop or background of the sky as before.

Title: *Les ballons/Los globos*
Alternatively this could be socks on a line (*les chaussettes/los calcetines*), pencils in a pot (*les crayons/los lápices*), flowers in a vase (*les fleurs/las flores*).

Food

Draw round a dinner plate on a sheet of A4 card to make a pizza shape. Divide it into three or four segments and draw/colour different ingredients in each segment, for example, cheese, ham, sausage, etc. Label the segments on the outside of the pizza ring so that they stand out.

Title: *J'ai faim! J'aime les pizzas!/¡Tengo hambre! ¡Me gusta la pizza!/* I'm hungry! I like pizza!

French		**Spanish**	
le fromage:	cheese	*Queso*:	cheese
le jambon:	ham	*Jamón*:	ham
le saucisson:	sausage	*Salchicha*:	sausage
l'ananas:	pineapple	*Piña*:	pineapple
le thon:	tuna	*Atún*:	tuna
les tomates:	tomatoes	*Tomates*:	tomatoes

Breakfast

Investigate what a typical breakfast might be and illustrate a plate of food. An example of a completed display is included in the picture gallery on the accompanying DVD for this project.

French		**Spanish**	
le petit déjeuner:	breakfast	*el desayuno*:	breakfast
les céréales:	cereal	*los cereales*:	cereal
un croissant:	a croissant	*el pan*:	bread
un pain au chocolat:	a chocolate 'roll'	*la mantequilla*:	butter
du beurre:	some butter	*la mermelada*:	marmalade
de la confiture:	some jam	*el yogur*:	yoghurt
du yaourt:	some yoghurt		

Picnic or packed lunch box

Each child draws their own packed lunch box opened up to display the contents (or if they eat school dinners, their imaginary favourite box). They draw and label what's inside. This could be used as a good impetus for discussions about Healthy Eating or part of a science topic on food. *Note that in Spain and France children do not take packed lunch to school so the words for lunchbox are unusual and the concept very strange. This could be the start of an interesting cultural comparison about the importance of food in each country and about different aspects of school life.*

Title: *J'ai faim / Tengo hambre* – I'm hungry

French

une boîte à sandwiches:	lunchbox
un sandwich au fromage / au jambon:	a cheese/ham sandwich
des chips:	crisps
un biscuit:	biscuit
une pomme:	apple
une boisson:	drink

Spanish

un picnic:	lunch box
un bocadillo de queso / de jámon:	a cheese/ham sandwich
patatas fritas:	crisps
una galleta:	biscuit
una fruta:	piece of fruit
una manzana:	apple
una bebida:	drink

Weather

Set up a section for a weather forecast for the week ahead, complete with a map of France/Spain. Groups of students could take it in turns to give a daily forecast and could prepare a written report to be posted on the board.

Title: *Quel temps fait-il? / Qué tiempo hace?* – What's the weather like?

French		**Spanish**	
la météo:	forecast	*el tiempo*:	weather
il fait froid:	it's cold	*hace frío*:	it's cold
il fait chaud:	it's hot	*hace calor*:	it's hot
il neige:	it's snowing	*está nevando*:	it's snowing
il pleut:	it's raining	*está lloviendo*:	it's raining
il y a du vent:	it's windy	*hace viento*:	it's windy

il y a du soleil:	it's sunny	*hace sol*:	it's sunny
il y a un orage:	it's stormy	*hay tormenta*:	it's stormy

For the sake of simplicity, keep the forecast in the present tense as these are the most common phrases that primary students will encounter.

The snowman

Draw a snowman and label the clothing he may need. An example of a completed display is included in the picture gallery for this project on the accompanying DVD.

Title: *Le bonhomme de neige / La figura de nieve.*

French

une écharpe:	scarf
un chapeau:	hat
les gants:	gloves
les boutons:	buttons

Spanish

una bufanda:	scarf
un sombrero:	hat
los guantes:	gloves
los botones:	buttons

Travel

Place a map of Europe on the wall with countries labelled in French/Spanish. Children add their list of countries they have travelled to during an imagined week. Add appropriate flags.

Title: *Où vas-tu ? / ¿A dónde vas?* – Where are you going?

Days of the week and places to go

French

lundi, mardi, mercredi, jeudi, vendredi, samedi, dimanche

Je vais (I go) *en France; en Italie; en Allemagne; en Espagne; en Suisse; au Portugal; au Japon; au Danemark*

Spanish

lunes, martes, miércoles, jueves, viernes, sábado, domingo

Voy (I go) *a Francia; a Italia; a Alemania; a España; a Suiza; a Portugal; a Japón; a Dinamarca*

Holiday Suitcase

Each student draws the shape of a suitcase with a handle attached and draws a selection of labelled clothes they would take on holiday.

Title: *En vacances!/¡Vacaciones!* – On holiday.

French		**Spanish**	
ma valise:	my suitcase	*mi maleta*:	my suitcase
un pantalon:	trousers	*los pantalones*:	trousers
un short:	shorts	*los pantalones cortos*:	shorts
un tee-shirt:	T shirt	*la camiseta*:	T shirt
une robe:	dress	*el vestido*:	dress
une jupe:	skirt	*la falda*:	skirt
la chemise:	shirt	*la camisa*:	shirt
un chapeau:	hat	*el sombrero*:	hat

Animals and habitats

Collect a series of pictures of animals and their habitats. Group them according to their habitat and label them accordingly. Examples of completed displays are included in the picture gallery for this project on the accompanying DVD.

Title: *Où habites-tu? ¿Dónde vives?* –
Where do you live?

French

Où habites-tu?:
Where do you live?

J'habite dans la mer/dans la ferme/dans l'arbre/dans la jungle/dans la forêt:
I live in the sea/on the farm/in the tree/in the jungle/ in the forest.

Spanish

¿Donde vives?: Where do you live?

Vivo en el mar/la granja/el árbol/la selva/el bosque:
I live in the sea/on the farm/in the tree/in the jungle/in the forest.

Language displays for the classroom: additional DVD materials

1.   Picture gallery

3

Languages, celebrations and festivals

Introduction

It is easy to find a reason to celebrate – and celebrating in a foreign language can be just as much fun! There are seven reasons to celebrate presented in this third part, all of which seek to promote intercultural understanding and active language use. Whilst some of the projects are longer than others – for example, *It's Christmas* covers five sessions – all are bursting with fresh ideas and detailed information. In this part you can celebrate the *Day of the Dead* in Spanish, make a German nutcracker bookmark and do some cooking in French to name but a few of the things it contains. Two of the projects in this part (*Day of the Dead* and *It's Christmas*) derive from the work of *Routes into Languages*, a national initiative established in 2007 (www.routesintolanguages.ac.uk). *Routes into Languages* is designed to promote the take-up and continued study of foreign languages in the 14–19 age range by motivating students, particularly in secondary schools, to participate in a wide variety of events, projects and activities initiated by universities in discrete regions. The main aim of all the projects however, is to provide a taste of life in a different country through the foreign language – and have fun at the same time!

Project 1 It's Christmas!

Introduction

Christmas is always fun in the classroom, and this theme provides a wealth of materials for primary-school students to explore in German. After all, many of our own Christmas traditions and customs originate in German-speaking countries, several of which were brought to England by Prince Albert from Germany in the nineteenth century, such as the Christmas tree and the advent calendar. Christmas markets are frequently found in major English towns nowadays and often form the basis of secondary-school trips abroad if these are run. One of the oldest Christmas markets is to be found in Vienna (dating back to 1294), whilst the first Christmas market recorded in Germany was held in Bautzen, close to the border with the Czech Republic, in 1384 (Walker, Williams and Stewart 2009). Increasingly in England, people eat special foods that come to us from Germany at Christmas time, such as *Stollen* (for which the town of Dresden is famous), marzipan (associated with Lübeck) and spiced gingerbread biscuits or *Lebkuchen* (produced in Nürnberg since the fourteenth century).

Whilst many traditions are the same or similar in England and Germany, some are very different. In northern Germany, carp and potato salad are traditionally eaten on Christmas Eve, whereas we traditionally eat turkey on Christmas Day. German children put their shoes or boots outside their bedroom doors (or the front door to the house) on the night of December 5th ready for Saint Nikolaus, the patron saint of children, to pay them a visit in the night and help them celebrate Nikolaustag, St Nicholas Day, on December 6th by leaving sweets, nuts, oranges and small presents behind (but only if the children have been good!). Traditionally Saint Nikolaus is accompanied by his servant, Knecht Ruprecht, who leaves bundles of twigs in the shoes if the children have been naughty!

This project explores some of the language needed to bring a German Christmas alive in the classroom and presents five 40-minute lessons, which could run over as many weeks or take place at intervals throughout the autumn term, as appropriate. Each activity aims to present some relevant language and a motivating task, as well as some interesting background information to celebrating Christmas the German way! A special Christmas story is included at the end of the part too with its translation on the accompanying DVD for this project.

Session One: The Advent calendar

Aims: to introduce some background information; to establish numbers in German up to 24 and the letters of the German alphabet.

The Advent calendar as we know it today has its origins in Germany, with the first known example being handmade in 1851. The first printed Advent calendars were produced in Hamburg in 1902 or 1903 according to some sources, whilst others say that Herr Lang, a printer who worked in Munich, was responsible for printing the first Advent calendars in 1908. The first chocolate-filled Advent calendar was sold in Germany somewhat later, in 1958.

This Advent calendar comes from the German Embassy in London (see list of useful websites on the accompanying DVD materials), where it is presented in 3D. It was drawn by Bettina Mayer, and we are grateful to her for allowing us to use it here. This closed example can be adapted to suit your class with a new question posed each day.

Design: SAY HELLO! Graphic Design,
-www.bettinamayer.com-

Advent calendars are a good way to introduce your class to numbers in German up to twenty-four. Here they are:

eins	*zwei*	*drei*	*vier*
fünf	*sechs*	*sieben*	*acht*
neun	*zehn*	*elf*	*zwölf*
dreizehn	*vierzehn*	*fünfzehn*	*sechzehn*
siebzehn	*achtzehn*	*neunzehn*	*zwanzig*
einundzwanzig	*zweiundzwanzig*	*dreiundzwanzig*	*vierundzwanzig*

You could also use the Advent calendar to introduce the letters of the alphabet too, as a word can be hidden inside the calendar which has 24 letters. Ask your class to try to work out what the word is in German from the jumbled letters, one of which will appear each day behind the door; you can disclose the letters in any order. A suggested word (24 letters including the gender) for this example is *die Weihnachtssüßigkeiten* (the Christmas sweets).

It makes sense to introduce the letters in alphabetical order – perhaps a couple each day at registration time. Starting with 'a' (which is in the given example word), add 'b' in the same session, and move on to 'c' (in the example) and 'd' the next time. Gradually the complete alphabet is built up. The full alphabet in German could be displayed on your classroom wall, perhaps in a dedicated languages section (see also Project 7 in Part II *Language Displays for the Classroom*).

Das Alphabet

a = ah	b = bay	c = tsay	d = day
e = ay	f = eff	g = gay	h = hah
i = ee	j = yot	k = kah	l = ell
m = emm	n = enn	o = oh	p = pay
q = koo	r = air	s = ess	t = tay
u = ooh	v = fow	w = vay	x = ix
y = oopsillon	z = tset	ß = ess tset	

In the additional DVD section which accompanies this project there are three more Advent calendars. One is reproduced courtesy of the UK–German Connection and gives a taste of what can be found on their website. It includes instructions for making special Christmas stars. The second calendar is in French and can be found on a weblink, whilst the final link is to an online world advent calendar. All of them are lovely and well worth a visit!

Session Two: What can you see?

Aim: to introduce some Christmas-themed vocabulary through picture recognition.

Ask the students to look at the pictures and see whether they can work out what they can see first. They could work in small groups and use their imaginations; it is often easier to predict new vocabulary than might be imagined! Check the answers with the class afterwards.

Was siehst du hier? **1**

1) *einen Adventskalender*

2) *einen Lebkuchen*

3) *einen Schneemann*

Was siehst du hier? **2**

1) *eine Glocke*

2) *eine Kerze*

3) *eine Krippe*

Was siehst du hier? **3**

1) *ein Rentier*

2) *ein Geschenk*

3) *einen Weihnachtsbaum*

Was siehst du hier? **4**

1) *eine Weihnachtsgans*

2) *einen Weihnachtsmann*

3) *eine Christbaumkugel*

Was siehst du hier? **5**

1) *einen Weihnachtsstern*

2) *einen Adventskranz*

3) *einen Engel*

Was siehst du hier? **6**

1) *eine Kerze*

2) *einen Lebkuchen*

3) *ein Rentier*

Was siehst du hier? **7**	*Was siehst du hier?* **8**	*Was siehst du hier?* **9**
1) *einen Adventskalender* 2) *einen Lebkuchen* 3) *einen Schneemann*	1) *eine Glocke* 2) *eine Kerze* 3) *eine Krippe*	1) *ein Rentier* 2) *ein Geschenk* 3) *einen Weihnachtsbaum*
Was siehst du hier? **10**	Was siehst du hier? **11**	Was siehst du hier? **12**

1) *eine Weihnachtsgans* 2) *einen Weihnachtsmann* 3) *eine Christbaumkugel*	1) *einen Weihnachtsstern* 2) *einen Adventskranz* 3) *einen Engel*	1) *eine Kerze* 2) *einen Lebkuchen* 3) *ein Rentier*
Was siehst du hier? **13**	*Was siehst du hier?* **14**	*Was siehst du hier?* **15**

1) *einen Adventskalender* 2) *einen Lebkuchen* 3) *einen Schneemann*	1) *eine Glocke* 2) *eine Kerze* 3) *einen Weihnachtsstern*	1) *ein Rentier* 2) *eine Christbaumkugel* 3) *einen Weihnachtsbaum*

Answers

Picture 1: *der Adventskalender*	Picture 9: *der Weihnachtsbaum*
Picture 2: *die Krippe*	Picture 10: *die Weihnachtsgans*
Picture 3: *das Geschenk*	Picture 11: *der Adventskranz*
Picture 4: *der Weihnachtsmann*	Picture 12: *das Rentier*
Picture 5: *der Engel*	Picture 13: *der Lebkuchen*
Picture 6: *die Kerze*	Picture 14: *der Weihnachtsstern*
Picture 7: *der Schneemann*	Picture 15: *die Christbaumkugel*
Picture 8: *die Glocke*	

Tip: It is a good idea to learn the gender of the noun along with the word right from the start. In this way patterns are formed.

An extension to this vocabulary activity is to play Bingo with the following clues. Read out the clues and ask the students to tick the corresponding picture each time. The winner is the first person to tick all the pictures correctly and shout out BINGO! The pictures could be displayed on the whiteboard with or without the vocabulary (it is obviously easier if the words are visible). You can mime/gesture some of the words to teach the concepts (for example: make antlers with your hands on the reindeer; flap your hands behind your back to make the angel's wings; smack your lips to show how tasty the Lebkuchen are; open and close the classroom door to demonstrate a door; point to the picture of the candle: hold up four fingers to show the advent wreath etc).

Clues/Hinweise
Ich habe 24 Türen (der Adventskalender)
Ich schmecke lecker! (der Lebkuchen)
Ich habe vier Kerzen (der Adventskranz)
Ich habe Geweihe auf meinem Kopf (das Rentier)
Man hängt mich auf den Weihnachtsbaum (die Christbaumkugel)
Ich bin aus Schnee gebaut (der Schneemann)
Ich habe Flügel (der Engel)
Man hört mich überall (die Glocke)
Unter mir liegen oft Geschenke (der Weihnachtsbaum)
Man öffnet mich am 24sten Dezember in Deutschland (das Geschenk)
Ich bin das Weihnachtsmahl (die Weihnachtsgans)
Ich bringe die Geschenke (der Weihnachtsmann)
Normalerweise bin ich aus Wachs gemacht (die Kerze)
Man kann mich oft am Himmel sehen (der Weihnachtsstern)
Hier kannst du auch Tiere finden (die Krippe)

Session Three: A German Christmas carol

Aims: to learn a traditional German Christmas carol and to have some fun with music.

Most people enjoy singing, and learning a Christmas carol in a different language is good fun. This is a very popular German Christmas carol, which was written by Joseph Mohr in 1816. It has been translated into over 300 languages and is well-known all over the world. You can play your class a recording of the first verse from Austrian Public Television ORF by looking at the useful websites on the additional DVD. You can also download the sheet music. Your class might like to learn *Silent Night* in German to sing in a whole-school assembly, perhaps near to the end of the Christmas term!

Stille Nacht
DEUTSCH

Music: Franz Xaver Gruber, 1818
Words: Joseph Mohr, 1816/1818

Stille Nacht, heilige Nacht,
Alles schläft; einsam wacht
Nur das traute hochheilige Paar.
Holder Knabe im lockigen Haar,
Schlaf in himmlischer Ruh!
Schlaf in himmlischer Ruh!

Stille Nacht, heilige Nacht,
Hirten erst kundgemacht
Durch der Engel Halleluja,
Tönt es laut von fern und nah:
Christ, der Retter ist da!
Christ, der Retter ist da!

Stille Nacht, heilige Nacht,
Gottes Sohn, o wie lacht
Lieb' aus deinem göttlichen Mund,
Da uns schlägt die rettende Stund'.
Christ, in deiner Geburt!
Christ, in deiner Geburt!

Heute singt man nur die Strophen 1, 6
und 2 (oben) von der originellen
Joseph-Mohr-Version (1816).

Silent Night
ENGLISH

Music: Franz Xaver Gruber, 1818
Words: John Freeman Young, 1863

Silent night, holy night,
All is calm all is bright
'Round yon virgin Mother and Child
Holy infant so tender and mild
Sleep in heavenly peace
Sleep in heavenly peace

Silent night, holy night,
Shepherds quake at the sight.
Glories stream from heaven afar,
Heav'nly hosts sing Alleluia;
Christ the Savior is born
Christ the Savior is born

Silent night, holy night,
Son of God, love's pure light.
Radiant beams from Thy holy face,
With the dawn of redeeming grace,
Jesus, Lord, at Thy birth
Jesus, Lord, at Thy birth

Today only verses 1, 6 and 2 (above)
from the original Joseph Mohr
version (1816) are sung.

Session Four: The preposition game

Aim: to focus attention on different German prepositions through a game.

This game is very simple to organise. Copy six of the pictures from Session Two and enlarge them (if you then laminate them, they will last longer!). Hide the pictures in six different places around the classroom. For example, you could take the reindeer (*das Rentier*), the angel (*der Engel*), the bell (*die Glocke*), the Christmas goose (*die Weihnachtsgans*), the snowman (*der Schneemann*) and Father Christmas (*der Weihnachtsmann*) and place one in a corner, one on a chair, one on the floor, one under the table, one on the table and one behind the door. Ask your students to work in small groups and find the six hidden pictures. They should then complete the sentences on the following handout (or you could display the sentences on the whiteboard and complete them together).

Preposition game/Präpositionenspiel

Six pictures are hidden somewhere in the classroom. But where? Find the pictures and complete the following sentences.

Sechs Bilder sind irgendwo im Klassenzimmer versteckt. Aber wo? Findet die Bilder und ergänzt die folgenden Sätze.

Clues/Hinweise			
in the corner:	*in der Ecke*	on a chair:	*auf einem Stuhl*
on the floor:	*auf dem Boden*	under the table:	*unter dem Tisch*
on the table:	*auf dem Tisch*	behind the door:	*hinter der Tür*

1. *Das Rentier ist _____ der Ecke.*
2. *Der Engel befindet sich _____ einem Stuhl.*
3. *Die Glocke ist _____ dem Boden.*
4. *Die Weihnachtsgans ist _____ dem Tisch.*
5. *Der Schneemann ist _____ dem Tisch.*
6. *Der Weihnachtsmann ist _____ der Tür.*

Answers

1. *Das Rentier ist in der Ecke.*
2. *Der Engel befindet sich auf einem Stuhl.*
3. *Die Glocke ist auf dem Boden.*
4. *Die Weihnachtsgans ist unter dem Tisch.*
5. *Der Schneemann ist auf dem Tisch.*
6. *Der Weihnachtsmann ist hinter der Tür.*

Can your students remember the words in German for: the chair (*der Stuhl*); the table (*der Tisch*); the door (*die Tür*); the floor (*der Boden*); the corner (*die Ecke*)?

You may notice that the words following these prepositions are indirect objects and take the dative case in German. It is not important to point this out to your students, but they should learn the correct patterns, for example, in **der** *Ecke*, etc.

Session Five: German nutcrackers

Aims: to introduce colours and body parts/items of clothing in the context of the German nutcracker.

People have eaten nuts for many hundreds if not thousands of years. Indeed, the tools for opening nuts have been around for at least 2,000 years. According to German folklore, nutcrackers are a popular gift at Christmas time, as they are supposed to bring good luck and protect the home from evil spirits and danger. The typical German nutcracker (or *Nußknacker*) doesn't look very pretty! It comes in the form of a misshapen little man who often has a grim look and an angry mouth – presumably to help chase away evil spirits and protect the home. Traditionally, German nutcrackers were in the form of a policeman, a king or a soldier – all figures of authority which can protect the people. The nutcracker in the picture is a lawyer and nowadays you can buy all sorts of nutcrackers doing all sorts of jobs! But they all typically have a lever in their backs to open the nuts.

The centre of nutcracker production in Germany is in the Erzgebirge region, which lies in the east of the country close to the border with the Czech Republic. This area was once an important mining region, but when supplies of ore to mine became scarcer, the miners turned to making hand-carved nutcrackers from the wood that surrounded them instead.

The first Erzgebirge nutcracker was crafted in 1865 in the workshop of a family named Füchtner. There are many people who collect nutcrackers today and each year interest in nutcrackers is renewed as Tchaikovsky's ballet *The Nutcracker* come to towns throughout the world as part of the Christmas holiday tradition. Perhaps someone in your class has seen it?

The nutcracker on the left is based around a design by the German company Käthe Wohlfahrt GmbH & Co. OHG, which sells all sorts of traditional German Christmas items (see list of useful websites on the accompanying DVD).

Your students could colour in the picture which also presents a good opportunity to learn some colours in German and items of clothing/parts of the body. Here is some vocabulary you could use:

Colours		Clothes/body parts	
red:	*rot*	hat:	*der Hut*
green:	*grün*	shirt:	*das Hemd*
white:	*weiß*	trousers:	*die Hose*
black:	*schwarz*	sleeves:	*die Ärmel*
blue:	*blau*	hair:	*die Haare*
yellow:	*gelb*	eyes:	*die Augen*
brown:	*braun*	beard:	*der Bart*
gold:	*gold*	face:	*das Gesicht*
silver:	*silber*	hands:	*die Hände*
pink:	*rosa*	teeth:	*die Zähne*

After the students have coloured in the picture, they could form simple sentences along these lines:

Der Hut is rot und gold.

Das Gesicht is rosa.

Die Zähne sind gelb.

Der Bart is braun.

Die Augen sind blau.

Die Hose ist silber (note the singular verb needed).

Das Hemd ist grün und gold.

Die Ärmel sind schwarz.

Die Haare sind weiß (note the plural verb needed).

A lovely soldier nutcracker is pictured with the lawyer nutcracker in the additional DVD materials to this project.

Here is a different nutcracker which could also be coloured in by your students. This one makes a good bookmark.

Ask your class to colour in the nutcracker. Then stick the nutcracker onto cardboard. Your students could write 'Happy Christmas and Happy New Year' in German on the back (*Frohe Weihnachten und ein gutes neues Jahr!*). Then laminate the bookmark. Using a hole punch, make a hole in the top of the bookmark above the nutcracker's head. Tie some ribbon through the hole and display the finished book mark. It will certainly make an unusual Christmas present!

Session Six: A Christmas story

German families often read stories and poems to each other at Christmas time. In some homes it is traditional for the parents to keep a room locked until Christmas Eve, when it is opened and the children can then enjoy the presents around the tree and all the decorations on it. There are also fruit and nuts and Christmas biscuits – see Project 3 in Part II (*In the kitchen*) for how to make some – as well as carols and the Christmas story, which is read by a member of the family each year.

The three trolls is a special Christmas story written in English with a German translation included on the additional DVD materials for this part. The German translation will probably be too difficult for your students to understand, but you may like to read it yourself! First you might like to do some simple sentence-building with your class, using the picture of the three trolls and the gap-fill activity before you read the Christmas story.

Task

Fill in the gaps in the story with the correct word in German to complete the sentence. All the missing words have been presented in previous lessons.

Vocabulary			
kleiner(e):	smaller	*die Zauberaxt*:	a magic axe
trägt from *tragen*:	to carry/to wear	*kommt* from *kommen*:	to come
hält from *halten*:	to hold	*die Spitze*:	the top
die Laterne:	lantern		

Hier sind die ___ **(three)** *kleinen Wichtelmännchen. Der erste heißt Heinzl. Er hat einen* ____ **(gingerbread)** *und eine Laterne. Der zweite heißt Berndl, der eine kleinere Laterne und eine Zauberaxt trägt. Dann kommt Fritzl, der in einer Hand zwei* _____ **(presents)** *hat und in der anderen Hand einen* **(Christmas tree)** *hält. Der Weihnachtsbaum hat einen goldenen* _____ **(star)** *auf der Spitze.*

Answers

Hier sind die **drei** *kleinen Wichtelmännchen. Der erste heißt Heinzl. Er hat einen* **Lebkuchen** *und eine Laterne. Der zweite heißt Berndl, der eine kleinere Laterne und eine Zauberaxt trägt. Dann kommt Fritzl, der in einer Hand zwei* **Geschenke** *hat und in der anderen Hand einen Weihnachtsbaum hält. Der* **Weihnachtsbaum** *hat einen goldenen* **Stern** *auf der Spitze.*

And now here is the story.

The three trolls/Die drei Wichtelmännchen

(written by Cathy Watts and illustrated by Nicola Goodland)

The three tiny trolls came out of the woods on that freezing December night and walked down the hillside towards the village that crouched at the bottom of the valley. Despite the small size of their feet, their wooden-soled leather shoes crunched through the ice which had formed in the grooves along the pathway. It had been a long, hard winter that year, and there were still no signs of a thaw. A million stars twinkled overhead in the icy black night sky, and a new moon cast a thin strip of silver light in front of them as they walked along.

All was silent on that magical night, the night when the three trolls were to complete their separate tasks. Heinzl came first along the track, holding a piece of never-ending gingerbread and a lantern on the end of a long pole. His gifts could feed the hungriest human and light up the humblest cottage. Berndl came next, and he carried a smaller lantern and a magical axe which could split any tree into as many logs as were needed. And then there was Fritzl, who held two presents in one hand and in the other a tiny Christmas tree which even had a golden star on the top. He was looking to bring Christmas into the house of a family who had nothing at all.

The street lights from the village in the valley below seemed to beckon to Heinzl,

Berndl and Fritzl as they crunched through the icy night, leaving the dark pinewoods behind them. Each troll had the friendliest face you could possibly imagine, and all wore hats over their hair. Their clothes were different shades of brown, and Berndl and Fritzl sported the most magnificent silvery-grey beards which matched their long, wispy hair. Berndl's beard tumbled around his face in beautiful, silvery-grey curls of which he was enormously proud. Heinzl wore a brown scarf instead of a beard, as he was the youngest. On his head perched a light-brown, knitted bobble hat which stood up straight and tall above his dark-brown hair. The other two trolls also wore hats. Fritzl's was the same as Heinzl's, only edged with fur, but he wore it folded down across one shoulder and had fastened a sprig of holly to the front. Berndl wore a beret made of brown felt, which gave him quite a jaunty look, he thought.

As the three friends tramped along the frozen path towards the village in the valley below, they came to a humble cottage set back in the trees on one side of the pathway. Peering in through a low window the trolls saw a very faint glimmer from a very weak fire and a boy dressed in rags weeping silently and sitting at a bare, wooden table. The three friendly trolls approached the young boy who was a woodcutter's son and asked him what was wrong.

"All our logs are frozen," he said sadly, "and we can't even heat our own cottage, let alone sell any logs to anyone in the village. Our tools simply can't split the logs, and the whole village depends on us." And he wept in utter despair as he thought of his parents out feeding the chickens in that freezing December night and the folk in the village who could not get warm enough even to celebrate Christmas.

"Come outside with me to your log pile," said Berndl in a kindly voice and the boy, wiping the tears from his pale, cold cheeks, followed him meekly. Once outside, Berndl raised his axe which gleamed silver in the moonlight and split all the logs with twenty blows

"Wow!" breathed the woodcutter's son in wondermentand, gathering up an armful of logs, he returned to his cottage to build up the fire. Inside the cottage Heinzl had placed his magical gingerbread on the table next to three platesand Fritzl had put two Christmas presents on the hearth next to the crackling fire. Berndl stood his smaller lantern on the mantelpiece above the fireplace, and when the woodcutter and his wife eventually returned from feeding the chickens outside, they found warmth and light from the roaring log fire and Berndl's lamp, with food on the table and even two Christmas presents to open. Leaving the magical axe for the woodcutter to keep, Heinzl, Berndl and Fritzl slipped silently away and carried on their way along the frozen path towards the village down in the valley. All they had left now was the Christmas tree and the lantern on the end of Heinzl's tall pole.

As they approached the outskirts of the village, not a soul appeared. The street lights flickered overhead, and the trolls' wooden-soled leather shoes made tiny scratching noises over the ice. They could see their breath before them like three small puffs of dragon smoke. But there were no signs of any living creature: all the shutters on the houses were closed, and everyone seemed to have locked themselves away. Fritzl, Heinzl and Berndl walked on in silence until they came to the main square. There they stopped and set down the Christmas tree, which twinkled and sparkled in the moonlight. Next to it they placed the large lantern on the end of Heinzl's pole. And all around the tree, lit up by the lantern, appeared piles and piles of logs as if by magic, all different shapes and sizes and all of them dry and ready for burning.

As Fritzl, Heinzl and Berndl turned to go back up the icy pathway towards the pinewoods ahead, they heard the front door of a cottage open and a shout of joy as the logs were found. Then more voices joined in and the lights in the village glowed more brightly as the villagers stoked up their fires and enjoyed the warmth. And then the three tiny trolls heard the sound of singing and, when they looked back down the path, they saw maybe one hundred people gathered around the Christmas tree and the lantern in the main square all holding hands and singing together. Smiling to themselves as their tasks were now complete, the trolls continued their climb back up the frozen pathway until the darkness of the pinewoods embraced them and they disappeared from view.

It's Christmas! Additional DVD materials

1.   Advent calendars

2.   Nutcrackers

3.   Small classroom market ideas

4.   The three trolls in German

5.   Useful websites

Project 2   Day of the Dead

routes into
LANGUAGES

Project outline

Requirements: classroom or hall (depending on number of students taking part)
Event time: various, depending on how the activities are used: i.e. spread out, or presented together as part of an afternoon event.
Language targeted: Spanish

Introduction

This project combines learning about the traditional Day of the Dead festivals in countries such as Mexico and Spain with taking part in some of the customary cultural activities associated with the event. The project presented here is structured as a basic model to help promote Spanish to new learners in the primary school environment. The whole project was first developed in 2008 by the University of Brighton under the auspices of Routes South.

The additional materials that accompany this section include: a Day of the Dead presentation in Spanish, two picture galleries of decorating sugar and paper skulls, a Day of the Dead quiz, a recipe for *pan de muerto* (bread of the dead) and a list of useful websites.

Organisation

This project is flexible and can be reduced or extended, depending on the time available. The basic outline presented here comprises two sections, with the first part covering target language tasks and the second part devoted to cultural activities. The project could be run over a number of weeks during the autumn term, for example, or different activities can be used as time permits.

Part One: Language activities

It is useful to begin the session with a short presentation about the Day of the Dead festival. This can include showing short video clips of typical celebrations and parades (*desfiles*) in Mexico and other Latin American countries (see list of useful websites in the additional DVD materials for this project). The following presentation in English is also available in Spanish in the additional materials section on the DVD. After the presentation, students can take part in various activities which are designed to help reinforce new vocabulary. Three such activities are presented after the presentation: picture/word matching, themed anagrams and a word search.

El Día de los Muertos, vocabulario – *Day of the Dead, vocabulary*

Here is some useful vocabulary to support the project as a whole:

el altar de la ofrenda:	altar (of the offering)
el ataúd:	coffin
la calaca:	skeleton (see also *el esqueleto*)
la calavera:	skull
la calavera de azúcar:	sugar skull
el candelero:	candlestick
las Calaveras:	poems and songs written during El Día de los Muertos
las caretas:	masks (see also la máscara)
las Catrinas:	female skeletons
el cementerio:	cemetery
la cruz:	cross
el cempasúchil (cempazúchil):	marigold
el desfile:	parade
la flor de muertos:	flower of the dead
los dulces:	sweets
el Día Todos los Santos:	All Saints' Day
la máscara:	mask

el esqueleto:	skeleton
las ofrendas:	offerings
el pan de los muertos:	bread of the dead
la tumba:	grave
el papel picado:	cut-out paper decorations
la vela:	candle

English presentation

This presentation can be used to introduce the session. Vocabulary related to the presentation can be put on the board before the lesson or can be used as homework or for a quiz. There is a lovely video clip which may help your introduction. Links to this can be found on the additional DVD materials for this project under 'useful websites'.

El Día de los Muertos, or Day of the Dead, is a traditional holiday celebrated in Mexico and other Latin American countries on November 2nd every year. It is linked to All Saints' Day (1st November) and All Souls' Day (2nd November) and dates back to the Aztecs.

In Mexico people usually get together with their friends and families to remember other friends and relatives who have passed away. These gatherings are not intended to be sad and serious, instead they are a time for honouring the dead as well as celebrating and partying whilst eating and drinking the food and drink enjoyed by the deceased. Gifts and flowers are taken to grave sites and cemeteries, often after a parade. Grave sites are cleaned and tidied, and sometimes people spend the whole night at the cemetery.

Many people build altars at the cemeteries or at their homes or offices. Photographs of loved ones, candles, decorations – including marigolds, painted oilcloths and paper decorations – are placed upon the altars alongside the person's favourite food and drinks. Typical offerings might include candied pumpkin, 'bread of the dead', sugar skulls and other sweets. Some people also leave a bowl of water and a blanket or pillow, in case the soul of the departed is thirsty or tired. Families sit together around the altar, where they pray as well as tell stories about those who have died. In some areas people often attach shells to their clothes. This is so that when they dance the shells make a noise, which they hope will wake up the dead.

Skulls are popular at this time – whether edible ones made out of sugar paste or chocolate, or ones that are used for decoration, or masks made out of wood, card or paper. These skulls often have the name of the dead person written on them, and the edible ones may be eaten by friends or relatives to show that they are not afraid of death. Full skeletons also feature prominently, as well as coffins, which can be made out of card, papier-mâché or chocolate. The skeletons are often dressed as rich women, known as '*Catrinas*' and are a very popular symbol of the festival.

Other traditions also include: writing short poems, known as '*calaveras*', about the dead or death itself; wearing skull masks; creating elaborate paper decorations; singing songs and playing music.

Activity One: Picture/word matching

Match the words to the pictures:

1. *Catrina*
2. *Calaca*
3. *Ataúd*
4. *Cempasúchil*
5. *Cruz*
6. *Calavera de azúcar*

 A
 B

 C
 D
 E
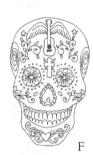 F

Answers: 1 = B, 2 = C, 3 = A, 4 = D, 5 = E, 6 = F

Activity Two: Themed anagrams

Unscramble the letters to make Spanish words relating to *El Día de los Muertos*

ANAGRAMA	ESPAÑOL	INGLÉS
smrtoeu	....	....
darnerof	....	....
alacsac	....	....
sacmraá	....	....
vrsacaela	....	....
zúarca	....	....
adí	....	....
xiémoc	....	....
poñeasl	....	....
orlf	....	....

sanictra	....	....
zucr	....	....
daaút	....	....

Spanish answers

muertos, ofrenda, calacas, máscara, calaveras, azúcar, día, México, español, flor, Catrinas, cruz, ataúd

English answers

dead, offering, skeletons, mask, skulls, sugar, day, Mexico, Spanish, flower, female skeletons (Catrinas), cross, coffin

---

Activity Three: Word search

Look for the following Spanish words which are hidden in the word square:

Ataúd / Azúcar / Calaca / Calavera / Candelero / Catrina / Cruz / Desfile / Día / Dulces Español / Fiesta / Flor / Máscara / México / Muertos / Ofrenda / Tequila / Vela

```
S  O  Z  Y  N  E  G  X  W  O  N  R  S  P  J  T
E  F  L  B  U  G  Z  P  T  H  O  W  A  N  E  R
S  D  E  S  F  I  L  E  V  L  G  L  R  V  J  Q
E  C  I  D  Ú  A  T  A  F  E  Y  W  E  R  P  L
C  Y  A  C  A  T  R  I  N  A  T  Y  V  C  V  M
L  E  M  N  A  P  I  U  C  R  E  C  A  R  F  U
U  I  É  R  D  L  G  A  Z  A  Q  E  L  U  L  E
D  T  X  E  I  E  A  C  M  C  U  L  A  Z  H  R
S  C  I  T  L  R  L  C  V  Ú  I  O  C  O  E  T
X  E  C  O  Y  I  C  E  A  Z  L  Ñ  F  Y  M  O
J  X  O  N  Q  Q  A  Q  R  A  A  A  P  H  A  S
A  D  N  E  R  F  O  I  J  O  X  P  L  T  L  V
W  D  T  R  E  E  K  Q  C  W  E  S  S  W  I  E
N  S  A  M  Á  S  C  A  R  A  P  E  A  C  C  L
M  N  F  E  C  S  Y  O  Z  D  Í  A  R  G  D  A
T  C  X  B  V  L  Q  Y  D  F  W  Q  K  J  P  B
```

Answers:

Part Two: Cultural activities

These cultural activities are all fun and help bring your Day of the Dead celebrations to life! Depending on the time available, students can take part in any number of the following tasks.

Calaveras de azúcar (sugar skull decorating)

This is a fun activity for learners of all ages. It involves decorating pre-made sugar skulls which can then be placed on an *ofrendra* (altar). Skulls can be decorated with a variety of materials, such as sweets, icing, glitter and sequins★. Prizes can be awarded for the best-looking skulls. It is advisable that the skulls are made well in advance of the event, so that they have time to dry and harden before decoration. Internet sites selling skull moulds can be found in the list of useful websites in the accompanying DVD materials, as can a selection of photographs of the best-decorated sugar skulls (in our opinion!).

Basic recipe (makes one skull):
- 450g granulated sugar
- 2 full teaspoons meringue powder
- Water to add

Directions (Skulls can also be made out of jelly, plaster of Paris or chocolate).

1. Put the sugar and meringue powder into a large bowl and mix together.

2. Gradually add drops of water until the mixture becomes moist and similar to the texture of wet beach sand.

★ Please note that whilst the skulls are made with sugar and can be decorated with sweets, they are not intended to be eaten.

3.   Once the mixture resembles sand it is ready to mould – press it firmly into the skull mould, ensuring all indentations are properly filled.

4.   Smooth the back of the mould and ensure it is filled right to the top.

5.   Place a square of cardboard on top of the mould then turn it over (as removing a cake from a tin).

6.   Gently remove the mould and set the sugar skull aside to dry and harden.

Note: depending on the type of mould you use, you can either make the skulls in two halves and sandwich them together using icing (so that you have a full skull) or, to save time, you can make just the 'face' half of the skull, leaving the reverse side flat to lay on plates or pieces of card for ease of decorating.

Máscara de calaveras (skull mask making)

If making sugar skulls as described above is not possible, students can make and decorate their own skull mask. Here is a template which can be copied onto cardboard and then decorated. In the accompanying DVD materials there is a picture gallery of skull masks made by Year Seven students.

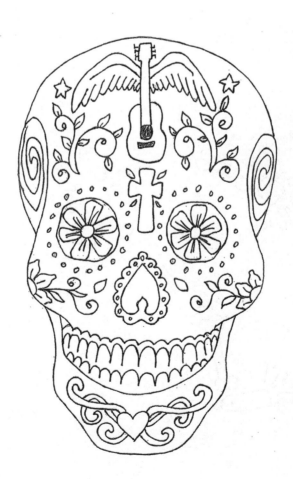

Ofrenda (altar)

Students can work together to construct an altar upon which items such as sugar skulls and masks can be placed. Altars are usually brightly decorated with crosses, candles and flowers – typically the marigold (*flor de muerto or cempasúchil*) – although religious artefacts can be omitted if necessary. The *ofrenda* can be a decorated table, or it can be specifically constructed using items such as cardboard boxes.

Calacas (skeletons)

Skeletons are typical symbols commonly seen throughout the festival. Students can make and decorate individual skeletons, and these can be hung up on the *ofrendra* or throughout the room as decorations. Skeletons can be made as follows.

1. Using the template shown here, draw a skeleton onto thick paper or cardboard.

2. Paint the skeleton in bright colours and leave to dry.

3. Cut around the outline of the shapes. The feet and hands can be kept as one section each (i.e., do not cut out each finger or toe).

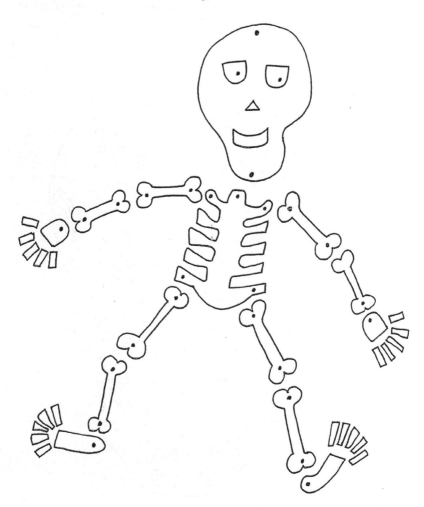

4.   Make a small hole on each spot, using a needle (or hole puncher if the skeleton is large enough).

5.   Tie the bones together using white thread and knot securely.

6.   Finally draw a face on the skeleton and hang it up with a loop of thread in the top hole on the head.

Traditional food and drink tasting

A very popular part of this event involves tasting food and drink traditionally consumed during the Day of the Dead festival. This can be kept quite simple, by choosing only one or two items from the list below, or can be extended to include all of them.

Cucumber and lime: sticks of cucumber drizzled with fresh lime juice

Salsa or guacamole with tortilla chips

Chilli-flavoured chocolate (available at most supermarkets)

Hot chocolate with mild or strong chilli powder added to taste

A recipe for 'bread of the dead' is also included in the materials for this section on the accompanying DVD.

Tips

A charge of 50p–£1 can be applied to help cover the costs of materials or ingredients. Students can be asked to collect cardboard boxes in advance of the event to help construct the *ofrenda*.

Shopping list

Sugar skull ingredients:

- Granulated sugar
- Meringue powder
- Prizes for best sugar skull or mask

Sugar skull moulds

- Decorating items, such as small sweets, icing, cake decorations, glitter, sequins, glue, etc.
- Paper plates to put skulls on
- Paper bowls for decorating items
- Cucumber
- Limes
- Salsa
- Guacamole
- Tortilla chips
- Chilli-flavoured chocolate
- Hot chocolate powder
- Mild and/or hot chilli powder
- Flowers for the *ofrenda* (marigolds if possible)

Calaveras poem task

Another traditional activity during this festival is writing short poems. Here is a traditional one which your students may like to listen to.

Calavera	**Skull**
Ahi viene el agua	Here comes the water
Por la ladera,	Down the slop,
Y se me moja	And my skull
Mi calavera.	Is getting wet.
La muerte calaca,	Death, a skeleton,
Ni gorda, ni flaca.	Neither fat, nor skinny.
La muerte casera,	A homemade skeleton,
Pegada con cera.	Stuck together with wax.

Reflections

The sugar skulls are certainly a very entertaining and successful part of the event but can be time-consuming to prepare. Be sure to leave enough time to practise making a skull as well as enough time for them to dry once they have been made (at least eight hours or more). The addition of wallpaper paste certainly helps stick the skull together but care must be taken to ensure no one eats the finished product!

Day of the Dead: additional materials

1. *El Día de los Muertos* presentation in Spanish
2. Picture gallery: decorating sugar skulls; decorating paper skulls; completing a worksheet; working with Fimo®; enjoying some Mexican food.
3. *El Día de los Muertos* quiz
4. *Una receta para pan de muertos*
5. Useful websites

Project 3   European Day of Languages

Project outline

Requirements: a few words of any language
Event time: any time available on September 26th, from 10 minutes to a whole day
Languages used: any

Introduction

Did you know that there are over 6,000 languages spoken in the world, and yet most of us can only muster a smattering of words in another tongue? Help is at hand! At the beginning of the school year, there is a chance to bring the subject to the fore and to give students a little taster of the diversity of other languages and cultures. In 2001 the date of September 26th was chosen by the Council of Europe to be the European Day of Languages, when schools can demonstrate how important languages are and what fun everyone can have learning them. If this date falls on a weekend, then the Monday closest to the 26th is chosen for the celebrations.

The European Day of Languages is a Europe-wide celebration of language and culture and involves 47 countries. The Council of Europe, together with the European Union, initiated the concept over ten years ago, and the celebration is co-ordinated in the UK by CILT, the National Centre for Languages, part of CfBT Education Trust (see useful web addresses in the accompanying DVD materials). The first European Day of Languages was held in 2011, which was the European Year of Languages. All languages are involved in the celebration, not just European ones and the day has its own dedicated website (see list of useful websites on the accompanying DVD for this project).

The idea is simple but effective and each year all participants have great fun celebrating the language(s) of their choice. The European Day of Languages has three main objectives, as stated by the Council of Europe, which are to raise awareness of:

■ Europe's rich linguistic diversity, which must be preserved and enhanced;
■ the need to diversify the range of languages people learn (to include less widely used languages), which results in plurilingualism;
■ the need for people to develop some degree of proficiency in two languages or more to be able to play their full part in democratic citizenship in Europe.

An excellent place to begin with exciting activities for the day is the CILT website, which has ideas and resources to help you to plan an event lasting anything from 10 minutes to a whole day.

Organisation

You might choose to invite a teacher and past students from your local secondary school to help or to run an event yourself with your colleagues. You might consider whole-school events such as *Fly the world from your own school airport* (Project 1 in Part VII) or a year-group celebration such as a food making and tasting session (for example, Project 3 *In the kitchen* in Part II) or a Key Stage event such as putting on a play (there are several ideas in Part V: *Languages and Performance*).

In addition, there are many simple ideas which require little preparation and just a DVD or a few resources to inspire students. The following are some of the most popular events recommended by CILT to get your school buzzing with language learning.

- Find out as many greetings in other languages as you can. Make a lively poster for the classroom and use a different greeting each day.
- Compile a song book with songs from around the world and sing along with them. A useful website is www.mamalisa.com.
- Make a passport giving your name, age, appearance, languages spoken. This could be set out in the language that the class is learning or in a home language.
- Use ICT and other reference materials to make fact files on countries of the world. Each file could include *hello* in the main language of the country (Project 6 below, *World Hello Day*, has a lot of this information), the capital city, population, currency, and so on.
- Where would you like to go? Plan a trip around the world and find out some greetings, food choices, tourist destinations, and so on, for each country.
- On a world map put a coloured sticker on each country that a child or adult has a connection to. What language is spoken there, and can they share any words or phrases in that language?
- Learn numbers one to ten in another language and play Bingo or some simple Maths warm-up games in them. Try Japanese numbers and learn the actions which help you to remember them.
- Investigate the etymology or origin of words which have been 'loaned' from other countries such as: Parliament; denim; hospital; carnival; berserk; abacus; ketchup; hazard.
- Collect travel brochures and make a collage including greetings or other useful phrases.
- Listen to some songs on a CD from another country and learn a dance to fit the music.
- Sing a song from another country. This example is a popular and easy German song *Mein Hut*, given below.

Mein Hut

(Sung to the tune of *The three-cornered Hat*):

> *Mein Hut, er hat drei Ecken, drei Ecken hat mein Hut;*
> *Und hätt' er nicht drei Ecken*
> *Dann wär' er nicht mein Hut!*

The song is sung three times.

- First, just as it is.
- Second, with actions. For **mein,** students point to themselves. For **Hut** they point to an imaginary hat. For **drei** they show three fingers and for **Ecken** they form their fingers into the shape of a triangle
- Finally they sing the song a last time but when they do an action they just hum the word.
- Children can also wear funny hats for the song while performing.

How to make a very simple three-cornered hat.

1. Take two sheets of A4 white paper.
2. Fold each piece of paper diagonally to form a square with an extra bit left over.

3. Cut the extra bit off on both pieces of paper. You now have two triangles which are the two halves of a hat.
4. Staple the two pieces together at the top and the centre bottom.
5. Tape over the centre line to join the two halves together.
6. Decorate to suit.

European Day of Languages: Additional DVD materials

1. Electronic version of the CILT logo
2. The CILT EDL characters
3. Useful web sites

Project 4   International Tongue-Twister Day

Project outline

Requirements: normal classroom
Event time: up to 20-minutes
Languages used: German, French and Spanish

Introduction

November 7th is International Tongue-Twister Day! To celebrate it you could read a rhyming book in class or practise some of your favourite tongue-twisters with your students. Tongue-twisters have fascinated people throughout history, and everyone just seems to love them! A famous one in English, *Peter Piper picked a peck of pickled peppers*, is based on an historical figure: a one-armed French horticulturalist (Pierre Poivre). Pierre was notorious for arranging clandestine smuggling forays to obtain seeds and plants as well as spice nuts (known as 'peppers') from the East Indies, to plant in his botanical garden in Mauritius. Once he even stole half a bushel of nutmegs, which inspired the tongue twister we know today.

Tongue twisters in German are known as 'tongue breakers' literally (*Zungenbrecher*), and many do just that! Four examples each in German, French and Spanish follow in this short project which aims to provide a bit of fun in your classroom if you have any spare time. Of course, you don't have to keep your tongue twisters just for November 7th. They are a great way to practise pronunciation and play with language together.

Four examples in German

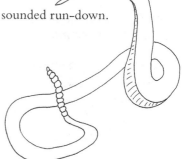

1. *Acht alte Ameisen assen am Abend Ananas.*
    Eight old ants ate pineapple in the evening.

2. *Esel essen Nesseln nicht, Nesseln essen Esel nicht.*
    Donkeys don't eat nettles, nettles don't eat donkeys.

3. *Es klapperten die Klapperschlangen,*
    bis ihre Klappern schlapper klangen.
    The rattlesnakes rattled until their rattles sounded run-down.

4. *Bäcker Braun bäckt braune Brezeln. Braune*
    Brezeln bäckt Bäcker Braun.
    Baker Brown bakes brown pretzels.
    Brown pretzels bakes Baker Brown.

Four examples in Spanish

1. *Como poco coco como, poco coco compro.*
   Since I eat little coconut, little coconut I buy.

2. *Una cacatrepa trepa tiene tres cacatrepitos. Cuando la cacatrepa trepa trepan los tres cacatrepitos.*
   A climbing caterpillar has three baby caterpillars. When the climbing caterpillar climbs, the three baby caterpillars climb.

3. *Del pelo al codo y del codo al pelo, del codo al pelo y del pelo al codo.*
   From hair to elbow and from elbow to hair, from elbow to hair and from hair to elbow

4. *El perro de Roque no tiene rabo porque el travieso de Roque se lo ha cortado*
   Roque's dog has no tail because naughty Roque cut if off

Four examples in French

1. *Un chasseur sachant chasser sait chasser sans son chien de chasse.*
   A hunter who knows how to hunt knows how to hunt without his hunting dog.

2. *Où niche la pie? La pie niche haut. Où niche l'oie? L'oie niche bas. Où niche l'hibou? L'hibou niche ni haut ni bas!*
   Where does the magpie nest? The magpie nests high. Where does the goose nest? The goose nests low. Where does the owl nest? The owl nests neither high nor low.

3. *Trois tortues trottent sur un trottoir très étroit.*
   Three turtles trot along a very narrow pavement.

4. *Cinq chiens chassent six chats.*
   Five dogs chase six cats.

DIY

You could have even more fun with your class by making up your own! This is a brilliant way to revise vocabulary. Here are two examples:

1. *Sept serpents sont sur sa chaise!*
   Seven snakes are on her chair!

2. *Meine Mutter macht mehere Mandeln*
   My mother makes several almonds

International Tongue Twister Day: Additional DVD materials

1. Useful websites

Project 5   Celebrating Mardi Gras

Project outline

Requirements: classroom space; hall for possible subsequent assembly performance
Event time: whole morning or afternoon
Languages used: French

Introduction

Mardi Gras, or Shrove Tuesday, is frequently celebrated in primary schools, so why not give it a French twist for a change with very little extra preparation. This project involves a chance to open a *Crêperie* in the classroom for a morning or afternoon session and is followed by an assembly script, song and instructions to show off the cooking skills acquired when preparing the *crêpes*. It involves cooking and tasting pancakes/*crêpes* in the classroom according to a simple French recipe and setting up the classroom as a café. However, although the cooking itself, ordering food and eating in a classroom café are great fun and the recipe-deciphering a useful task, one unusual focus for this project is to carry out an assembly performance where students can re-enact the preparation and cooking. If the assembly seems too daunting, just sing the song or do part of the performance below with hats or aprons and actions.

For any cooking event, risk assessments need to be thought through, especially if heating on a hotplate is required or sharp knives are used for cutting. These days, most schools have portable hotplates which are used to spread the word about healthy eating, so cooking pancakes is quite a common occurrence, especially on Shrove Tuesday! You may like to display 'The Golden Rules' (*les règles d'or!*) which are contained in the third project in Part II (*In the Kitchen*). The accompanying DVD contains all the signs you need to turn your classroom into a *Crêperie* for this project, including opening hours, menu of the day and drinks menu. *Bon Appétit!*

Organisation

1.   Decide first if just adults will do the cooking, or how you will manage it safely. It should be perfectly possible to have students preparing the mixture at their tables, as this only involves stirring and whisking ingredients, but think carefully about your set-up for the cooking in hot fat in the frying pan! You don't want students to miss out on tossing a pancake, so factor this in for everyone to try if possible, away from the heat.

2.   Set the classroom up before starting to cook. Show the students the French recipe first and encourage them to work out what it means. Then check it out with the English version.

3. A class *Crêperie* could be set up with some students' tables converted to a dining area. Each student could design their own place mat using an A3 piece of paper decorated with pictures of pancakes, fruit. etc,. labelled in French and the words *Bon appétit!* Alternatively, it could picture a plate, knife, fork and spoon with place for a cup, all suitably labelled.

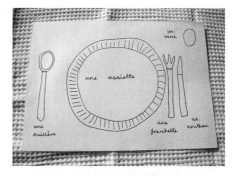

4. A French menu could be put up on the whiteboard with different options for fillings which students could choose from, priced in Euros.

5. Students would be expected to ask politely in French for their finished pancake and chosen filling. They would ask how much it cost and pretend to hand over the money.

6. A confident Year 6 student or bilingual student in the school could be at the till and respond with the price in French.

7. If you have a favourite, unbeatable recipe for pancakes that you have tried before, use your own for the cooking itself, especially because the sizes involved in the French one are for a small family. Just use this one for reading and getting the main points across.

Useful Vocabulary

la confiture:	jam
le citron:	lemon
le chocolat:	chocolate
les fraises:	strawberries
le miel:	honey
le sucre:	sugar
la crêperie:	Pancake shop/café
menu du jour:	Today's menu
je voudrais une crêpe au citron:	I'd like a lemon pancake
une crêpe au chocolat, une crêpe au sucre, une crêpe aux fraises, une crêpe à la confiture:	chocolat, sugar, strawberry, jam pancake
s'il vous plaît:	please
merci beaucoup:	Thank you very much
c'est combien, s'il vous plaît?:	How much is it please?
c'est deux euros, s'il vous plaît:	It's 2 euros please

La recette: Des crêpes	Recipe: Pancakes
(Pour 2 adultes et 2 enfants)	(Serves 2 adults and 2 children)
Ingrédients	**Ingredients**
200 g de farine prête à lever	200 grams self-raising flour
2 oeufs	2 eggs
25 centilitres de lait	25 centilitres of milk
un peu de beurre	A bit of butter
un peu de sucre	A little sugar
Comment faire?	**How to do it**
Prenez le bol.	Take the bowl.
Mettez la farine dans le bol.	Put the flour in the bowl.
Cassez les oeufs.	Break the eggs.
Versez le lait.	Pour the milk.
Mélangez!	Mix!
Fouettez!	Whisk!
Prenez la poêle.	Pick up the frying pan.
Ajoutez le beurre et chauffez-le.	Add the butter and heat it.
Versez le tout dans la poêle.	Pour the mixture into the pan.
Faîtes cuire la crêpe.	Cook the pancake.
Secouez la crêpe!	Shake the pancake!
Ajoutez du sucre.	Add some sugar.
Bon appétit!	Enjoy it!

Assembly celebration

Students could re-enact the stages of cooking the *crêpes*, responding to the teacher's instructions in French, as part of a whole-school celebration of the day. Parents could also be invited to catch a glimpse of the exciting primary languages work done in school.

- Students sit in rows of about ten facing the audience (three rows is the ideal). One student or adult calls out instructions in the target language for each row to mime.
- One or two volunteers at the front hold up the real ingredients and equipment so that people can see what is being mimed.
- The first row stand up to mime instructions to wash hands, put on an apron and hat and then sit down again, so the next row can be seen.
- The second row mime taking a bowl and pouring flour in it while one student holds up real food. The third row take a bowl and break an egg into it, etc.
- Rotate the three rows to tell the story.
- When the *crêpes* are "made", individuals could say what they kind of *crêpe* they ate.

Simple assembly text

Préparons une crêpe!	**Let's make a pancake!**
Voici la farine.	Here's the flour.
Voici les oeufs.	Here are the eggs.
Voici le lait.	Here's the milk.
Voici du sucre.	Here's some sugar.
Voici du beurre.	Here's some butter.
Voici un peu de sel.	Here's a bit of salt.

More complex assembly text

Cuire la crêpe	**Cooking the Pancake**
Voici un bol.	Here's a bowl.
Voici un fouet.	Here's a whisk.
Voici une poêle.	Here's a frying pan.
Lavez-vous les mains.	Wash your hands.
Mettez un tablier.	Put on an apron.
Et un chapeau de chef!	And a chef's hat!
Prenez le bol.	Take the bowl.
Mettez la farine dans le bol.	Put the flour in the bowl.
Cassez les oeufs.	Break the eggs.
Versez le lait.	Pour the milk.
Et le sel.	And the salt.
Mélangez!	Mix
Fouettez!	Whisk!
Prenez la poêle.	Pick up the frying pan.
Versez le tout dans la poêle.	Pour the mixture into the pan.
Faîtes cuire la crêpe.	Cook the pancake.
Faîtes sauter la crêpe!	Toss the pancake!
Secouez la crêpe!	Shake the pancake!
Ajoutez du sucre.	Add some sugar.
Bon appétit!	Enjoy it!

Add a little cooking song to go with it!

Why not sing a little song together afterwards, reinforcing the language practised? Work out some actions and everyone put on their Chef's hats. This song could either be sung entirely by the whole class or with different rows singing a line at a time as outlined overleaf.

Crêpe song (to the tune of *London's Burning*)	
(1st row):	*Prenez du sucre, prenez la farine,*
(2nd row):	*Cassez les oeufs, cassez les oeufs,*
(All together):	*Mélangez, Mélangez!*
(All together):	*Bon appétit!* × 2
(3rd row):	*Versez du lait, Versez du lait,*
(1st row):	*Prenez la poêle, prenez la poêle,*
(All together):	*Fouettez, Fouettez!*
(All together):	*Bon appétit!* × 2
(2nd row):	*Versez la pâte, versez la pâte* (pour in the mixture),
(1st row):	*Secouez, secouez!*
(All together):	*Mangez vite!* × 2 (Eat quickly)
(All together):	*Bon appétit!* × 2

Celebrating Mardi Gras: Additional DVD materials

1. Selection of *Crêperie* signs

Project 6   World Hello Day

Project outline

Requirements: see below for requirements per activity
Event time: ten minutes to one hour depending on number of activities delivered
Languages targeted: any (or as many as possible!)

Introduction

World Hello Day is celebrated across the world on November 21st every year. It was established as a way of promoting peace in response to the 1973 conflict between Egypt and Israel (http://www.worldhelloday.org/) and, although this continues to be its main theme, it has since also become a simple means of introducing students to different cultures and languages.

On this day, people are encouraged to say *hello* to at least ten different people. In a language-learning context, this offers an excellent opportunity to encourage students to find ways of saying 'hello' in as many languages as possible. From there, these different languages can be further explored, as can their associated cultures. It also provides a platform for initiating simple class discussions about the concept of peace. Both of these strands link well with other curriculum areas, such as history (finding out about world conflict), citizenship (understanding different communities) and Personal, Social, Health and Economic Education (PSHE) (respecting difference) and also tie in with themes relating to the International Primary Curriculum.

Presented below is a range of activities that can be used in the classroom to celebrate *World Hello Day*. Each activity can be used individually or can be combined with others depending on your available time.

Activity 1: Saying 'hello' in other languages

This activity can be used as a warm-up or introductory activity to familiarise students with the idea of *World Hello Day*. Explain briefly what the day is about and why it is celebrated, and then ask the class how many different ways of saying 'hello' they can think of. Students can work in pairs or small groups to do this. Allow five minutes' thinking time and then go around the class to see how many different ways/languages they have come up with. Write each greeting on the board for everyone to see (if you have native-speaker students in your class, you could ask them to come up and write on the board instead). It is useful to have a pre-prepared list of greetings which can be used as prompts if the students get stuck or if only a few are thought of. Here are a few to help.

Different (informal) ways of saying 'hello'!

Marhaban (Mar-ha-ban):	Arabic
Grüßgott (gruess-got, formal) or *Servus* (informal):	Austrian German
Kaixo (kai-show):	Basque
Namaskar:	Bengali
N h o (nee how):	Mandarin Chinese
Ahoj (ahoy):	Czech
Hej (hai):	Danish
Salut:	French
Hallo:	German
Namaste/Kemcho:	Gujarati
Aloha:	Hawaiian (also means 'goodbye'!)
Szervusz (sairvoose):	Hungarian
Dia duit (deah duit):	Irish
Ciào:	Italian (also means 'goodbye'!)
Konnichi wa (kon-nee-chee-wa):	Japanese
Sveiki (svay-ki):	Latvian
Kia ora (kia o-ra):	Maori
Boas:	Portuguese
Privet (pree-vyet):	Russian
Hola:	Spanish
Jambo:	Swahili
Selam:	Turkish
Xin chào (sin chow):	Vietnamese
Shwame (shoe-my):	Welsh

You may wish to display these greetings on the board or flipchart. Ask students if they have heard any of the phrases before, or if they would like to try pronouncing one. Then run through the list and read each one aloud, asking the class to repeat the words back to you. Discuss whether any of them sound similar or like English. Students could also be asked if they have been to anywhere where these languages are spoken.

A way of extending this activity can be to book the computer room and ask students to conduct an online web-quest to find out how other words relating to the peace theme of *World Hello Day* are said in other languages. Ask students what other words they think they could look up (for example, 'peace', 'community', 'harmony', 'world', etc.), and see who can find the highest number of words in other languages in the given time.

Activity 2: Matching words to languages

Worksheets for a word–language matching game can be prepared using the list of greetings above. Depending on the group's age/ability, the task can be differentiated by giving clues to the answers. For higher-ability groups/older students use the worksheet below (answers are in bold) and for lower-ability groups/younger students use the worksheet found on the DVD of additional materials.

Task: Can you match the greeting to the language? Circle the language you think the word belongs to.

Marhaban:	Is this **Arabic**, French or Vietnamese?
Grüßgott or *Servus*:	Is this Italian, Swedish or **Austrian German**?
Kaixo:	Is this Welsh, **Basque** or Japanese?
Namaskar:	Is this **Bengali**, Gujarati or German?
N h o:	Is this Spanish, **Mandarin Chinese** or English?
Ahoj:	Is this Irish, Latvian or **Czech**?
Hej:	Is this **Danish**, Hawaiian or Maori?
Salut:	Is this Hungarian, **French** or Swahili?
Hallo:	Is this Turkish, Portuguese or **German**?
Namaste/Kemcho:	Is this **Gujarati**, Welsh or Russian?
Aloha:	Is this Vietnamese, **Hawaiian** or Irish?
Szervusz:	Is this Spanish, Swahili or **Hungarian**?
Dia duit:	Is this **Irish**, Italian or Portuguese?
Ciào:	Is this French, **Italian** or Danish?
Konnichi wa:	Is this Bengali, Arabic or **Japanese**?
Sveiki:	Is this **Latvian**, Spanish or Turkish?
Kia ora:	Is this Vietnamese, **Maori** or German?
Boas:	Is this Gujarati, Italian or **Portuguese**?
Privet:	Is this **Russian**, Mandarin Chinese or Hungarian?

Hola:	Is this French, **Spanish** or Basque?
Jambo:	Is this Danish, **Swahili** or Czech?
Selam:	Is this Austrian German, Maori or **Turkish**?
Xin chào:	Is this **Vietnamese**, Arabic or Portuguese?
Shwame:	Is this Bengali, **Welsh** or Irish?

Give the class ten minutes to match the words to the languages and then call out the answers, or ask students to swap their worksheets with each other for marking. This provides another opportunity for you to call out the greetings and have the students repeat them back.

Activity 3: Making Cards (see also Part II, Project 6)

A good way of reinforcing the premise of *World Hello Day* (saying 'hello' to at least ten different people) is to encourage students to make greetings cards which they can give or send to family and friends. In keeping with the peace theme, international peace symbols could be displayed for students to copy onto the front of their cards (a simple Google search will bring up many examples) and they can then choose a greeting in a foreign language to go inside. Alternatively students could draw national flags or anything else which symbolises 'peace' to them. Depending on available time, students can make more than one card, so that they have enough to hand out at the end of the day. Once everyone has finished their cards they can be displayed at the front of the classroom before being taken home.

This activity can be extended by asking students to report back in the next lesson what their friends and family thought of the card(s) and *World Hello Day* in general. Did the students ask their friends and family to also say 'hello' to ten other people? How many people did they say 'hello' to in the end? Did others say 'hello' in return?

Activity 4: Posters

Another way of engaging students in *World Hello Day*, as well as of promoting it beyond the classroom, is to ask students to make posters. Students can work independently or in groups to depict their view of *World Hello Day* and what it means to them. These can then be displayed in the classroom or even in the corridor or school entrance, thus giving others the chance to find out more about it.

This is just a selection of activities related to *World Hello Day*. Further ideas can be found in the additional materials on the accompanying DVD.

Reflections

World Hello Day offers an interesting platform for learning a few words in a variety of languages as well as inspiring students' interests in other countries and cultures. It also presents a way of introducing links to other subjects, such as history, citizenship and PSHE and familiarising students with the basic concepts of 'peace' and 'conflict'. As a result, a wider curriculum project could be developed on the basis of the ideas presented above. From a learning perspective, new languages are situated in the context of other subjects and ideas, thus providing students with a clear rationale for learning them.

World Hello Day: Additional DVD materials

1. Worksheet for lower-ability or younger students
2. World Hello Day poems and songs
3. Useful websites

Project 7   St Martin's Day

Project outline

Requirements: a normal classroom, an area for the procession and craft materials for making lanterns
Event time: one lesson for the song and the story. A further lesson to make the lanterns is needed
Languages targeted: German

Introduction

The project is based around the St Martin's Day celebrations which take place in Germany on November 11th each year. This project presents several things you can do with your class to celebrate this traditional German custom. It starts with a short story about St Martin and goes on to present a traditional song. This is followed by instructions telling you how to make a lantern and then how to join in a traditional procession.

The story of St Martin

St Martin of Tours was a Roman soldier who became a monk later in life. He was a kind man who led a quiet and simple life. One cold winter's evening Martin rode into town on his white horse. The roads were covered with thick snow, and it was bitterly cold. All of a sudden, Martin's horse reared up and Martin saw a strange lump in the snow.

"Is it an animal or a man?" thought Martin to himself as he approached carefully. Then he heard a soft groan coming from the lump. It was a beggar, dressed only in rags and obviously freezing cold. Martin did not hesitate. He pulled out his sword and cut his cloak in half to share with the beggar and keep him a bit warmer. Then he took the other half of his cloak, threw it over one shoulder and rode away into the night at top speed before the beggar could even thank him.

Later that night Martin had a dream in which Jesus appeared, wearing the half-cloak that Martin had given to the beggar. Soon after this Martin left the army and became a monk. He was popular with the townsfolk where he lived (Tours), and the people wanted him to become their bishop. Martin hid in a goose pen to try to escape from everyone, as he was not sure he really wanted to be a bishop. But the geese made such a noise with their cackling that Martin was discovered. He was made a bishop, and to this day people traditionally eat roast goose with red cabbage and dumplings on St Martin's Day!

St Martin died on November 11th and this is the day, called *Martinstag* in Germany, which is celebrated every year. In many countries, including Germany, *Martinstag* begins at the eleventh minute of the eleventh hour of the eleventh day of the eleventh month: i.e., at eleven minutes past eleven on the eleventh of November!

Learn a traditional song

Here is an example which is often sung on St Martin's Day, and which the whole class can learn and sing together:

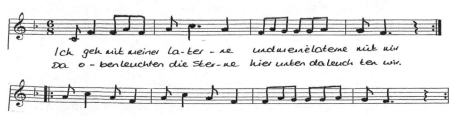

Ich geh' mit meiner Laterne	**Lantern, Lantern**
Ich geh' mit meiner Laterne	I'm going with my lantern
Und meine Laterne mit mir.	And my lantern goes with me.
Dort oben leuchten die Sterne,	Up above the stars are glowing,
Hier unten, da leuchten wir.	And glowing, too, are we.
Mein Licht ist aus,	My light is out,
Wir geh'n nach Haus,	We're going home,
Rabimmel, rabammel, rabum.	Rabimmel, rabammel, rabum.

Make a St Martin's Day Lantern

After school when it gets dark, the children go outside in a procession, carrying home-made lanterns and singing traditional songs like the one above. You can make a St Martin's Day lantern with your class by following the instructions below. There are some lovely photographs of lanterns on the DVD which accompanies this project.

You will need:

- an old jam-jar (clean and empty)
- a sheet of transparent paper (flower shops are a good source)
- sheets of differently-coloured tissue paper
- a tea light (preferably battery-operated)
- string for the handle (or coat-hanger wire if you are using real candles)
- a stick to tie the lantern to the string/wire
- scissors
- glue

Instructions

1. Cut a piece of transparent paper 12cm × 26cm.

2. Make lots of shapes out of differently-coloured tissue paper. This is a good chance to learn the names of different shapes in German such as:

der Kreis: circle	*das Dreieck*: triangle
das Rechteck: rectangle	*das Quadrat*: square
das Oval: oval	*das Herz*: heart

3. Glue the shapes of tissue paper onto the rectangle of transparent paper. It doesn't matter if the shapes overlap, as the light will still shine through.

4. Leave the decorated paper to dry for a few minutes.

5. Wrap the transparent piece of paper with the shapes on it around the clean jam jar and attach one end to the other with tape.

6. Knot a piece of string around the neck of the jam jar to make a handle (you will need to use wire if you are using real tea lights).

7. Place a battery-operated tea light inside the jam jar and switch on. You are now ready to join in the St Martin's Day procession! Afterwards you can string up the lanterns across the classroom.

Take part in a procession

Traditionally one person dresses up as St Martin, wearing a long red cloak and riding a horse. One member of the class could be St Martin (on a hobby horse perhaps), and then your parade could go around the playground or in a local area near your school/home. Songs such as the one above can be sung, and the procession can end with a traditional St Martin's bread man, a *Weckmann*, (see photo gallery on the accompanying DVD) and a cup of *Kinderpunsch* or hot chocolate, perhaps around a bonfire if appropriate (a *Martinsfeuer*)! A *Weckmann* is a sweet type of bread baked in the shape of a man with raisins for eyes and often with a white clay pipe in his mouth. They taste delicious!

Recipe for Kinderpunsch

Ingredients

225ml (8 fl oz) water

2 pinches ground cloves

750ml (1.25 pints) apple juice

150g (5 oz) caster sugar

1 cinnamon stick

1 lemon, sliced

Method

In a large saucepan, bring the water, sugar, cloves and cinnamon to the boil. Stir in the juice and heat through. Do not let the liquid boil. Take the spices out and pour the liquid over lemon slices in a serving bowl. Serve warm. Enjoy!

Invite other people to your celebration

Why not invite another class or school to help you celebrate *Martinstag*? Here is an invitation you could adapt:

Herzliche Einladung zum

Martinstag-Laternen-Umzug

Wann? Am elften November

Wo: (Schule X/Treffpunkt X)

Wie: Bitte bringen Sie und die Kinder

eine Laterne mit

(und auch eine Tasse für den Kinderpunsch!)

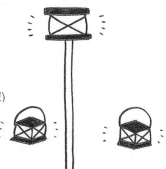

St Martin's Day: Additional DVD materials

1. Picture gallery
2. Useful websites

Project 8   Quizzing about languages

Project outline

Requirements: Powerpoint slides of language words

Event time: one lesson with opportunities for follow up and homework or competition

Languages targeted: French, German, Spanish, Italian

Introduction

When time is short and the school day is very busy, you may want a simple event to raise the status of languages spoken in nearby European countries which students are likely to visit. It could be used to mark *European Day of Languages* (see Project 3 in this Part) or to stimulate interest at the beginning or end of a term. This activity involves presenting the students with common and useful words in four foreign languages (and English) and asking them to guess which language is which. The National Framework for Primary Languages gives importance to investigating similarities and differences between English and other languages. Moreover, connections between languages, the derivation of English words and their historical roots is a fascinating subject which should be part of any student's learning experience. With a little encouragement, even Year Three students (age eight) find these comparisons intriguing and are keen to continue this exploration out of school, perhaps for a poster competition or for a piece of homework.

Organisation

There are several ways to organise this event. You could have a whole-class activity in the form of a discussion, where everyone offers ideas about the identity of each word; there could be a proper quiz, where small groups or pairs compete against each other to guess the answer; there could be two teams which compete. It is easy to add more rounds to the examples given or to change the languages chosen to suit different circumstances: for example, if you have a large group of Polish- or Portuguese-speaking students in the class, you might add a column for their language. You may want the class to record the words in a table as they go along, so that they can identify language patterns and draw conclusions about their findings.

Recent experience of this activity has revealed a strong spirit of enquiry in students about language links and culminated in a series of multilingual posters and mini class dictionaries being made. All year groups in Key Stage Two requested more activities investigating links between countries, their cultures and languages.

uno, dos, tres
un, deux, trois
eins , zwei, drei
uno, due, tre

Steps

1. First decide on the vocabulary you want to cover. This will depend on the age and experience of your class. Obvious words to consider would be:

hello/goodbye	welcome
please/thank you	good morning/afternoon/evening/night
numbers one to five or ten	country names
family names	days of the week
pets	colours
school subject names	

Another interesting possibility is to give each country's own word for their name – for example, España, Italia – or the way each language expresses the name England. A different theme to investigate subsequently is the cultural and geographical difference between countries for example, the name of their capital city, Prime Minister, their Parliament building, name for their national flag, longest river, best known food, range of mountains, most famous cheese, most famous artist, etc.

2. Present the class with a Powerpoint collection of five words for (for example) hello, using different colours for each language. For the first slide, include the English word to act as a baseline, then for subsequent slides omit the English word, so that they have to work out the meaning of the words too.

3. Proceed through the remaining slides in whichever way you choose, whether as a collective or a competitive exercise. Either give the answers to each slide as you go along or save all the answers to the end.

4. Record the words in a language table, either as you go along or at the end.

5. Have a class discussion: what similarities have they found? For example, what links are there between Spanish and Italian words? Which languages seem not to conform to any pattern found? Can they spot any common features about word endings in a language? Is there a language which seems easier to pick up? Which one would they like to learn?

Further steps

1. For homework, ask students to investigate the origins of the languages chosen *via* the internet. Why are Spanish, French and Italian so similar? This can lead to a fascinating discussion about settlers and invaders, migration.

2. Invite them to find the same words in two other languages for example, Danish, Portuguese.

3. Ask them to make up a poster to say *Hello* or *Welcome* or *Good morning* in as many languages as possible (see also the *World Hello Day* project in this chapter).

4. Make up a class mini multi-lingual dictionary of common words.

5. Teach your class a few Latin words so that they can see the root of many of the words investigated for example, numbers one to ten

Unus, duo, tres, quattuor, quinque, sex, septem, octo, novem, decem.
Look at these Latin words and work out some English derivatives.

amicus:	friend	*pater*:	father	*mater*:	mother
domus:	home	*dono*:	I give	*manus*:	hand
felis:	cat	*canis*:	dog	*miles*:	soldier
corpus:	body	*primus*:	first	*ultimus*:	last
crux:	cross	*sordidus*:	dirty	*civis*:	citizen

Project 9 Vive la cuisine!

Project outline

Requirements: classroom space for food preparation, ingredients, chopping equipment, liquidiser
Event time: a whole morning for both recipes or one hour for each
Languages targeted: French

Introduction

There are many opportunities in the primary curriculum to experiment with tasting or preparing delicious food from other countries on our doorstep and it's a chance to have some fun and learn about other cultures in addition. This could be the culmination of a topic on food shopping, going to a restaurant, visiting French markets or a taster session before a school trip to France. On the other hand, most schools operate a continuous stream of work about healthy eating and this activity could fit neatly into a day or week of projects. There may be alternative ways of introducing an expert to lead some food preparation. You could invite a Home Economics teacher from your local secondary school who would be willing to come for a morning to instruct the students in making sushi and organise the ingredients for you, as long as you cover the food cost. Alternatively, you could see if you have any parents with restaurant connections who could make pizza or noodles recipes. The project presented here consists of an easy food preparation and tasting occasion with two straightforward child-friendly recipes.

Organisation

Tasting food from other countries is a great starter for a special event, but even better is the possibility of making your own nibbles. A carousel of simple recipes which students can follow under the supervision of an adult could be extended over several classes in a year group or over a morning in one classroom. Risk assessments need to be thought through, especially if sharp knives are used for cutting. If you are cooking pizza or any other hot food, some schools have a helpful cook in the kitchen who will obligingly pop the food in the industrial oven, saving much time and anxiety. Think ahead about whether to confine the food to a single country, for example, lots of Italian pizza. Alternatively you could follow these two simple recipes in French which require no cooking and contain healthy combinations of vegetables and fruit.

In advance

- Ask for a small contribution from the families of the class to buy the ingredients, or ask students to bring in ingredients on the day.
- Collect chopping boards, knives, aprons, spoons, bowls for Recipe 1 and in addition liquidiser, drinking straws and glasses for Recipe 2.
- Prepare risk assessments for chopping ingredients and discuss how to do this safely with the class.

On the day

- Prepare food preparation space with a suitable table covering.
- All wash hands before starting.
- Read and decipher the French ingredients list together. Keep the English translation to one side until you have worked through the list.
- Encourage students to read the French version of the recipe instructions and use the English only as a fallback.

Recipe 1: Un dip d'été	**Recipe 1: A summer dip**
Les Ingrédients	**Ingredients**
Un grand pot de yaourt	Big pot of yoghurt
Du persil frais	Some fresh parsley
De la menthe fraîche	Fresh mint
Deux petits oignons doux	Two mild spring onions
Un petit concombre	One small cucumber
Un peu de paprika, du sel et du poivre	A pinch of paprika, salt and pepper
Deux ou trois carottes, un poivron	Two or three carrots and a pepper

Comment faire? / Method

Rincez le persil, la menthe, le concombre et les oignons
Rinse the parsley, mint, cucumber and onions

Coupez très fin le persil et la menthe
Chop the parsley and mint very finely

Coupez le concombre et les oignons en petits morceaux
Cut the cucumber and onions into small pieces

Versez le yaourt dans un bol avec soin
Pour the yoghurt carefully into a bowl

Ajoutez le concombre, les oignons et les herbes
Add the cucumber, onions and herbs

Ajoutez un peu de sel et de poivre
Add a pinch of salt and pepper

Mélangez bien, ajoutez un peu de paprika et tenez au froid
Mix together well, add a pinch of paprika and put the dish somewhere cool

Servez avec des bâtonnets de carottes et de poivrons
Serve with little sticks of carrot and peppers

Recipe 2: Un milk-shake à la fraise	Recipe 2: Strawberry milkshake
Les Ingrédients	**Ingredients**
Un demi -litre de lait	Half a litre of milk
Trois fruits bien mûrs au choix	Three very ripe pieces of fruit from
une banane, une pêche, une nectarine	a choice of a banana or peach or
six fraises, une petite mangue	nectarine, six strawberries or a small mango

Comment faire? / Method

Rincez et coupez les fruits en tranches
Rinse the fruit and cut into chunks

Mettez toutes les tranches dans un robot ménager
Put all the chunks into a liquidiser

Ajoutez le lait et mixez
Add the yoghurt and mix well

Versez le mélange dans un grand verre
Pour the mixture into a big glass

Décorez avec des fraises coupées
Decorate with strawberries cut in half

Sirotez avec une paille!
Sip with a straw!

Follow-up activities

1. Students could write out the recipe used in French and illustrate it.
2. Take photos of the cooking event and make a display with the recipes and captions.
3. Students draw a picture of their own face or use a photograph and add a speech bubble with a comment in French about the food.
4. As a class, make up some more recipes in French with slightly different ingredients but the same basic foundation and create a French cookery book.

Vive la cuisine: Additional DVD materials

1. Picture gallery

PART

Inspiring language learning and teaching

Preface

This Part has a different format to the others, as it presents in detail ways in which we can inspire language teaching and learning within the primary school context. It offers a refreshing overview of a variety of different aspects of primary language teaching and considers in turn: the role of the foreign language assistant; how to adopt a whole-school approach to language learning; ways of involving students from reception class (aged five) upwards; ways to involve the whole-school community; how to encourage staff members and use them as role models; ways of involving parents and helpers; how to motivate boys to learn languages. This chapter ends with some exciting ideas for making the best use of 'just thirty minutes of lesson time' in terms of small games and activities you can easily present in the target language.

Introduction

It is often said that younger students tend to embrace the idea of learning a new language or languages and need little encouraging to try out the different words and phrases they have learnt. However, as many primary language teachers will attest, this is not always the case. Sometimes the reticence and lack of interest in foreign languages often displayed in secondary school classrooms can also be found amongst primary students. Given that current National Curriculum guidelines stipulate compulsory language learning up until the end of Key Stage Three (when students are approximately 14 years old), developing students' interest in foreign language learning from the outset is crucial.

It is also important to take into account those who are charged with delivering primary language lessons. Some schools will engage language specialists and/or native speakers who are comfortable with and confident in introducing a new language to young learners and are armed with a wealth of teaching ideas. Conversely, teachers in other schools may be thrust into the role of languages teacher, relying only on rusty skills quickly remembered from their own school days and wondering how best they might convey them.

Whatever position you are in as a teacher, and whatever the attitudes of your students towards foreign language learning, this Part will provide a variety of ideas to help inspire language teaching and learning. In comparison to others in this book, it does not offer discrete projects or activities. Instead it explores the roles various people can play in motivating and inspiring young people and their teachers in a language-learning context and suggests ways of implementing new ideas. Consideration of the involvement of foreign language assistants is included, as is a section on adopting a whole-school approach to language learning. Special attention is given to motivating boys and, finally, ways of making the most of your language lessons are discussed. These ideas are not prescriptive and may not always be applicable, or even possible, in every school. However, they are intended to provide food for thought, especially for those striving to offer a fun and innovative languages curriculum.

Foreign Language Assistants

We have chosen to look at foreign language assistants (FLAs) here because they are an excellent resource that many teachers are not often aware of. This section explains what a foreign language assistant is, the potential cost to your school, the benefits of engaging an FLA, how to go about applying for an assistant, and the support available should you decide to host one.

What is a foreign language assistant?

Foreign language assistants are native or near-native speakers of the foreign language(s) you teach or are hoping to teach in your school. They are commonly aged between 20 and 30 years and will have a keen interest in living and working in the United Kingdom. Most will likely be seeking to improve their own language skills, as they will be either studying English or undergoing training to become English teachers in their own country. Appointing an FLA is an excellent way of enlivening the languages classroom and also helps to provide students with an authentic 'voice' of the language they are learning. These are extremely valuable aspects of the learning process and can contribute to increased student confidence and interest.

How much does it cost?

Foreign language assistants typically work a minimum of 12 hours per week but this can be extended to a maximum of 18 hours per week depending on negotiations between the school and the assistant (http://schoolsonline.britishcouncil.org/funding/language-assistants)[1]. They usually stay in post for an eight-month period (1st October–31st May). Schools pay the FLA's salary, which is dependent on where the school is located (see the British Council's 'how much will it cost?' page: http://www.british-council.org/languageassistants-how-much-will-it-cost.htm). It is easy to keep these costs to a minimum by sharing your FLA with another school. This could be your partner secondary school or another primary school in your area.

---

1   Note that FLAs from non-EU countries may not extend their working week beyond 12 hours.

What are the benefits?

Investing in a foreign language assistant can bring a number of benefits to the languages classroom and the wider school environment. FLAs are keen to share their knowledge of, and passion for, their language and culture, and thus inject enthusiasm and fun into language lessons. They are usually armed with a good array of materials and resources which help make lessons authentic, relevant and interesting. As a result, learner confidence increases, as does motivation and competence. By the same token, these benefits can also be extended to the languages teacher and to other teachers in the school who may perhaps be considering adding language teaching to their portfolio. In terms of wider school advantages, hosting an FLA contributes towards gaining or sustaining international status via the International School Award (http://schoolsonline.british-council.org/International-School-Award).

How do I apply to host an FLA?

Applications for hosting foreign language assistants are managed *via* the British Council. Schools are usually invited to apply for an assistant some months in advance of when the post would be taken up: i.e., applications are made in January–February for posts starting in October. In the first instance, applications are sent to your Local Authority's Modern Languages Advisor or Co-ordinator (if you are unsure whom to contact in this regard, a list is usually provided by the British Council).

Is there any support available?

Plenty of support is available to you and your foreign language assistant *via* the British Council. They offer useful downloadable guides on topics such as making the best use of your assistant and finance. Of particular use in this context is the Primary FLA starter pack, which is full of information about teaching strategies, resources and classroom management (http://www.britishcouncil.org/languageassistants-schools-primary-starter-pack.pdf) and is free to download. The British Council also provides links to induction courses held by Local Authorities and cultural institutes. Schools should encourage their assistants to attend such events, as they are a good way of getting to know other locally based FLAs and, from there, developing social and professional networks.

In terms of supporting your FLA locally, you should ensure they are settled in, both at school and at home. At school they should be introduced to the whole staff team and involved in general day-to-day school activities, as well as events such as staff meetings and parents' evenings. Where possible, assign them a buddy or mentor who will be the first person to whom they can ask questions or raise concerns. Introduce them to the students and ensure they understand that the FLA should be treated like any other member of staff. On a more personal level, be prepared to help them with domestic arrangements, such as registering with a doctor, finding accommodation or sorting out household bills.

These are the principal things to think about and be aware of when considering appointing a foreign language assistant. Of course, this is only a basic framework of ideas and much more detailed information can be found via the British Council website (see list of useful websites at the end of this chapter). If you have never had an FLA at your school it is also worth talking to colleagues from other schools about their experiences. This may also provide you with an opportunity to discuss sharing an assistant, as mentioned above.

Reflections

Organising a foreign language assistant for your school may seem like a complicated endeavour. However with a well-planned support structure in place, hosting an FLA can be one of the most valuable assets for the languages classroom and the wider school. Bringing with them invaluable enthusiasm and target language knowledge, along with authentic materials and fresh ideas, FLAs can truly transform both language learning and language teaching.

Adopting a whole-school approach to language learning

We all face the task of ensuring that language learning is not an isolated part of the school curriculum, restricted to a brief weekly session and with little relevance to daily life. How can you involve adults working in school in a broader way, to suggest that a foreign language is an essential tool for students? The ideas presented below are intended to get the whole school involved in language learning, from the youngest students in reception class to parents and helpers. It should be quite achievable to walk along a school corridor first thing in the morning and hear every class using another language to start the day and for daily routines to be taught in French, Spanish, German or any other language.

Ideas to involve students from reception class upwards

The suggestions and ideas presented here are given in French, but can be easily adapted for other languages.

Speech bubbles

Young children are very open and curious about new sounds and words, even at the age of four or five. Most teachers are keen to discover the range of languages spoken at home by their class and could be encouraged to put up photographs of individuals with a speech bubble in that language, saying hello/welcome/good morning/my name is … or an appropriate phrase which fits in with a topic being taught. Use the display to choose a different student each day or week to introduce their words and expect everyone in the class to greet each other the same way. Older students might write a dual-language paragraph about themselves.

Class registers

The simplest and most practical use of a new language is to establish a routine in every class of a formal greeting and response when the students are sitting ready for the register. This could be:

Bonjour les enfants/ la classe	*Bonjour Madame/Monsieur*
Comment ça va?	*Ça va bien merci!*

It is simple then to carry on calling out the register by greeting each student in the same way: *Bonjour Millie* and expecting the reply, *Bonjour Madame/Monsieur*. Continue this with the dinner registers by teaching the words: *la cantine* (school dinner) and *les sandwiches* (packed lunch) and expecting the students to say one or the other each day when their name is called, for example, *la cantine ou les sandwiches, Millie? La cantine.* Older students could add *s'il vous plaît* to say please. Before going off to lunch, a useful way to leave the classroom would be to wish the class *Bon Appétit!* They could chorus the phrase in return.

Counting

It is easy for young learners to pick up numbers to five or ten, but keep your counting within reasonable limits. While you are waiting for routines to be finished, such as coats to be hung up, PE bags to be put away, and so on, count in another language, using a clapping rhythm to provide a steady beat. Look for other opportunities to count, for example, the number of students having *les sandwiches* each day by asking them to stand up and you all count them in a line; the number of people on the green table; the number of students away; those with a January birthday.

Classroom instructions

Incorporate languages into the normal daily school procedures. With younger students, start with simple everyday routines, for example, *Levez-vous* – stand up; *Asseyez-vous* – sit down. The whole school could gradually adopt instructions such as:

Mettez-vous en ligne:	Get into a line
Mettez-vous en cercle:	Get into a circle
Regardez-moi:	Look at me
Ecoutez-moi:	Listen to me
Rangez vos affaires:	Tidy up your things
Allons-y:	Let's go!
J'arrive:	I'm coming!
Ouvrez la porte/ la fenêtre/les cahiers:	Open the door/window/workbooks
Fermez la porte/ la fenêtre/les cahiers:	Close the door/window/ workbooks
S'il vous plaît:	Please
Merci:	Thank you

Physical Eduction Instructions

Why not have a few phrases for a PE lesson in French? Start in the classroom and sing a French song while they get ready. Choose one of the simplest songs from Project 4, *Sing up for languages*, in Part V.

Changez pour le sport:	Get changed
Courez /Marchez/Sautez/Dansez/Arrêtez:	Run/Walk/Jump/Dance/Stop
Allez les bleus/ les rouges/ les verts/ les jaunes!:	Come on blues/reds/greens/yellows
Les bleus ont gagné:	The blues have won!
Tu as gagné:	You (one person) have won!

Using Photographs

Students love having their picture incorporated into a poster or message. If you are teaching an instruction such as *Mettez-vous en ligne*, take a picture of a group of students and attach it to the words to display in school corridors. Don't forget to check that you have permission to use each child's image in the photos. A sample consent form can be found in Appendix One.

Praise words

Use a thumbs–up to convey the meaning of these words. Keep a favourite for a very special achievement.

Super!/Chouette!/Merveilleux!/ Fantastique!/Excellent!/Bravo!

Tu es doué/Vous êtes doués:

You are clever (to one person/ to more than one person)

Chouette!

Tu es doué!

Classroom display

Aim for a language display in each classroom, even if it's as simple as a series of flashcards of numbers or praise words. Ideas for easy displays can be found in Project 7 in Part II entitled *Language displays for the classroom*.

Involving the whole school community

Using school assembly

When the whole school is together, a great start could be made to the occasion with the now familiar greeting from a teacher: *Bonjour les enfants!* And the reply could be *Bonjour tout le monde!* Hello everybody!

Song assembly

If you have a regular assembly when all teachers are present and the students sing, introduce a new simple song for everyone to learn each week. Choose one of the simplest songs from Project 4, *Sing up for languages*, in Part V as a starting point and encourage the teachers to practise singing with their class during the week in spare moments. This is an ideal opportunity to train both staff and students at the same time and to make sure that everyone knows how to pronounce key vocabulary.

Christmas time

Try to squeeze a language song into a Christmas assembly. It could be the well-known traditional French song *Vive le Vent* to the tune of *Jingle Bells* (available on many commercial CDs) or any way of singing about Christmas, for example, to the tune of *We wish you a Merry Christmas:*

Bonne Année et Joyeux Noël × 3

Bonne Année à vous!

Phrase of the week

Choose a phrase of the week for the whole school to learn and practise in the classroom. Introduce the phrase in the first school assembly of the week when everyone (including teachers) is present. If you have a newsletter which goes home each week, have a section to highlight the phrase and its meaning and encourage families to learn together. Keep it simple and you are more likely to achieve good participation. For example:

Week One:	*Bonjour Madame, Bonjour Monsieur*
Week Two:	*Comment ça va? Ça va bien!*
Week Three:	*Je m'appelle …*
Week Four:	*Levez vous, Asseyez- vous*
Week Five:	*Ecoutez bien.*

Labels for rooms

Create or buy labels for the rooms in the school, including a picture of the room and its name in the language. You could ask the class to make their own pictures and labels, laminate them and stick them up outside the rooms. If this goes well, label parts of the classroom too. For example: *la table/l'évier/l'ordinateur* – table/sink/computer. Further labels could include:

la salle de classe:	classroom
le bureau:	office
la bibliothèque:	library
la cantine:	canteen
la cour:	playground
la salle d'informatique:	computer suite
le hall:	hall

le bureau du Directeur/de la Directrice: Head master's/ Headmistress' office

le couloir: corridor

les toilettes: toilets

le vestiaire: cloakroom

le bureau du concierge: caretaker's office

Welcome signs

Each class could design a *Welcome* sign and place it outside the door. For example, *Bienvenue dans la classe six!*

Posters

Students could design posters about how great/useful languages are. Laminate them and place them in the corridors around the school.

Learning French is really useful. I can talk to people when I'm on holiday in France.

Encouraging staff and using them as role models

Prepare flashcards

Make life easier for other less confident teachers by preparing laminated flashcards of the phrase of the week to be put up in each classroom. Put classroom instruction words up on the school's central server for everyone to access.

Bonjour tout le monde! Moi, j'adore visiter la France pour parler en français!

Teach a game

At the end of each staff meeting, ask to have a five-minute slot where you can teach everyone a new, easy game to practise vocabulary. Make it fun as a bit of light relief and make it easily transferable to use in a classroom. For example:

- you say a word. They repeat in low voice, high voice, whisper, loudly, scared voice and so on;
- you mouth a word or phrase silently; they guess which word you've said;
- guess which word I'm thinking of. They put up their hands to suggest what your word might be;
- choose someone to come out to the front. Place a flashcard of a word over their head where they can't see. They guess which word it is;
- fruit salad with four or so words they need to know. Give everyone in rotation a word to remember; you call out a word, those people change places. Call out all words on the last go and everyone changes place;
- play *Silent If I'm Wrong*. Go over the new phrases learned. You say a phrase. If it's correct, they repeat it after you; if it's incorrect, they keep silent;
- choose two words or phrases which they need to know. Make a circle. One person goes round tapping the back of each person in turn, saying the word chosen. After

about three goes, they get to someone, tap them on the back and unexpectedly say the second word instead. Both the 'tapper' and the person tapped then race round the circle to get back to the tapped person's place first;

■ two teams game. Stick up all new phrases/words on the wall. Get two rulers, fly swatters or similar, and give one to a volunteer from each team. Choose another person from each team to add up the score in the language. You call out a word/phrase. They have to hit it with the ruler before their opponent to get a point;

■ play the mini Mexican wave game to practise a useful phrase or sentence. Everyone stands in a circle. Each person in rotation says a word from the phrase as fast as possible. The person to say the final word of the phrase has to sit down (they are out) once they have spoken. This game is fun as it progresses, as everyone tries to work out who will be the last person standing.

Bonjour les efants! J'adore les moules et j'aime boire du vin français!

Teacher models

Use your colleagues as language speaking role models around the school. Take photos of them and place speech bubbles of what they might say appropriately! For example, a sporty teacher might say *J'aime jouer au foot!* Laminate photos and place on the walls around the school.

Involving parents and helpers

Home languages

Contact parents and carers to find out what languages may be spoken at home and to explore ways to bring those languages into school on a regular basis. Investigate how they might support language work done at school or complement it in a different way, such as by talking about cultural experiences or helping to prepare displays or food about their country.

Story-reading

You may discover a rich resource of language speakers who may be willing to come into school and read a simple story to a class. Consider setting up monthly or termly story-reading sessions, where parents prepare a story in advance and rotate around different classes. Bear in mind that parents are sometimes overawed by the prospect of reading to 30 students at once and need some guidelines to help to make the experience meaningful for everyone. Useful guidance would include:

■ choose a story from a book with some pictures to show, perhaps a folk tale;

■ choose a story which is not too long or complicated, even for KS2 learners;

■ look for repetition in the story, so that students can listen for these words or a character's name;

- teach everyone the repeated words first and explain how the story goes in English;
- give some students (or all of them if possible) a home-made prop – for example, a tiny coloured flag or feather or picture of fruit – to represent something in the story. They will wave this when they hear the key words read from the story;
- read the story in the language, showing the pictures, with the students responding by waving props;
- discuss together what they found out about the country, or the moral of the story;
- perhaps the parent could record their reading onto a CD and lend the book to the class who could keep it in the Book Corner for a while;
- take photos of the event to make a display to encourage other parents and to put in a display book near the front entrance of the school to show visitors.

Home reading project

Follow this project about creating reading materials to take home, as set out in Part VII, Project 2, *Home Reading Scheme*). This forms a strong connection between home and school and enables parents and whole families to share in language learning.

Reflections

The above examples show the wide variety of ways in which language learning can be infused into the whole school. It would be ambitious to embark on all of these projects in one go, but they mark the extent to which you could go to promote language learning to students, teachers, parents and others. Some of the ideas can be used as platforms for implementing the more detailed activities, but all should be looked upon as a library of ideas into which you can dip at any time.

It is a wise idea to keep evidence of all the initiatives you adopt in school to promote languages. They might be photos, written work, recordings of oral work, DVDs of performances, letters of thanks, etc. Keep them in a file to show inspection teams or any other interested visitors, such as student teachers. It is useful to keep a consolidated record, because it is impossible to remember everything you have done and a photo might just act as a reminder of something crucial.

Motivating boys to learn languages

It has been a cause for concern for some years that, on the whole, boys are less keen on learning a language, more reluctant to join in and less likely to make good progress. Even in the later primary years, boys become more self-conscious about pronouncing foreign words and less involved in active, lively language lessons, while girls generally maintain their interest and participate enthusiastically in a wide range of activities. Are there lessons to be learned about this division and what action can be taken by teachers? How can we provide a structure and activities which will encourage more boys to appreciate language learning?

Broadly speaking, experience and research has shown that boys react better to the following:

- good pace and variety in lessons;
- having a purpose. they need to see why they are learning a particular topic and where it is leading;
- breaking work into manageable chunks;
- competition (whereas many girls prefer to collaborate and not outdo each other);
- moving around;
- being noisy;
- playing running or chase games;
- making things;
- technology;
- acting;
- having a laugh;
- working with a friend of their choice;
- cartoons and comics;
- monsters, dinosaurs, aliens, animals;
- horror, adventure, mystery, sci-fi, fantasy;
- rewards;
- being the best;
- male role models;
- seeing the big picture.

Some of these issues can be addressed by planning lessons carefully. Spending a few moments thinking about what might be appropriate for the boys in your class can lead to many happy language lessons for students and teachers alike. It is important to note that, in focusing on what motivates and engages male learners, we are not ignoring the girls in the classroom; rather we are endeavouring to find approaches and activities which will bring the subject alive for everyone.

Activities, resources and materials

Am I thinking about boys when I'm planning?

This section provides a raft of ideas that will help you to plan lessons that will engage and motivate your male learners.

- **Check that lessons provide a good balance** of active parts and more formal instruction. Look for starter games to play on the floor space of the room or occasionally in the hall or playground. Have a loud and noisy game as an incentive for good participation for the last five minutes of the lesson. Find opportunities for partner work and small-group games where students can choose their own partners.

- **Find imaginative ways to break down writing tasks.** This could include storyboarding a set of sentences rather than expecting a longer piece of writing in one go. Teach the vocabulary and context for each part of the storyboard and then give time for students to complete that part.

- **Think about varying the writing tasks given as part of the lesson.** Ask the class to write speech bubbles rather than a dialogue. Students can work as a whole class, performing a shared writing task as they might in a literacy lesson. They can also be encouraged to work with a partner to write alternately a set of descriptive sentences in the form of the Consequences game, folding the paper over each person's sentence and passing it on for the next. Students can also be asked to write emails and notes, warnings and rules so that the style of writing is varied.

- **Explore the technology available in school.** Give students the chance to film their group's role play of: visiting a shop; going to the doctor; ordering in a café; going to the zoo; meeting someone in the street. Create mini dramas to be filmed and looked at together to make improvements: for example, visiting a haunted house; swimming in a dangerous sea; a birthday party. There may be a microphone system, allowing children to read a commentary on an event performed by others in the class, such as a fashion parade where each item of clothing is described.

- **Extend the use of computer software for language work.** Most primary children become well acquainted with PowerPoint and make their own presentations about a favourite topic. They could rewrite in their own words a simple story, such as *Handa's Surprise* by Eileen Browne (a story of an African girl who sets out to take a surprise gift to her friend. It is useful for counting, sequencing and so on). They could change the setting and characters or rewrite the words to fit the tune of a well-known traditional song such as *Sur le pont d'Avignon*.

- **Create interactive displays**, highlighting everyone's work and setting a challenge or competition for the children to participate in. Attach a box for entries to the competition and award a mini prize for the winner. For example: How many owls are hiding in the trees? *Il y a combien d'hiboux dans les arbres?*

A wide selection of tried and tested games and activities for motivating boys can be found in the additional materials on the accompanying DVD.

Exploring the context of learning another language

Am I helping boys to see the bigger picture?

- **Help students to be aware of the context and advantages of languages.** Investigate where French/German/Spanish-speaking countries are situated and their historical significance. Look at links to the rest of the world with pen pals, *via* a school link, school trips to the target country, internet links and so on. Use the trusted internet sites to see what school life is like in other parts of Europe. Exploit all the sporting and cultural occasions which bring countries of the world together.

- **Look out for male role models to show that languages are not exclusively a female preserve.** There may be male teachers who excel at language speaking or a caretaker or visiting music teacher who has a second language. In the local secondary school there may be former pupils who have gone on to learn Mandarin or Japanese and would be willing to come back to speak to a class. Politicians can sometimes demonstrate the value of being proficient in languages and children's family members are often keen to share their knowledge. Take photos of these males to display in corridors with catchy slogans.

- **Look for examples of careers or job opportunities enhanced by speaking another language.** These could include: being an interpreter at the Olympics; working abroad as a travel courier; doing voluntary work in a Francophone country; studying at a European university.

- **Host an inter-school general-knowledge quiz about international languages and cultures.** Organise a whole-school competition for posters to say *Welcome* or *Hello* in as many languages as possible (see Part III, on World Hello Day, for an example). Send home a language questionnaire for homework to celebrate the European Day of Languages with a prize for the best entry.

Celebrating achievement

Am I encouraging boys to achieve?

Encouraging boys to achieve in language learning can be done in many ways. Think about establishing rewards for good participation and results with reward stickers, team points and winning privileges, such as going out to playtime first, no homework, having five minutes extra play/a longer PE session. In the longer term, presenting termly certificates and prizes for good achievement and effort is a good way to recognise achievement. Organise regular assemblies where language work can be showcased and students can receive applause and admiration from their friends, class, the whole school and parents.

Assessment

How do I know that I'm being boy-friendly?

Carry out student evaluations at the end of an activity or lesson or topic; this could be in the form of a tick list or speech bubble colouring, for instance. Discuss with the class the different elements of the lessons and their opinions about their effectiveness. Encourage students to think about the strategies that suit their own learning style and to expand their range. Also encourage different methods of self-assessment, as boys in particular respond well to these. Self-assessments at the end of a lesson which would suit boys might include:

- showing thumbs up for good understanding of the Learning Intentions, thumbs in the middle for moderate understanding, and thumbs down for poor understanding. This is a quick and unobtrusive way of revealing a student's confidence;

- using arms to show understanding. Spread arms out as widely as possible for good understanding and progressively smaller as this diminishes, until you reach a tiny space for poor understanding;

- using a traffic-light system, where each student is given three colour cards: amber, green and red and shows the appropriate colour for their understanding at a given signal;

- if the class is particularly football crazy, suggest that the classroom is a football pitch and ask students to position themselves in a particular part of the room to show their understanding. A defence position at the back would reflect poor understanding; a midfield position in the centre area would reflect moderate understanding; an attacking position at the front would reflect good understanding;

- after a written exercise, ask those who feel that their work fits all the success criteria to stand in a particular place (with their work); the moderate group stands in another place and the least confident in a third. When they reach that place they must compare their work with others in that place and see if they can justify their place. The teacher will also come to each group and help to moderate;

- help students to make a written assessment of their progress or understanding by preparing a structured approach for them, with Sentence Starts to get them going: for example, *One thing I have learned today is…; One thing I don't understand is…; Something I have enjoyed is…; I would like to do more …because …; I would do better at French if I ….*

Reflections

Ensuring that boys in particular are engaged in language lessons may seem like a daunting task in the first instance. However, careful planning and being aware of how boys tend to behave and respond in the languages classroom can lead to successful and positive lessons for all involved. None of the suggestions above require vastly different materials or techniques, merely a sharper focus on how boys like to learn languages. The majority of these suggestions will no doubt appeal to female students as much as male learners and, as a result, it is hoped a strong grounding in language learning can be provided for everyone.

Just thirty minutes: making the most of your language lessons

When you only have half an hour or 45 minutes for a weekly language lesson in primary school, how can you make the best use of your time and reach out to all the children in your class? It is almost certain that your class will be mixed-ability, so how can your lesson be inclusive of all levels of ability? How can you inspire students with the excitement of learning a language in such a short time? How can you be certain that you plan for progression over a year?

This section contains some ideas to remind you of key objectives and to make language lessons meaningful for every learner. Again, examples are given in French but could be applied in any language.

As you plan your lessons a useful checklist might include:

- careful and systematic reference to the Primary Framework for Languages (for more details, see here: http://primarylanguages.org.uk/policy_and_research/policy_ and _reform/ key_stage_2_framework.aspx);
- links to other parts of the curriculum;
- ensuring progression over a school year and from one year group to the next;
- opportunities for self-assessment;
- recognition of different types of learning styles;
- differentiation of activities and expectations;
- setting out learning intentions and recapping at the end;
- a balance of lively activities and thought-provoking sessions;
- scope for individual work, pair work and group work;
- focus on oracy with growing development of literacy;
- giving students the chance to communicate with each other;
- suggesting follow-ups for home learning or later in the week in school.

From a different perspective, every teacher would hope to engage their class in a challenging but enjoyable lesson by considering the following:

- encouraging good listening and looking;
- setting a good, lively pace;
- ensuring that every child participates;
- maintaining good control;
- establishing a good relationship with the class;
- encouraging a sociable, co-operative atmosphere in the classroom where 'having a go' is encouraged;
- setting up rewards and incentives;
- assessing the teaching and learning from the lesson.

Starting the lesson

Make it obvious from the start of the lesson that this is a new subject, not Maths or Literacy, and that different things happen here. Do not start the lesson until every pair of eyes are on you and a couple of essential rules are complied with, for example, looking at the teacher and listening carefully. Encourage everyone to sit where they will be sensible. If you have to move someone, try to do so in a positive way by suggesting that they will be able to join in more successfully elsewhere. Try to use the space you occupy imaginatively: if you are lucky enough to have a large space for your lesson, move the group from one part of the room to another at different stages of the lesson, so that they will have a fresh start each time they swivel round or face a new direction.

Have a set routine of interaction with the class, so that this tunes them in straight away to the language. It could be:

Bonjour les enfants!   Reply: *Bonjour Madame/ Monsieur.*

Comment ça va?   *Ça va bien merci, et vous?*

Establish a set of short phrases which the students repeat with actions, which can act as a quick chanting signal later in the lesson if you need to get their attention: for example,

Touchez les yeux: they repeat while touching their eyes

Touchez le nez: as above, touching their nose

Touchez la bouche: as above, touching their mouth

Un, deux, trois!:   clap hands with the numbers and then hold both hands up in the air

Introductory activities

After reading the Learning Intentions together, breaking them down and relating them to work from previous weeks and cross-curricular links, look for a positive, lively start to the lesson which might have a co-operative feel to it. This could be a favourite rhyme, with actions which children could stand up to perform with a partner and then, on a count of three, change to a different partner or group several times.

You may like to have a regular slot at this stage for continuous assessment of the whole class, where three or four individual students each week practise a particular routine: the weather forecast for the week ahead; a diary report on what they do at the weekend. Set up any flashcards or whiteboard display to support the students, keep a class list handy to write comments about the volunteers, and ask three or four volunteers to present their impromptu information. This might take the form of:

> *La Météo: lundi il fait froid; mardi il fait chaud; mercredi il pleut; jeudi il y a du vent; vendredi il y a un orage; samedi il neige; dimanche il y a du soleil.*
>
> The weather: it will be cold on Monday; hot on Tuesday; rainy on Wednesday; windy on Thursday; stormy on Friday; snowing on Saturday; sunny on Sunday.

This can be adapted simply to provide opportunities for progression. Some students may take an easier option of using a limited number of two or three weather expressions; others may choose two or three for each day of the week linking them with *mais* or *et*. Invite applause for each brave person, no matter how faltering and award stickers or other rewards. You will soon see patterns emerge and be able to make useful notes about relative confidence and accuracy.

Plan a short exercise next in which students have a snappy grammar session for a few moments, where they find out about word classes and link them with Literacy work on a similar subject. For example, they could read aloud a list of frequently used imperatives (part of the verb used as a command) which you and the class have been accumulating over the term, such as *regardez, écoutez, montrez,* etc. Now teach them how to make these negative instead: i.e., *don't listen.* Explain that you put *ne* in front of the imperative and *pas* afterwards, making a sandwich around it. Play a quick game where you call out the imperative and students shout back the negative, for example, you call *regardez*; They shout back *ne regardez pas!* Invite someone to take your place calling the imperative, and then ask the children to do the exercise in pairs. Students enjoy calling out in a way they do not normally behave in school and understand more about grammatical structures at the same time.

New learning

Next, recap on the main stage of learning from the previous week, asking everyone to recall from a few prompts what was taught. As usual, target students with differentiated questions, so that everyone feels involved in learning a language and praise good recall and interest.

Teach the next step in your Learning Intention with a whole-class approach, then look for an opportunity for pair work, where students can practise securely with a friend. For a whole-class approach, effective games for reinforcement include: holding a flash card over the head of a volunteer who has to guess which word has been chosen; Guess Which Word I'm Thinking Of, where students put up their hands to guess the word you have secretly chosen; mouth a word silently and they guess which one; play Word Tennis by 'hitting' a new word to the class, and they hit it back (or its opposite, if appropriate); spell out a word with *voyelle, consonne* (vowel, consonant), and they decipher which one it is. For example, *le chien* would be *consonne, voyelle, consonne, consonne, voyelle, voyelle, consonne.*

Paired work could be with a vocabulary fan where each pair has a fan of pictures of the new vocabulary or words and pictures on different sides. They could play: I say, you show me the picture; I show the picture, you say the word; I say the word, you show the written word; I mouth a word silently, you show the picture and so on. Ask for volunteer pairs to show an example of their fan work.

Useful tips for inclusion

- Always display the text of songs, rhymes, new vocabulary in full view of the class, even if they know them off by heart.
- Use as wide a variety of visual prompts, picture clues and hand and body actions as possible to reinforce vocabulary.
- Break down new words to make them more manageable by repeating them in numerous ways: loudly/softly/dramatically/emotionally, beating out the rhythm or the syllables with fingers on your palm/hands tapping on your head and shoulders/hands in the air then out at the side, singing them high and low, etc.
- Encourage students to practise new words or phrases by repeating them and counting them off on each finger of a hand (i.e. five times each hand), then holding up their hand to you.
- Those with special needs are familiar with these techniques and often assimilate new words more quickly than other students as a result. Look out for this and reward effort promptly.

Planning Progression

At all costs, avoid merely teaching lists of nouns to the class. Where possible, look for ways to develop progression, building up from a new phrase or noun to a longer, scaffolded sentence by adding other phrases, such as a useful verb and an adverb, or a set phrase, such as a day of the week. In this way you could start with: teaching vocabulary about hobbies one week; teach likes and dislikes the next week; put them together and then put the days of the week at the beginning of the sentence. You could extend this further by qualifying the part of the day immediately after the day of the week. For example:

First week: *Faire du sport/lire,* etc;

Second week: *J'aime/je n'aime pas,* plus the hobbies from the previous week;

Third week: *lundi, mardi, mercredi, matin, après-midi, soir,* etc.

Put them together, and students can say:

lundi soir je n'aime pas faire du sport

mardi matin j'aime lire

Don't forget to teach the question needed to turn this into a conversation, with phrases like *Que fais-tu lundi soir?* Students often know responses but not always the questions that prompt them, so make a point of teaching them formally. One very popular way is to use the Mexican wave game. Everyone stands in a circle or distinct rows and each person in turn says one word of the phrase as fast as possible in rotation. The person saying the final word has to sit down once their word is said. Speed it up as the sentence becomes familiar; students love the suspense of working out who will be the last out.

Alternatively, the Human Sentence Game works well. Write each word of your chosen sentence onto a separate card (add any punctuation too, on separate cards). Jumble up the words and invite volunteers to come out to the front and hold a card in any order. Ask them to get into the right order and discuss possible alternative orders and their implications. Ask the whole class to read aloud the sentence displayed – time after time. As they read aloud together, you gradually turn down random word cards, one after the other, until the class is still reading the sentence aloud with all the cards showing a blank face. This is very effective for memorizing a long sentence. Finally, ask the group if they could think of any other vocabulary which could be added or replaced in the sentence. This game often seems like magic to students, as they keep reading the blank words which have disappeared in front of their eyes.

Practise this new vocabulary in several ways: with a made-up song modified to fit the content of the lesson; with a commercial song on the same theme. The first time it is sung, ask everyone to raise their hands for a given word or phrase, or count how many times it is sung. Ask them to match written words on a strip of paper to each line, wave them in the air when they hear them and then reassemble the song lyrics on the table in front of them. Finally, sing the song in parts, or as a round, or as two teams, one line softly and the next loudly, or any other interesting way.

To put the new vocabulary into practice, devise a way that students can get up and have a conversation with each other around the room. Make sure that your visual prompts are clearly visible as pupils move about. One way is for each pair to have a questioner and a responder; they raise their hands to show you which person has each role. Questioners work out their own question such as: *Que fais-tu samedi après-midi?* while responders work out their possible response, for example: *j'aime jouer au foot*. Teach everyone to listen out for the special day and time of day in the question so that they can start their answer appropriately, for example: *samedi après-midi je joue au foot*.

Before they choose, ask students as a group to identify the most complicated sentence they could make up using the possible permutations practised and, conversely, the simplest alternative. This can be helpful guidance for less confident and very confident members of the class. Encourage each student to assess their own strength in maintaining a conversation: if they feel confident, they could vary their reply for each new questioner; if they feel less sure, they could keep to the complete sentence they have thought up with each new person. They can also choose either a complicated version or a simple one (there is always at least one child who goes for the most complicated one imaginable). Set them off to approach any child in the room, maybe keeping the questioners in a line at the side or wearing a red PE band, so that they can be identified. As they walk around the room, join in the conversations, looking out for stray students who need help and keep a mental tally of the choices made. Repeat the phrases for those who are hesitant and always praise effort. At the end, ask for volunteers to re-enact their conversations in front of the class and expect everyone to applaud.

Change of pace

At this stage, if you have space, incorporate a lively running game to introduce new vocabulary or a phrase which is useful for general conversation. This could be a team game, such as ladders or fruit salad, or it could be a circle game, where one student is chosen to run round the outside of the seated circle tapping each person on the shoulder while saying the chosen word (for example, *s'il vous plaît*) to each one, and then changing this to another word (such as *merci beaucoup!*) when they reach a friend of their choice. The two students then race back to see who will be the first person to sit in the empty place. If there is no space for running, look for a lively song or dance with a cultural emphasis in which everyone can stand up and do actions on the spot. If your class is already overexcited, a drawing game might settle them and prompt good teamwork and listening skills. One popular game involves each group sending one person at a time to the teacher who secretly reveals a noun, such as *un lion*. The student has to go back and draw a picture of the noun on their mini whiteboard for their team to guess and they must write the French word correctly on their whiteboard.

Finishing the lesson

Bring the class back to a milder pitch with a familiar song, which could be sung progressively more quietly. Return to your Learning Intentions and ask everyone to assess their understanding *via* the success criteria, to help you to plan ahead. This is a good point to award stickers for good effort or an unexpected perceptive comment or making a connection linking grammatical points.

Suggest a task or challenge for the class to try before the next lesson: for example, timing themselves to count up to 20 in the language as fast as they can, so that you can have a quick competition the next lesson. Or practise saying *j'ai soif* (I'm thirsty) ten times (using their fingers to count) like a tongue twister. Or find out the words for the days of the week in another language. Offer a sticker for each child who has a go.

Finish with *Au Revoir* or *Bon Appétit* or *A Bientôt* and expect a similar reply from the class.

As they get up to leave the room or return to their table, ask each student to say a word or phrase which they have practised during the lesson. Repeat what each person says so that less confident learners can hear an example to follow. If you do this regularly, you will soon notice who experiments with more complex language or remembers obscure phrases. It is these students whom you can target with more advanced questions the following week.

Your aim is that each student leaves the lesson with a sense of achievement, keen to come back for more, feeling that language learning is sometimes complicated but always fun.

Reflections

Teaching a language to young students can be challenging. Teaching it in only a small space of time can certainly intensify that challenge! Structuring your available time sounds obvious but may not always be practised. Refocusing your ideas for planning, teaching and assessing your foreign language lessons will enable you to make the most of the time in the classroom and will help turn the challenge into a productive and enjoyable task.

Inspiring language learning and teaching: Additional DVD materials

1. Games and activities for motivating boys
2. Useful websites

5

Languages and performance

Introduction

Many primary school students love to perform in front of an audience and the seven Projects included in this chapter encourage them to do so – in the foreign language, of course. A colourful array of suggestions for different assembly performances are presented in the first Project which draw on ideas for songs, actions, rhymes and raps contained in Projects 4 and 6 among others. Many ideas are included for adapting a story and turning it into a playscript, with The Three Little Pigs used as an example in German in Project 3 and an adaptation of an animal tale in Spanish presented in Project 5. A haunted house is the spooky setting for a step-by-step drama performance in French in Project 2, whilst a magic mouse stars in a poem in German in the final Project. All in all, this Part can not fail to tempt you to try out your theatre and performance skills with your class – and fun, together with effective language learning, is almost certain to ensue!

Project 1   Being creative in assembly

Project outline

Requirements: hall space for performance
Event time: an hour to rehearse; 20–30 minutes for the final performance
Language used: any language; examples given in French

Introduction

Sharing ideas and achievements is part and parcel of life in primary school and it makes sense to use an outlet such a school assembly to display what students have been learning. This might be simply to teach a few songs to a parallel class or a different Key Stage, or it could be to present the culmination of a term's work to the whole school and parents too. If you have a visiting Inspector or visitor in school, this is a great chance to demonstrate the confidence and versatility of your students, daunting though it might seem at first.

Organisation

We are all accustomed to a theatre set-up for most assemblies, with members of a class at the front of the hall and an audience facing them. Why not try a different way to showcase your work: set the hall up in a new way; have more interaction between the audience and performers; process from different parts of the room.

One possibility is to set your assembly in the round, with a central area for the performers and the audience seated around the circumference. This has the great advantage that everyone in the audience has a good view of the action, rather than having to crane their necks to spot someone in the distance. It also gives a chance to do unusual items for performance. The following ideas have all been tried in school and provide a refreshing new angle for language display.

In-the-round assembly

Start with some action rhymes, with students standing in a circle facing outwards to the audience. Wow the audience with a very lively starter which you call and they repeat and perform such as *Voici ma main* (see the accompanying DVD for the text and instructions) and *Comptez jusqu'à huit* (from *Take 10 en français*).

Next, they could turn to the person beside them to recite and act out a series of partner rhymes (see Project 6 in this chapter: *Action, rhymes and raps*) or sing an easy *Bonjour* song (see Project 4 in this chapter: *Sing up for languages*) shaking hands with their partner as they sing.

Alternatively, you could arrange the students in two concentric circles and ask the outer ring to face the inner ring to make pairs. Organise songs or rhymes where the outer ring move to the left, changing from one partner to the next while the inner ring stand still in their places. In this way, everyone changes partner for each verse or repetition with minimal disruption and it gives the audience a good view of many different performers. Make sure you accustom the students to this format in advance, but it will prove to be a useful and versatile vehicle for practising vocabulary in lessons and always looks impressive. Working with a partner helps everyone to feel more relaxed, so that they sing up and join in more enthusiastically, giving a more vibrant performance in public.

Follow on with some songs in the round such as the skipping song *De quelle couleur est mon écharpe* (see the accompanying DVD for the text) to the tune of *Here we go gathering nuts in May*, requiring a few scarves and other items of clothing in different colours. Another might be *Si tu aimes les bananes, tape les mains* (see the accompanying DVD for the text), a version of the traditional song *If you're happy and you know it...* which you can adapt to suit your class.

Games could follow such as an easy Fruit Salad (see also Project 6 in Part I: *Playing Games*), where children are given a noun to remember and swap places when their word is called, maybe calling out their word as they run. Space in the circle will be limited, so moving will be restricted to just a few people at a time. The Hot Potato singing game *Un, deux, trois, passez vite* also works well and is designed to be used in a circle with minimal space (see Project 4 in this chapter: *Sing up for languages*).

The central point of this assembly will be to demonstrate some parachute games (see Part I, Project 1 *Fun with Parachutes*, for a range of different games). Parents, in particular, have rarely seen this type of activity and raising the colourful canopy for the first time always brings gasps of amazement. A good starter is the Champignon game. This involves calling out *un, deux, trois, champignon*, and then everyone raises the parachute. Tease the children by calling out alternative words beginning with the *ch...* sound (for example, *chou, chocolat*), to encourage them to concentrate and listen out for the key word *champignon*, before they can lift the parachute in the air. Then you could play a few games under the parachute itself. Make sure that you have at least two additional adults holding the parachute, so that the audience can see what is going on under the canopy. Firm favourites for an assembly would be *La Tempête* and *Cache-cache*, but if time allows most games would work well in this arena. You could even demonstrate sitting under the parachute for Silent Statements, but keep this very brief, as the only thing the audience will see is the outer cocoon shape of the parachute. Once you have the idea of working in the round, many other ideas will pop up to add to the performance.

Show-them assembly

A different approach could be to re-enact a special event with appropriate props and actions. Most people in the class sit in a semi-circle and speak in groups while others re-enact the event. This fits the theme of *Mardi Gras* (Shrove Tuesday) where everyone could pretend to mix pancakes, toss them and add fillings, with a few chefs acting as compères. A song, instructions and script can be found in Part III, Project 5 *Celebrating Mardi Gras*, which could be performed by Years Three or Four.

Another short play to illustrate a topic can be found in Part I, Project 2 *Florence Nightingale*, where the class can re-enact the situation in Scutari Hospital, complete with some easy songs and a short drama. The story of the *Three Little Pigs* (see Project 3 in this chapter) lends itself well to a performance too and is presented in the form of a playscript.

Parade assembly

Using the central aisle of a hall works well at Christmas for the grand entrance of the Three Kings, so use it for your language performance too. This assembly could be based on the theme of *seasons, travel* and *clothes* and involve students from Years Five or Six (ages ten and eleven), who are more confident about moving about, speaking on their own and acting with some verve.

Start with a song from a dozen or so students walking up the centre chanting or singing a song about the months of the year (this is a popular subject found in many commercial CDs). Continue with a different group taking it in turns to give the weather forecast using a map and a pointing stick, describing one season of the year, followed by another group showing the contents of their suitcases, packed for that season's holidays. Here are some examples.

> *La Météo pour janvier: dans le nord il fait froid. Dans le sud il neige, etc.*

Three students could then share speaking this item:

> *Je vais en vacances en hiver. Je vais faire du ski. Dans ma valise je mets mes bottes chaudes et une écharpe*

A different weather forecast could then be read:

> *La Météo pour juillet: dans le nord il fait chaud. Dans le sud il y a du soleil, etc.*

Another threesome would say:

> *Je vais en vacances en été. Je vais au bord de la mer. Dans ma valise je mets les lunettes de soleil et mon maillot.*

Continue through each of the four seasons in the same way, involving more students in turn. The aim is to bring all the class up to the front and to give each person a speaking part.

Students could then conduct a fashion parade, with a few commentators introducing the 'models' and describing the clothes they are wearing, for example:

> *Je vous présente… Alice qui va en vacances…. Voici la mode pour le ski cet hiver/La plage cet été.*

Several volunteers could introduce their own clothes or nominate a braver friend.

> *Pour aller à la plage… je porte un pantalon rouge et un tee-shirt bleu clair.*

A group could then perform a Snowman routine.

Il fait froid	Make shivering movements with hands
Il neige	Make snow falling movements with hands
Je mets mon chapeau melon	Put on your bowler hat
Je prends ma pipe	Mime taking a pipe and putting it in your mouth
Je mets mes boutons noirs	Mime putting buttons on your body, counting aloud
Un, deux, trois…	
Je mets ma belle écharpe	Mime putting on a scarf
Je mets mes gants d'hiver	Mime putting on winter gloves
Et je dors	Mime sleeping

This could be extended by having the sun coming out and each item of clothing being taken off in reverse order: for example,

> *il fait chaud … j'enlève mon chapeau ….*

As a finale, the entire class could sing a song to the tune of *We wish you a merry Christmas*:

First verse:
> *Je vais en vacances en été,*
> *Je vais en vacances en été*
> *Je vais en vacances en été,*
> *Je mets un maillot* (I put on a swimming costume)
> (Someone show one or wear one or wiggle in one!)

Second verse:
> *Je vais en vacances en hiver,*
> *Je vais en vacances en hiver*
> *Je vais en vacances en hiver,*
> *Je mets mon écharpe* (I put on a scarf)
> (Someone holds up a scarf)

Third verse:	*Je vais en vacances au printemps,*
	Je vais en vacances au printemps
	Je vais en vacances au printemps,
	Je mets un chapeau (I put on a hat)
	(Someone holds up a spring-time-looking hat or cap, etc.)
Fourth verse:	*Je vais en vacances en automne,*
	Je vais en vacances en automne,
	Je vais en vacances en automne,
	Je mets mes gants chauds (I put on warm gloves)
	(Someone holds up warm gloves)

Teach-the-audience assembly

The point of this next assembly is for students to show how they learn a language at school and at the same time teach their parents a few songs, rhymes etc. to continue to play at home. Although there may be an initial reluctance from the audience to join in, the introduction of a simple, familiar song will get most people joining in and then they are usually hooked! Remember to put up words and prompts on the whiteboard or other display, so that the audience don't have to remember everything.

For this assembly, the whole class would demonstrate some of their songs, games, etc., and then invite the audience to take part from their seats. Usually there is an outgoing student who can act as a compère to goad the audience when teaching them by saying *You can do better than that, etc., …One more time …, I'm going to ask you again in a few minutes …, We're going to show you how and then it will be your turn…*

One easy thing to teach and play would be a finger rhyme. A student or the teacher shows how to do this, with the class demonstrating and the audience repeating words and actions. Do the rhyme a couple of times to get into the spirit of the occasion, for example:

Deux petits lapins	Two little rabbits	Keep both hands behind your back
Cachés dans l'herbe	Hidden in the grass	Keep behind you
Je m'appelle Mimi	My name is Mimi	Bring one hand in front with finger in air
Je m'appelle Yves	My name is Yves	Bring the other in front to do the same
Bonjour Mimi!	One finger moves up and down facing the other	
Bonjour Yves!	The other finger says Hello the same way	
Au Revoir Mimi!	Say goodbye and go behind your back again	
Au Revoir Yves!	The second does the same	

Next could be a couple of Action Rhymes taken from Project 6 in this chapter, *Action, rhymes and raps* – such as *la semaine* or *à gauche, à droite*.

Two or three lively songs could be taught either from a commercial CD or from Project 4 in this chapter, *Sing up for languages*, and it would even be possible to tell a short story, with the audience waving their hands in the air when they hear a particular word or making an animal sound when the name of the animal is mentioned.

One way to remind parents of the difficulties and fun of learning new words in another language is to try an experiment where the teacher or a student introduces a limited number of words in a totally different language to the audience with a mime or action for each. This has been done very successfully with Japanese numbers up to five or ten, each of which has an action relating to the sound of the word. Everyone learns together, plays a mini Bingo game and is 'tested' by a student at the end of the assembly to see what people can remember.

For a finale, try to incorporate a dance from the DVD *Take 10 en français*, which has a brilliant array of traditional and familiar songs to move about to. Any dance is bound to get the audience on their feet and demonstrates to parents the enormous changes in teaching methodology for languages in primary schools over the last few years.

Being creative in assembly: Additional DVD materials

1. Text and instructions for action rhyme: *voici ma main*

2. Text and instructions for song: *de quelle couleur est mon écharpe?*

3. Text for song: *si tu aimes les bananes …*

Project 2   Creating a short drama performance (*La Maison Hantée*)

Project outline

Requirements: classroom space or hall area with rows of seats for students; some scary props (for example, a bat, a spider, a white floaty sheet), soundtrack of squeaky door or scary sounds (for example, Michael Jackson's *Thriller* opening track)
Event time: half-an-hour to practise, ten minutes to perform in public
Language: French

Introduction

Injecting a sense of excitement and suspense or fun is a great asset when you want to showcase the language work done in school. The class can make suitable background sounds with their hands, fingers, etc., to add to this performance of a story about fear and

bravado during a visit to a haunted house. This drama originated in childhood memories of family performances at Christmas, when simple stories were re-enacted with an adult narrator and a chorus of sounds and words from the audience echoing events, for example, by rubbing hands together to make the sound of a stream.

Organistion

Think up ideas with the students about how they can make imaginative sounds with their body parts to accompany a story. They might include: rubbing hands together; clicking fingers; rubbing a finger up and down on lips, etc.

Read some easy scary stories in French such as *Une histoire sombre, très sombre* (Brown, 1981); *Va-t'en, grand monstre vert* (Emberley, 2012); *Bernard et le monstre* (McKee, 2002); *Les Bizardos* (Ahlberg, 1996). Many of these books will be familiar to you and to the children from their original English editions.

Collect suitable phrases from the books and the reactions expected. Here are some examples and useful vocabulary.

Vocabulary

J'ai peur!:	I'm scared
Je n'ai pas peur:	I'm not scared
Va-t'en!:	Go away
Une nuit sombre:	a dark night
Une chauve-souris:	a bat
Une araignée:	a spider
Une toile d'araignée:	a cobweb
Un fantôme:	a ghost
Un château:	a castle
Une maison hantée:	a haunted house
Il est minuit:	it's midnight
Derrière la porte:	behind the door
Dans la cave:	in the cellar

- Practise pointing to different scary flash cards or plastic toys of spiders, bats etc with the class saying their names and also saying *J'ai peur* and, more defiantly, *Je n'ai pas peur!*
- Teach everyone the question *Qu'est-ce que c'est?* (What is it?). And have fun in the classroom placing the scary items behind cupboards or doors etc and inviting the class to guess what is there.

How to perform La maison hantée

Everyone, including the teacher, sits in rows in a semi-circle, preferably on chairs so that they are visible to the audience. The teacher acts as the narrator, telling a simple story with repetitive stages. Students repeat some lines and make sounds with their body parts to add to the atmosphere. Some of the class hold up plastic props or flash cards of cobwebs, etc., when appropriate to the story. One reliable volunteer has the special task of shouting *BOO!* at the required moment. Recite the story with a regular clapping beat of the hands, clapping the rhythm on your knees where possible, especially on the refrain: *mais je n'ai pas peur!*

Props: Cards/toys of spiders, bats, cobwebs, Haunted House, skeletons, clock face, ghost sheet.

A brave student is needed to introduce the drama: *Bienvenue à notre histoire sombre, très sombre.*

The teacher starts to clap a steady beat softly with hands on knees as a background sound. Whole class joins in.

Teacher:	*Je vais à la Maison Hantée* (show card of house) *mais JE N'AI PAS PEUR!* (Shake head, look bold)
Class:	JE N'AI PAS PEUR!
Teacher:	*Il est minuit* (show clock with time) *mais JE N'AI PAS PEUR!*
Class:	*JE N'AI PAS PEUR!*
Teacher:	*Il y du vent* (make a wind noise and action with hands and whistling), *Il pleut* (click fingers fast for raindrops) *JE N'AI PAS PEUR!*
Class:	*JE N'AI PAS PEUR!*
Teacher:	*Je traverse la rivière* (rub hands to make swishing river sound). *Je m'approche de la maison. Mais JE N'AI PAS PEUR!*
Class:	*JE N'AI PAS PEUR!*
Teacher:	*J'ouvre la porte* (squeaky door sound, old door picture held up) *j'entre dans la maison* (big intake of breath, look all around) *Mais JE N'AI PAS PEUR!*
Class:	*JE N'AI PAS PEUR!*
Teacher:	*Je monte l'escalier* (faster bangs on knees to make sound of going upstairs) *J'entends quelque chose!* (woooooo noise) *Mais JE N'AI PAS PEUR!* (Sound less confident)
Class:	(less confident) *JE N'AI PAS PEUR!*
Teacher:	*Je vois une grande araignée* (show spider picture, make scuttling noise and movement). *Il y a quelque chose sur ma tête* (show cobweb picture, make scuttling movements on top of head). *Mais JE N'AI PAS PEUR* (very softly now).
Teacher:	*Et derrière l'armoire – Qu'est-ce que c'est?!!* (Intake of breath, fear on face)
	Secret child in class, in ghost clothes maybe, gives a big *BOO!*
Teacher:	*J'AI PEUR!* (One child screams)
Children:	*J'AI PEUR!*
Teacher:	*Je cours le long du couloir* (running feet on knees)
Teacher:	*J'entends quelque chose derrière moi* (lots of woooooo noises)
	J'AI PEUR! (repeated by children)
	Je descends l'escalier (clap hands furiously for going downstairs)

J'ouvre la porte (squeaky door opens and hand movement to open door)

Je traverse la rivière (rub hands for river)

Je rentre chez moi (puffing with exhaustion, quick tapping on knees)

Je vois ma mère! Ah Bonjour Maman! (kiss on each cheek)

MAIS JE N'AI PAS PEUR!!! (great bravado, shaking of head, etc.)

Class repeat: *JE N'AI PAS PEUR!!!!*

Top tip

This is even better if you perform in low light, or with some carefully placed and protected candles (check risk assessments). Alternatively, battery-operated tea lights create an equally good effect.

Start the story with a tiny extract from a haunted-house-sounding music track: for example, Michael Jackson's *Thriller* to set the scene.

Project 3   The three little pigs

Project outline

Requirements: preparation time to enlarge and laminate the artwork; wooden lollipop sticks
Event time: one 40-minute lesson
Language targeted: German

Introduction

Most primary students will know the story of *The Three Little Pigs* who build different houses and are chased by the big, bad wolf. It is a simple story with lots of repetition, which is why it has been chosen to form the heart of this project. It lends itself well to whole-class performance, perhaps in assembly (see also Project 1 in this Part *Being creative in assembly*) or for *The European Day of Languages* (see Project 3 in Part III), as everyone can have a part, be it a wolf, a pig, a house or one of the chorus. The story is presented first and new vocabulary introduced. This is followed by the playscript of *The Three Little Pigs*, which can be performed using simple props and flashcards.

Organisation

Step One

Introduce the key vocabulary items that the students will need by showing the pictures and saying the word in German at the same time. Interestingly, the words in German and English are very similar in most cases and this connection forms part of a possible extension activity after the story has been read aloud and the play performed.

Vocabulary 1

Das Schwein: pig (cf. swine)	Das Schweinchen: piglet
Der Wolf: wolf	Das Haus: house
Das Haus aus ... the house made of ...	Das Stroh: straw
Das Holz: wood	Der Stein: stone
Der/die/das erste ...:	the first/second/third ...

Show your students the following pictures. Can they match them to the vocabulary items above?

Answers

Picture 1:	Der Wolf
Picture 2:	Das erste Schwein
Picture 3:	Das zweite Schwein
Picture 4:	Das dritte Schwein
Picture 5:	Das Haus aus Stroh
Picture 6:	Das Haus aus Stein
Picture 7:	Das Haus aus Holz

Step Two

Talk about the beginnings and endings to fairy tales in English. They normally start with 'Once upon a time ...' and end with ... 'and they all lived happily ever after'. In German there are two set phrases as well. At the beginning the phrase is *Es war einmal ...* , and at the end it is *... und wenn sie nicht gestorben sind, dann leben sie noch heute*. Practise saying the German ending with the class as this is part of the chorus in the play later.

Step Three

Some more chorus work is needed before you read the story. This is what the big, bad wolf says in German when the pigs won't let him come into their house: *dann huste ich und puste ich, bis dein Haus kaputt ist!* ('Then I'll huff and puff until your house is broken!'). Try to get your students to roar this out like a big, bad wolf – the louder the better! The phrase which triggers this is often repeated by the wolf: *liebes, gutes Schwein, lass mich doch zu dir hinein* ('Dear, good piglet, do let me come in'). You could write this phrase up, together with the beginning and the ending of the story, where everyone can see it. The students can practise it when it needs to be said during the story.

There are some lovely images in colour of the big, bad wolf and the three little pigs on a website listed on the accompanying DVD. They will help you to explain the five items of vocabulary that follow, which are needed for the story.

Vocabulary 2

Der Bruder: brother	*Das Dach*: roof
Der Wald: wood	*Das Feuer*: fire
Der Schornstein: chimney	

Step Four

Now it is time to read your class the story. Using the pictures presented earlier and the ones from the weblink mentioned in the previous section, as well as the words to the chorus taught in Steps Two and Three, tell the story slowly and clearly whilst your students listen quietly, unless they are joining in with the chorus parts. Some of the verbs your students will not know, but you can mine these or make gestures to explain them. For example, the verb *klettern* (to climb) can be demonstrated with two fingers climbing up just like the wolf on the roof, as can the verb *laufen* (to run) with your two fingers running along the page perhaps.

Die Geschichte von den drei kleinen Schweinchen

Translated by Monika Lind

Es waren einmal drei kleine Schweinchen. Jedes baute sich ein Haus. Das erste baute sich ein Haus aus Stroh. Das zweite baute sich ein Haus aus Holz und das dritte Haus war aus Stein.

Im Wald lebte der böse Wolf. Eines Tages war er sehr hungrig.

Er geht zum Haus des ersten Schweinchens und ruft:

"Liebes, gutes Schwein, lass mich doch zu dir hinein."

Aber das Schweinchen sagt: "Nein!"

Da ruft der Wolf:

"Dann huste ich und puste ich, bis dein Haus kaputt ist!"

Das Schweinchen läuft in das Haus seines Bruders.

Nun geht der Wolf zum Holzhaus und sagt:

"Liebes, gutes Schwein, lass mich doch zu dir hinein."

Aber das Schweinchen sagt: "Nein!"

Da ruft der Wolf:

"Dann huste ich und puste ich, bis dein Haus kaputt ist!"

Die zwei Schweinchen laufen zum dritten Haus.

Der Wolf kommt zum Steinhaus und sagt:

"Liebes, gutes Schwein, lass mich doch zu dir hinein."

Aber das Schweinchen sagt: "Nein!"

Da ruft der Wolf:

"Dann huste ich und puste ich, bis dein Haus kaputt ist!"

Und er hustet und er pustet aber das Haus geht nicht kaputt.

Er klettert auf das Dach und durch den Schornstein und fällt in das Feuer.

Nun rennt er schnell davon.

Jetzt waren die drei Schweinchen wieder glücklich und wenn sie nicht gestorben sind, dann leben sie noch heute.

Step Five

Now it's time to turn the story into a playscript. This was done by following the advice suggested in Project 5 in this Part (*Adapting a story to make a play*), which is well worth reading before you begin.

Roles:

Piglet 1	House 1 (straw)
Piglet 2	House 2 (wood)
Piglet 3	House 3 (stone)
The wolf	Narrator

If you have a class of thirty, there are obviously not enough parts for each student to have one alone. But you can double up the parts, or even triple them (i.e., two students can be the wolf, or three students can take it in turn to be each pig). The houses do not have speaking parts and are made purely by two children forming an arch with their arms to make a bridge underneath which the piglets sit. The narrator can be played by two or more students, whilst others may be happier not speaking alone at all but being part of the chorus and helping with the artwork/props.

Props

These should be kept as simple as possible. The pictures presented earlier, laminated and pasted onto lollipop sticks, can be used to indicate what is going on, and the students themselves can dress the parts too. Dungarees are effective for the three pigs, perhaps with stripey T-shirts underneath and spotted handkerchiefs at the beginning. The wolf can wear brown or black with a large furry tail (a scarf?) and a top hat, whilst the two (or more) narrators can dress alike, so as to make their separate roles come together.

Playscript of The Three Little Pigs

By Cathy Watts

Narrator *es waren einmal drei kleine Schweinchen.*

Piglet 1 *Ich bin das erste Schwein.*

Piglet 2 *Ich bin das zweite Schwein.*

Piglet 3 *Und ich bin das dritte Schwein.*

Narrator *Jedes Schweinchen baute sich ein Haus.*

Piglet 1 *Mein Haus ist aus Stroh* (points to house – i.e., 2 students forming an arch and one student holding up the picture).

Piglet 2 *Mein Haus ist aus Holz* (points to house – i.e., 2 students forming an arch and one student holding up the picture).

Piglet 3 *Und mein Haus ist aus Stein* (points to house – i.e., 2 students forming an arch and one student holding up the picture).

Narrator *Im Wald lebte der böse Wolf.*

Wolf *Ich bin der Wolf. Ich bin sehr böse* (spoken with a deep, growly voice). *Ich bin auch sehr hungrig* (the three pigs squeak with terror).

Narrator *Der Wolf ging zum ersten Haus.*

Wolf *Liebes, gutes Schwein, lass mich doch zu dir hinein!*

Piglet 1 *Nein!!* (stamps foot).

Wolf (and chorus of students) *Dann huste ich und puste ich, bis dein Haus kaputt ist!* (Students forming bridge for first house fall on the floor).

Narrator *Das Schweinchen läuft in das Haus seines Bruders* (first piglet runs to second house made by the bridge of students).

Narrator *Nun geht der Wolf zum Holzhaus.*

Wolf Liebes, gutes Schwein, lass mich doch zu dir hinein.

Piglet 2 *Nein!!* (makes a fist).

Wolf (and chorus of students) *Dann huste ich und puste ich, bis dein Haus kaputt ist!* (Students forming bridge for second house fall on the floor).

Narrator *Die zwei Schweinchen laufen zum dritten Haus* (first piglet and second piglet run to third house made by the bridge of students).

Wolf (knocks on door of house made of stone) *Liebes, gutes Schwein, lass mich doch zu dir hinein.*

Piglet 3 *Nein!!* (makes a fist and stamps foot. The two other pigs shake and tremble in the background).

Wolf (and chorus of students) *Dann huste ich und puste ich, bis dein Haus kaputt ist!*

Narrator *Und er hustet und er pustet aber das Haus geht nicht kaputt. Er klettert auf das Dach* (Wolf climbs up on top of the bridge of students using a chair) *und durch den Schornstein* (Wolf falls through the arch of students) *und fällt in das Feuer.*

Nun rennt er schnell davon (Wolf runs away holding his bottom and howling).

Narrator *Jetzt waren die drei Schweinchen wieder glücklich* (three pigs dance for joy).

Whole class together *Und wenn sie nicht gestorben sind, dann leben sie noch heute!*

Extension

It is amazing how many animals in German have very similar names to their English counterparts. You might like to point this out to your class and introduce them to a few.

das Schwein:	pig (cf swine)	*die Giraffe*:	giraffe
der Wolf:	wolf	*die Maus*:	mouse
die Katze:	cat	*der Hund*:	dog (cf hound)
der Tiger:	tiger	*der Fuchs*:	fox
der Bär:	bear	*der Frosch*:	frog

The three little pigs: Additional DVD materials

1.   Useful websites

Project 4   Sing up for languages

Project outline

Requirements: song words displayed; willingness to sing or hum a tune on your own
Event time: ten minutes to learn each song
Language used: French

Introduction

Singing is a lively, active way to teach vocabulary in class, and most students love to sing in the safety of a group if it's fun. You can vary how loudly they sing, the actions they add, whether they are sitting, standing or moving about, whether they sing in one, two or three groups, in a circle or rows, or at their tables. If you turn the song into a round, where each group starts in rotation, a simple song can sound instantly quite professional, and certainly good enough for an assembly presentation.

Of course there are plenty of excellent CDs to buy with great songs to fit every topic, but maybe you could make up some of your own too. They can fit your class and circumstances exactly, and students can help fit the words to the tune with you. Record the class or the whole Key Stage singing on a CD and maybe you've got a fundraising opportunity ahead, or a classroom resource to play at wet playtimes or lining up for Assembly.

Organisation

Traditional, well-known tunes are a good starting point; students know them, the lines aren't too long, and they are catchy too. Make a list of tunes which you and your class are comfortable with. The following are suggestions to start you off.

- London's Burning/ *Frère Jacques*
- She'll be coming round the mountain
- Jingle bells
- Three blind mice
- Here we go round the mulberry bush
- Polly put the kettle on
- If you're happy and you know it…
- London Bridge is falling down
- Bobby Shaftoe
- Sur le pont d'Avignon
- There's a hole in my bucket

How to teach songs

Use a familiar tune and add words.

Hum the tune first and use your hands to encourage everyone to hum with you, so that they've got past the embarrassment of singing!

Then *you* show how to sing the song on your own, all the way through with the words.

Teach it line by line, with lots of praise.

If you can, add actions or get them to lift up a picture, get up and turn around, etc.

Make it as lively and fun as you can.

Use as much repetition as possible so that it's accessible to everyone.

Consider whether it could be sung in two or three parts, as a round. If so, establish a rule that you always sing a round through twice. It sounds extra special and a good show-off for a visitor.

Ideas for using authentic French traditional songs

Example: *savez-vous planter les choux?*

- Set scene by using props, such as wellies, spade, cabbage, etc.
- Students listen for one word or phrase and respond with action or card.

- Give out lines of song on strips of paper in envelopes. As the song is played, sequence strips of paper.
- Sing the song together using written words.

Top tip

Follow this up with some Literacy links: for example, ask students to identify and investigate the sounds in the song which are different in French, like the sounds *oi*, as in *doigt*, or *ou*, as in *genou*

Using a familiar tune: London's Burning

These first songs keep to simple language, so that even the youngest class can sing with meaning.

Écoutez-moi ×2	(Hands to ears)
Regardez-moi ×2	(Hands to eyes)
Levez-vous ×2	(Get up)
Asseyez-vous ×2	(Sit down)
Voici ma tête ×2	(Touch head)
Voici mon nez ×2	(Touch nose)
Voici ma bouche ×2	(Touch mouth)
Voici mes yeux ×2	(Touch eyes)
Bonjour ×2	(Shake hands)
Au revoir ×2	(Wave goodbye)
Bon appétit ×2	(Rub tummy)
Merci beaucoup ×2	(Thumbs up)
Jaune, bleu ×2	(Students stand at the front holding coloured cards, then swap places and form a new verse)
Rouge, vert ×2	
Orange, blanc ×2	
Marron, violet ×2	

Songs with a theme: Food and breakfast

Jingle Bells tune

Un croissant, un croissant
Un pain au chocolat
Des céréales, de la confiture
Un chocolat chaud pour moi!

Frère Jacques tune, briskly

Je bois du café ×2
Je mange un croissant chaud ×2
Je prends le petit déjeuner ×2
Bon appétit! ×2

London's Burning tune

J'ai un croissant ×2
J'ai du pain ×2
Encore du beurre ×2
Moi, j'ai faim ×2

More complicated songs about food

Here we go gathering nuts in May tune

Voici les poires et les bananes ×3
C'est combien s'il vous plaît?
(One student is chosen to call out the reply: e.g.
Cinq euros!)
Voici les pommes et les cerises ×3
C'est combien s'il vous plaît?
(Reply): *Huit euros*, etc.

She'll be coming round the mountain tune

Je voudrais une pomme, s'il vous plaît
Je voudrais une pomme, s'il vous plaît
Voici une pomme, voici une pomme.
Merci beaucoup, merci!

Je voudrais deux bananes, s'il vous plaît
Je voudrais deux bananes, s'il vous plaît
Voici deux bananes, voici deux bananes,
Merci beaucoup, merci!

Je voudrais trois pêches, s'il vous plaît
Je voudrais trois pêches, s'il vous plaît
Voici trois pêches, voici trois pêches,
Merci beaucoup, merci!

How much is that doggy in the window? tune

C'est combien les cerises et les oranges?
C'est combien un kilo de poires?
C'est combien les tomates et un chou-fleur?
C'est combien un litre de lait?

C'est combien une baguette et un croissant?
C'est combien un pain au chocolat?
C'est combien un gâteau au citron?
C'est combien une tarte aux fraises?

Oranges and lemons, say the bells of St Clements tune

Une pomme, une orange
Une banane, une poire.
Une petite cerise, un grand pamplemousse.

Une pêche, une framboise
Une fraise, un abricot.
Une petite mangue et un kilo de prunes.

More complicated songs with a weekly theme

She'll be coming round the mountain tune

Je voudrais des frites lundi soir ×2   (quiet echo: *lundi soir*)

Je voudrais des frites, je voudrais des frites,

Je voudrais des frites lundi soir   (full-blast echo: *lundi soir*)

Other verses beginning:

Je voudrais des escargots mardi matin

Je voudrais du rosbif dimanche soir

Je voudrais une glace jeudi après-midi, etc.

(For this song you can sing the same line all the way through, as in the first example, or, to make it more challenging when the students are used to the pattern, try a new type of food on each line.)

There's a hole in my bucket tune

Pour mon petit déjeuner

Le lundi, le lundi

Pour mon petit déjeuner

Je prends un croissant

Pour mon petit déjeuner,

Le mardi, le mardi

Pour mon petit déjeuner

Je prends une banane

Pour mon petit déjeuner

Le mercredi, le mercredi

Pour mon petit déjeuner

Je prends une tartine

For the song above, everyone can easily plan the next verses from the pattern and perform in groups. Adapt it for any meal, any day or describe drinks – *je bois du café*.

Here we go round the Mulberry Bush tune

Lundi je bois un chocolat chaud, un chocolat chaud, un chocolat chaud

Lundi je bois un chocolat chaud

A sept heures et demie

Mardi je bois du jus d'orange, du jus d'orange, du jus d'orange

Mardi je bois du jus d'orange

A huit heures et demie

(To continue this song, vary the days of the week, drinks and times.)

Sur le pont d'Avignon tune

(in this song you could change the name to an adult in school and a favourite food each day).

Monsieur Jacques mange les frites

Tous les lundis, tous les lundis

Monsieur Jacques mange les frites

Tous les lundis. Bon appétit!

Monsieur Jacques mange un oeuf

Tous les mardis, tous les mardis

Monsieur Jacques mange un oeuf

Tous les mardis. Bon Appétit!

Using songs to practise any new vocabulary

When you first introduce any new vocabulary – for example, food, classroom objects, animals, family members – choose the four most useful words and place them on flashcards or on the board, or ask for volunteers to hold them at the front of the class. Then sing the words to the tune of *London's Burning*, first repeating the same word all through the song, next verse add a second one, and finally change the words for every line. Here is an example:

Les frites (all the way through)

Les frites, les glaces (all the way through)

Les frites, les glaces, les fraises, les bananes

Students soon get the hang of this idea and, when they have sung all four words through a few times, play the game where you point to the next card at random, so they have to be on their toes. It's a good way of watching who can keep up and is quick to learn vocabulary.

As a next step, they could have the same four flashcards in a pair or small group and take it in turns to get their friends to sing in the same way.

You can extend this simply (still to the tune of *London's Burning*) with *J'aime* (I like) and a wider range of vocabulary. Again, add the new phrases in a structured way, increasing to a final flourish – for example:

J'aime les melons, j'aime les fraises,

J'aime les bananes, j'aime les pommes,

J'aime les poires, j'aime les pêches,

J'aime les citrons, j'aime les cerises.

Then ask everyone to help you to make a less healthy verse: for example, *les frites, les bonbons, les glaces, le chocolat*. As they sing, students could raise their hands when they get to a phrase they agree with, or you could distribute cards with food pictures on them which they wave when their word is sung.

The versatile verb phrase *Je voudrais* (I would like) is another useful starter for singing new vocabulary, with the addition of the tune *She'll be coming round the mountain*. Add a chorus with an action to make the song more exciting, for example:

Je voudrais un poisson, oui c'est vrai ×2 (thumbs up)

Je voudrais un hamster

Je voudrais un chat

Je voudrais un cheval, oui c'est vrai!

For this song, you could just sing the same line all the way through to keep it easy and rise to a crescendo on the final line *oui c'est vrai*, or students rise to their feet to call it and wave their hands vigorously in the air!

It's useful to teach a common question, such as *Qu'est-ce que?* (What?). Practise saying the phrase several times first, so that people get used to the sound. This song to the tune of *Polly put the kettle on* works well as question and answer. Everyone sings the line

Qu'est-ce que tu fais ce soir? ×3 (What are you doing this evening)

Have a series of cards about hobbies. Point to a card and the class sing a reply together, for example,

Je fais du sport or *je regarde la télé.*

This would work with drink or food too, for example:

Qu'est-ce que tu bois ce matin?

And the answer: *Je bois du lait* etc

Adapting familiar primary songs for language work

A popular song in primary school is *Hot potato, pass it round*, usually played with the class sitting in a circle on the floor passing a tambourine or drum and stopping at the end of the chorus to perform an action. Adapt this easily for a language singing game by placing four or so flash cards of phrases you've been learning in a drawstring bag or even a PE bag and pass it round as everyone sings to the *Hot Potato* tune:

Un, deux, trois, passez vite,

Passez vite, passez vite.

Un, deux, trois, passez vite,

Passez vi-te (two syllables on this last vite)

Sing this with a lively rhythm, so that the game is quick-moving. When you get to the end of the song the student holding the bag opens it, takes out a flashcard, calls out the word, passes the bag on around the circle and runs all the way round the outside of the circle back to their place, while everyone else sings the song again.

Another song that used to be sung widely in Key Stage One (ages five and six) and early Key Stage Two (up to age eight) is *one little, two little, three little Indians* .... Although the words in English might not be politically correct, the tune is a good basis for a song to get the class up in a line to sing and move around the classroom doing actions. Practise numbers up to three, teach *petit* (small) and a few common animal names: for example, *un poisson* (a fish); *un oiseau* (a bird); *un chat* (a chat).

Un petit, deux petits, trois petits poissons ×3

Trois petits poissons qui nagent   (three little fish who swim)

Un petit, deux petits, trois petits oiseaux ×3

Trois petits oiseaux qui volent   (three little birds who fly)

Un petit, deux petits, trois petits chats, ×3

Trois petits chats qui grimpent   (three little cats who climb)

Un petit, deux petits, trois petits lions ×3

Trois petits lions qui chassent   (three little lions who hunt)

Un petit, deux petits, trois petits hamsters ×3

Trois petits hamsters qui dorment   (three little hamsters who sleep)

As you sing, count out the numbers on your fingers, and bring out a volunteer to join a line by your side. The whole class, but particularly the students in the line, do the appropriate actions of counting and moving. For each verse, bring out a new group of three students. During your final verse, they could move around the classroom showing how their animals behave.

Project 5   Adapting a story to make a play

Project outline

Requirements: text suitable for age group; headbands or easy-to-make headgear
Event time: 30 minutes to rehearse and practise; 30 minutes to make headbands, etc.;
20 minutes to perform;
Language used: Spanish

Introduction

There are many inspirational texts in European languages available now which are simple enough for primary schools to use and which lend themselves to being turned into a short play. This could be used as the final outcome of a term's work. This project will take you through the stages which will help you to adapt a story to suit your class. An example of a project which was developed along these lines is *The Three Little Pigs* (see Project 3 in this Part).

Organistion

First choose a suitable text for the year group you teach. It is impossible to match the chronological age of your students with the equivalent text level in a foreign language at this stage of learning. Instead, look for a lively story which may be originally designed for a younger audience but makes up for this with humour, action or colour. Most students enjoy meeting a familiar text which they read in English a few years earlier, and now feel that they are one step ahead with understanding it in another language. It is particularly a bonus for students with special needs, who may have come across the story more recently and therefore feel at home with it.

How to choose the right text

Look for a story with lots of repetition: this could be characters asking the same question or going on the same journey or performing the same procedure. This will make the play more manageable, reduce the amount of vocabulary which has to be learned and help the audience to understand what is going on in another language.

Look for a useful question or turn of phrase which is practised – it makes sense to have a common, well-used phrase, rather than one that will never be needed again. This could be asking the time, your name or age, where or when you are going somewhere, what you are doing, etc.

Look also for a text which lends itself to a performance. This may involve having groups of children to represent different kinds of characters, or having an obvious narrator to tell the story. And make sure that students are speaking at the level which is appropriate for their stage of learning the language. There is no point putting into their mouths more advanced sentences which they have not understood or are unlikely to use in that school year.

Is the story adaptable, so that you could change the text to a slightly different theme which suits what you have been teaching? For example, focusing on different kinds of transport rather than places visited; talking about sports rather than hobbies.

Look for ways for pairs or groups, or even the whole class, to speak in unison. This is much more reassuring at this stage, although you may be lucky enough to find one or two confident speakers to act as narrators or lead the group.

Look for a visual aspect to the story theme which would enhance a performance. Could there be masks made, or bright colours used, so that groups wear the same colour T shirt? Is it possible to produce simple headdresses made of crêpe paper, or headbands with identifying symbols on the front?

Is there a way to add a dance, a home-made song, procession or action rhyme to bring the play to life?

Is it possible to have props or characters on sticks to represent parts of the story which are impossible to portray? Individuals or groups could raise these at appropriate moments.

Put up some text or pictures on a whiteboard overhead to help the audience understand what is being said.

Possible texts

Traditional tales are often used for play performance, and many are published in a wide variety of languages by Mantra Lingua (www.mantralingua.com) in dual-language format. These include: *Goldilocks and the Three Bears*; *Ali Baba*; *Billy Goats Gruff*; *The Little Red Hen*. Check that the text is suitable for your age group; you may need to simplify or reduce the language, as these books are particularly suited for bilingual readers, rather than beginners with a limited knowledge.

Popular children's books such as *The very hungry caterpillar* (Carle, 1969), *We're going on a bear hunt* (Rosen, 1989), *Farmer duck* (Waddell, 1991) *Brown bear, brown bear* (Martin & Carle, 1967) are also easily available and adapt well. The play example that follows is loosely based on *Oso pardo, oso pardo* by Bill Martin and Eric Carle (1998) and its partner book *Oso polar, oso polar* by the same authors (2000).

These books are based on a circular idea of one animal asking a question of another animal, who in turn asks a third, etc. At the end the teacher and class are brought into the final page. The books contain repetition, both in the animal name and in the familiar questions *¿Qué ves ahí?* (What can you see there?), *¿Qué es ese ruido?* (What is that noise?). Although this may not in itself be a common question, the construction *Qué es ese …* would be useful to learn. The stories contain golden opportunities for boldly-coloured costumes and easily identifiable groups for children to join. These texts would be very suitable for speaking in unison and for songs and actions.

The first way to use these texts would be to retell the story in quite a formal way, with a narrator, or group of narrators, giving the introduction and setting the scene. The rest of the class, in a semi-circle, would become groups of different kinds of animals who ask the repeated question to the next group until the finale, when all the class speak together. The words and story used could remain close to the text of the book.

Another way would be more visual and active, with the groups of animals suitably dressed and placed waiting in different areas of the space. When it is their turn, each group would process from their area, making appropriate movements and noises for their animal. They would approach the stage where the previous animal would ask the repeated question and after exchanging remarks, the group would move to the front to ask the next group of animals who emerge. This version would also use the text from the book as their dialogue. This version of the story gives more opportunities for drama with movement and costume. There could be a rap from each animal group as they arrive on stage (see Project 6 in this chapter *Action Rhymes and Raps*) and a chance for the whole class to sing a colour song at the end or to sing the names of the animals in a round to the tune of *London's Burning*.

A third and more ambitious method would be to use the context of the story as a chance to display the language which the class have been learning during the term or year, before re-enacting parts of the story. One group of animals at a time could come forward and have a little conversation using everyday language and asking each other their name, age, where they live, introducing their family. You could change the animals to insects, birds, farm animals or any others and change the colours too. This example has adapted the animals to insects and a set of birds, focusing on butterflies, ladybirds, spiders, bees and caterpillars. It begins with a group of green butterflies.

¡Hola, Mariposa verde! ¿Cómo estás?

¡Hola, Mariposa verde! Muy bien gracias.

¿Cómo te llamas? Me llamo Mariposa …(insert name) ¿Y tú?

Yo me llamo …¿Cuántos años tienes?

Tengo once años. ¿Y tú?

Tengo dorce años. ¿Tienes hermanos?

Sí, tengo dos hermanas. ¿Y tú?

Sí, tengo tres hermanas y dos hermanos.

Esta es mi familia – mi hermano, mi hermana, mi madre, mi padre, etc.

Each group could do a little rap or action rhyme about their family, for example:

Mi hermano pequeño

Mi hermana alta

Mi padre viejo

Mi madre joven

Esta es mi familia – ¡ uno dos tres!

They could sing to *London's Burning*, raising their hand in the air when their character is called.

Mi hermano × 2

Mi madre × 2

Mi padre × 2

Mi familia (everyone waves)

The main story could follow with students sitting in insect/animal groups (possibly six groups of insects/animals with five students in each, wearing appropriate clothing and masks) facing the audience and speaking in unison.

Class in unison: *Mariposa verde, mariposa verde, ¿Qué ves ahí?*

Mariposa group: *Veo una mariquita rosa* (ladybirds get up and flap about)

Class in unison: *Mariquita rosa, mariquita rosa, ¿Qué ves ahí?*

Mariquita group: *Veo una araña blanca* (spiders stand up and crawl about)

Class in unison: *Araña blanca, araña blanca, ¿Qué ves ahí?*

Araña group: *Veo una abeja naranja* (bees make buzzing noise and move around)

Class in unison: *Abeja naranja, abeja naranja, ¿Qué ves ahí?*

Abeja group: *Veo una oruga azul* (caterpillars squirm and move from side to side)

Class in unison: *Oruga azul, oruga azul, ¿Qué ves ahí?*

Oruga group: *Veo un pájaro amarillo* (birds perform, swooping down on the insects)

Class in unison: *Pájaro amarillo, pájaro amarillo, ¿Qué ves ahí?*

Pájaro group: *Veo a los niños* (point to the children in the class)

Class in unison, looking around at each other: *Niños, niños, ¿Qué vemos ahí?*

Class stand up and point to each group in turn who get up and move in their place: *Vemos una mariposa verde, una mariquita rosa, una araña blanca, una abeja naranja, una orega azul y un pájaro amarillo.*

The play could finish with a song of the animal or insect names sung to the tune of *Agadoo*:

Maripo-sa-sa

Mariquita ro-sa

A-a rañ-añ-a

Abeja naranja

Orega-ga-ga

Pájaro amarillo

Los ni-ños

Y los animales.

Project 6   Action, rhymes and raps

Project outline

Requirements: normal classroom space, some flash cards for the topic chosen
Event time: ten minutes or so to teach each item
Language targeted: French

Introduction

Why teach a language with a rhyme or action? Because it's an inclusive approach which encourages all students to feel that languages are for them. A kinaesthetic element helps learners to put actions and words together and often brings pupils with special needs to the fore. What other school subject invites everyone to get up in the middle of the lesson, dance around or act like a rocket? We want their language experience to be meaningful but also memorable, enjoyable and accessible. This approach also gives many opportunities for paired and partner work, where communication with others is the key. Subsequently these short items can be linked together to provide a non-threatening performance in front of family, peers and the whole school.

Organisation

Action Rhymes

These examples of action rhymes can be the starting point for a lesson to wake up a class and remind them of the fun in store in the next half hour or so, or a reward for great concentration and co-operation. When you make up your own, try to bear in mind the following useful steps:

- use the *I say, you repeat* format;
- look for repetition or a chorus;
- choose easy, memorable actions;
- establish a steady rhythm;
- look for an exciting finale;
- bring in an element of suspense to keep them guessing;
- establish a versatile model, so that Year Six (ages ten and eleven) do not feel too self-conscious.

Nounours (Teddy bear) rhyme

This is a good starter for beginners who have learned a few classroom instructions. Start with everyone sitting facing the teacher, hanging heads like sleeping teddy bears. As you say the instructions they copy the words and do the actions.

Nounours nounours, levez-vous!	Get up
Nounours nounours, tournez-vous!	Turn round in circle
Nounours nounours, dites bonjour!	Wave hand and say *Bonjour*
Nounours nounours, asseyez-vous!	Sit down
Nounours nounours, dormez bien.	Hang head, go back to sleep

La Fusée (The rocket)

This is a simple, fun way to practise numbers and to have a little performance. Even students who know their numbers need to practise saying them in reverse. You could demonstrate this first and then let them guess what the rhyme is about. Tantalise them by delaying saying the Zéro so they have to wait for the excitement.

All work in unison. Play a Beat the Teacher game to catch them out: for example, they look around, you call the title to surprise them and see if they can be ready before you.

Vocabulary: *dix, neuf, huit, sept, six, cinq, quatre, trois, deux, un, zéro*

Call out *La Fusée*. Stand absolutely still and put your hands together in front of you, as if in prayer. Insist on silence and complete attention.

Countdown from *dix* to *cinq* slowly with students repeating after you. Keep your hands still.

When you reach *cinq*, move your hands slightly upwards, still together.

When you get to *zéro*, call that number loudly all together, bringing your hands up and then down by your sides as if for a rocket taking off.

You could play it again with a volunteer calling out the numbers or a group taking it in turns.

La semaine (The week)

Make a collection of simple verbs which describe an action you might practise at school, in PE or in the classroom. Discuss which actions you might perform on different days. Look for an interesting culmination to the week for Sunday.

Use a steady rhythm. Everyone repeats after you and does an action for each verb. Have a dramatic action for the final line, for example:

Lundi je dors	On Monday I sleep
Mardi je cours	On Tuesday I run
Mercredi je marche	On Wednesday I walk
Jeudi je saute	On Thursday I jump
Vendredi je nage	On Friday I swim
Samedi je lis	On Saturday I read
Et dimanche je danse	And on Sunday I dance

Next steps

This simple rhyme works well with Years Three and Four (ages seven and eight). To make a more complicated rhyme, replace the verbs above by making a list together of hobbies or activities which students like doing: for example, *je joue au foot, je fais du sport, j'écoute de la musique, je joue du violon* (I play football, I do sport, I listen to music, I play the violin).

In pairs, students could make up their own rhyme and perform with a partner, performing an appropriate action for each phrase. They could announce the title: *la semaine de Hannah*, etc.

L'arc-en-ciel (The rainbow)

This is an easy rhyme for beginners in their first term, using some common colours. Have a set of colour flash cards for volunteers to hold up. Call out a colour name and choose a student to come to the front of the class to hold that card.

Select about six or seven colours, as far as possible, the colours of the rainbow.

You say each line of the rhyme, they repeat, and a student raises the card of that colour. On the last line, each person raises their card in turn to make the arc shape and everyone else slowly moves both their arms in the air from one side to the other to represent the arc and calls out the final words together.

Voici le bleu	Here's the blue
Voici le rouge	Here's the red
Voici le jaune	Here's the yellow
Voici le vert	Here's the green
Voici le violet	Here's the purple
Voici le rose	Here's the pink
Voici l'orange	Here's the orange
Et voilà! L'arc-en-ciel!	And there it is! The rainbow!

Le bonhomme de neige (The snowman)

This is an easy, useful rhyme for you to perform for the class without any prior explanation to start off a weather topic. Ask students to guess what the different actions indicate, especially when it gets to the snowman and his buttons. Then teach it to them line by line.

Oh là là! Il fait chaud!	Oh goodness! It's hot
	(hands in air in surprise, then right hand wipes forehead)
Oh là là! Il fait froid!	Oh goodness! It's cold
	(hands in air, then wrap arms around body to keep warm)

Oh là là! Il pleut!	Oh goodness! It's raining
	(hands in air, then fingers make twirly lines for rain)
Oh là là! Il neige!	Oh goodness! It's snowing.
	(hands in air, then fingers make zigzag lines for snowfall)

With both hands, make the shape of simple snowman's head and body in front of your face, then dot three buttons on his chest, saying....

Un, deux, trois!

Next steps

Add extra lines in the same format when you've got further with weather expressions: for example, *il y a du vent, il y a du brouillard, il y a un orage* (it's windy, it's foggy, it's stormy). Encourage everyone to find suitable actions.

Or bring out the sunshine and make your snowman melt: *il y a du soleil,* (It's sunny) count to five together and then you sink to the ground!

À gauche, à droite (To the left, to the right)

This action rhyme can be taught in the first term and still be useful a couple of years later as a reminder and a short lesson filler. Teach it line by line, with the class repeating. Do it first with the class facing you to learn the steps and then they can perform in pairs facing one another.

Students love it as a moving game that you can perform several times in succession. They can change partners each time you complete the rhyme, as you call out *Un, deux, trois, CHANGEZ!*

À gauche, à droite × 2	(stretch both their arms in each direction to the side)
En haut, en bas × 2	(raise and lower both arms)
En avant, en arrière × 2	(arms in front and then behind their heads)
Lentement, lentement	(slowly raise arms in front and then lower them)

Keep them waiting in suspense here, as this next bit is a favourite!

| *Vite, vite* | (quickly move arms up and down) |
| *Chouette, chouette!* | (both thumbs up in front of them in triumph) |

Performing a Rap

Raps are useful for encouraging pairs or groups to perform together after some exposure to a new topic. Everyone can add their own body music to make the performance more exciting and enjoy showing their work to the rest of the class. Look for groups with some musical expertise to perform first and to inspire less imaginative friends with an extra sense of rhythm or movement. Although older students might be more confident and knowledgeable about raps, younger classes can also enjoy the independence of adding their own rhythm and style. For an assembly performance, half the class could perform the favourite rap while the other half provide a strong beat by clapping, tapping their feet, clicking their fingers etc.

Animal rap

In advance, use a lesson to explore how animals move and play some language games to get the class moving around the room by instructing them to:

Courez comme un lion	run like a lion
Sautez comme un singe	jump like a monkey
Marchez comme un chameau	walk like a camel
Nagez comme un poisson	swim like a fish
Volez comme un oiseau	fly like a bird

Once they are familiar with these verbs of movement, introduce students to the third person singular part of the verbs above (to fit the pronouns *il* or *elle*) and encourage them to identify links between the different parts of the verbs, for example, *courez/court; sautez/saute; marchez/marche; nagez/nage; volez/vole*

Together work out a movement rap, using these new parts of the verbs, for example,

Un lion court	a lion runs
Un chameau marche	a camel walks
Un poisson nage	a fish swims
Un singe saute	a monkey jumps
Un oiseau vole	a bird flies

Perform the rap with suitable movements, and then add a final line:

Mais moi, je …

Choose a suitable verb to end the rap, preferably an interesting action that describes how a human could move: e.g. skate, dance, ski. A language dictionary could be used to search for a verb, and the class could then (with guidance) find the correct part of the verb to follow *je*:

je patine	I skate
je nage	I swim
je danse	I dance
je fais du ski	I ski
je dors	I sleep

Ask groups or pairs to make up their own rap, maybe with funny or silly possibilities: for example, *un poisson vole, un chameau saute.* If necessary, add extra animals or movements for them to choose, using a language dictionary to help. Each pair or group then performs their rap in turn, complete with rhythm.

Food Rap

Teach some basic foods and a selection of verbs to express a preference, such as:

J'aime	I like
Je n'aime pas	I don't like
J'adore	I love
Je déteste	I hate

Put together some combinations starting with *J'adore*, for example,

J'adore les frites

J'adore les glaces

J'adore les bonbons

J'adore le chocolat

Add a final line of an opposite, such as

Mais je déteste ça! (But I hate that!)

Perform with everyone pointing to a food card they hate at the end. Add appropriate actions, for example, rubbing tummy for pleasure, and a look and sound of horror on last line. Add rhythm.

Get students to work in pairs or groups to make up and perform their own food rap. This could be adapted for drinks, pets, sports, hobby names with suitable actions.

Project 7　　The magic mouse

Project outline

Requirements: preparation time to sew the mouse and make the masks. Felt, paper, scissors, lollipop sticks, googly eyes, needle and thread, stuffing
Event time: one 40-minute lesson
Language targeted: German

Introduction

It is hugely motivating to be able to understand a whole story in a foreign language. This project is based around a simple, very accessible story written by Katja Neubauer and reproduced here with permission from UK–German Connection (see useful weblinks in the material for this project on the accompanying DVD). The story concerns a little, grey mouse which wishes it could be a different animal and a different colour! The project involves simple language and can be enhanced by the use of a mouse soft toy and animal masks, for which instructions are given. Suggestions for extension activities are also provided and the additional DVD materials for this project contain a translation of the story in English as well as a list of useful websites.

Organisation

If you are working with your class using this story, it is fun to have a mouse to hand which you can use as a puppet to help illustrate the tale. You could either buy a mouse soft toy or puppet to enhance your story, or make one using the template that follows. Many primary schools have sewing clubs and you could perhaps ask some of your students, if they belong to such a club, to sew a mouse each as part of it. Or perhaps your whole class enjoys sewing, in which case you will have around thirty different mice to use in the lesson and later for your display (see also Project 7 in Part II *Language displays for the classroom*). The animal masks which follow the mouse instructions are easier to make and colour, so perhaps the more nimble-fingered students could make a mouse, whilst others colour in the masks. All contribute to the final result!

How to make a little grey mouse

Shopping list

Grey felt for the body and tail
Contrasting felt for the face
Googly eyes
Needle and thread
Black thread for whiskers
Stuffing

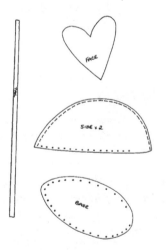

Templates

See opposite

Instructions

1. Cut your pieces out of grey felt to make the sides and the body. You could use a different shade of grey, or even another colour, for the face and tail. You need two side pieces and one each of the other pieces.
2. Sew your two sides together along the straight lines.
3. Sew your base to the sides along the dotted lines.
4. Turn your mouse the right way round through the gap in the base.
5. Poke the tail into the gap, together with enough stuffing to round out the body, and then sew up the hole.

6. Now glue two googly eyes onto your mouse's face (made from the heart shape).

7. Add some black wool whiskers.

Making masks

Your mouse is now ready to take part in the story – but you'll also need four other faces. These are the four animals that the mouse wishes it could be in the story: a cat; a duck; a snake; a giraffe. Here are four masks of these animals which you could make with your students. You could make small versions of the masks and glue these onto flat, wooden lollipop sticks to hold up in front of the mouse's face as you tell the story.

Or you could enlarge the patterns, divide your students into four groups, give each group the same animal to colour in the right colours based on the story (cat = blue; duck = green; snake = red; giraffe = yellow). As they hear their group's animal in the story, they can hold up a mask in front of their faces. If you laminate the masks when they are finished, they will not flop about. If you glue them onto lollipop sticks they will be easier for the students to hold.

Vocabulary

You will need to introduce the following vocabulary items to your class before you start reading the story. You can use your pre-prepared mouse and coloured masks to help.

Animals		Colours	
die Maus:	mouse	*grau*:	grey
die Katze:	cat	*blau*:	blue
die Ente:	duck	*grün*:	green
die Schlange:	snake	*rot*:	red
die Giraffe:	giraffe	*gelb*:	yellow

The story: Die Zaubermaus A story about a magical mouse!

© Katja Neubauer

Eine kleine graue Maus lebte auf einer Farm

Eines Tages wollte die keine kleine graue Maus mehr sein. Sie wünschte sich, eine blaue Katze zu sein. So wurde sie eine grau-blaue Maus-Katze.

UK-German Connection
Deutsch-Britische Schul- und Jugendbegegnungen
bringing young people together

    Eines Tages wollte sie keine grau-blaue Maus-Katze mehr sein. Sie wünschte sich, eine grüne Ente zu sein. So wurde sie eine grau-blau-grüne Maus-Katze-Ente.

    Eines Tages wollte sie keine grau-blau-grüne Maus-Katze-Ente mehr sein. Sie wünschte sich, eine rote Schlange zu sein. So wurde sie eine grau-blau-grün-rote Maus-Katze-Ente-Schlange.

    Eines Tages wollte sie keine grau-blau-grün-rote Maus-Katze-Ente-Schlange mehr sein. Sie wünschte sich, eine gelbe Giraffe zu sein. So wurde sie eine grau-blau-grün-rot-gelbe Maus-Katze-Ente-Schlange-Giraffe.

    Nun war sie so bunt, dass sich alle Tiere vor ihr fürchteten. Bald hatte sie keine Freunde mehr.

    Eines Tages wollte sie keine grau-blau-grün-rot-gelbe Maus-Katze-Ente-Schlange-Giraffe mehr sein. Sie wünschte sich, eine kleine graue Maus zu sein. So wurde sie wieder eine kleine graue Maus.

    Nun war sie sehr glücklich.

This text is an extract from UK–German Connection's *voyage kids* website. Interested in finding out more? Visit *voyage kids* for an audio recording of the *Zaubermaus* story, as well as useful vocabulary, an interactive colouring exercise and games and quizzes on colours, animals and many other topics! See useful websites on the accompanying DVD for UK–German Connection's website.

    Once the students have learnt the vocabulary, they could easily act out the story in assembly using the mouse puppet and the coloured masks, either holding these against the mouse's face or in front of their own faces – or both!

Extension

The story of the magic mouse lends itself beautifully to further work on colours and animals in German. Here are some more common colours.

braun:	brown	*weiß*:	white
schwarz:	black	*orange*:	orange
purpurrot:	purple	*rosa*:	pink

Here are some common animals. It is always a good idea to learn the gender of each animal as you learn the new word itself.

Der Hund:	dog	*das Pferd*:	horse
Die Kuh:	cow	*der Frosch*:	frog
Der Fisch:	fish	*der Vogel*:	bird
Das Nilpferd:	hippo	*der Tiger*:	tiger

You could try adding your own animals and colours to the story about the magic mouse. Or write your own version!

Note: the four animals used in the story are all feminine. It is easier if you stick to the same genders – i.e., all masculine, all feminine or all neuter – to allow the articles to agree.

Katja Neubauer also suggests the following extension activity, which we are delighted to include here.

1. Take four animals (such as the ones above), colour them each differently and stick them onto card.

2. Cut the animals in half.

3. The students, working in pairs, have to reassemble the four animals. First they need to work out which four animals and which colours they have (the German words for the animals and colours should be used).

4. Then students can make their own 'funny' animals by mixing and matching the halves in whichever order they choose. Again, they have to name them.

5. Finally students choose one animal and one colour each and create their own versions, which can be displayed in the classroom at the end of the session.

The magic mouse: Additional DVD materials

1. A hand-made mouse
2. Translation of the story into English
3. Useful websites

6

Languages and literacy

Introduction

Literacy work is the backbone of much classroom activity in primary schools and this Part feeds into this in a bright and refreshing way. It offers eight projects full of original and fresh ideas to help you adapt your classroom literacy work to foreign language learning. You can make your own mini-book with your class, write poetry, adapt a well-known fairy tale and much more besides. This Part gives you ideas for ways to make the most of links with literacy by using small, but manageable activities in the target language, some of which involve singing, some involve poems, some involve using parachutes – but all involve having fun and learning at the same time!

Project 1   Making the most of links with literacy

Project outline

Requirements: prior learning about similes in literacy poetry lessons
Event time: part of weekly language lesson over three or four weeks. Could be a focus for Mother's Day card or another special day
Languages targeted: French

Introduction

How can we build on skills developed in literacy lessons to find links when exploring a second language? Looking at poetry in literacy lessons in Key Stage Two is often lively and exciting, leading to students creating poems of their own which reflect their fresh, uninhibited approach. How can you use this freshness when experimenting with a second language?

Students in Key Stage Two are quite capable of writing simple comparison poems in another language as long as they are given a simple scaffold and clear step-by-step guidelines which can be built on week by week. It is important not to rush the different stages and to give the class enough time to enjoy and savour their achievements each week. Encourage them to experiment and make silly poems as well as thoughtful ones.

As a final touch, the poems written could be collected into a lively display, a classbook or to take home for a special birthday or Mother's Day.

The additional materials accompanying this section include two examples of simile books, together with some useful websites to inspire further writing.

Organisation

One straightforward way is to look at the use of poetic devices such as similes, where parallels can be drawn between an animal or living creature and a description, for example, as small as a mouse, as tall as a giraffe. These can be explored comfortably in a second language.

■ First, students can investigate a simple bilingual dictionary to make their own favourite animal lists books which could consist of farmyard/zoo/domestic/wild/desert/woodland/sea creatures.

■ Next, as part of a continuing classroom display, the class could collect adjectives. After all, we display adverbs and connectives for literacy, so why not collect and display similar parts of speech for language work? You could make webs of adjectives to describe a particular animal for a display or just collect words on a cupboard door. Useful adjectives describe size, for example, *petit, grand, gros, mince* or character, for example, *timide, tranquille, gentil, féroce, fatigué, fâché, méchant, sage, content* or appearance, for example, *beau, joli*.

■ Students can then select adjectives which seem the most appropriate for a particular animal or, conversely, the least likely. Using a scaffold, they can combine the two words, using *comme* (meaning *like, as*) as the link word and putting the adjective first, for example, *petit comme un rat, grand comme un tigre*. It works well to encourage children to assemble plausible descriptions first and then, when they've got the idea, to let them loose with the oddest, least likely comparisons, for example, *timide comme un lion, grand comme un chat*.

Grammatical Point

At this first stage, when you are simply comparing animals, you need to make sure that the **adjective** chosen **agrees with the gender of the animal** chosen. If you want to avoid complications of gender, just provide masculine animals, for example, *un lion, un chat, un cheval*, so that the adjectives can all be kept in the masculine form. For example, *petit come un chat, doux comme un lapin*. If you do use feminine animal names, then you would write *petite comme une souris, douce comme une vache*.

For Years Three and Four (ages seven and eight), this might be the place to stop. You could create interesting displays of animals and their descriptions, use the ideas as instructions for movement in Physical Education or have a daily favourite simile for the class to mime. With older or more advanced classes, the idea can be extended as below.

■ Next, teach the words *Je suis* (I am), place them in the centre of a page, and, in the shape of a topic web, write similes which could describe you, for example, *je suis grand comme un lion, je suis timide comme un lapin*.

- Now, because you have added a new subject (*je*) you need to make sure that the adjective agrees with the gender of *je*. So, if I am female, I would say *je suis petite comme un chat*. If I am male, I would say *je suis petit comme un chat*.
- If you find all this agreement too complicated, you could assume that everyone is masculine with corresponding agreements at this stage. To be accurate, you could place the name of a boy above *je suis* to show that you are speaking from his point of view.
- Students could decide either to do a sensible version of these similes or a wild and funny one, depending on the vocabulary you've assembled. So you might find *je suis doux comme un lion; je suis mince comme un éléphant*.
- At this stage it works well to read aloud and show the pictures of the inspiring and beautiful books *My Dad* (Browne, 2000) and *My Mum* (Browne, 2005a). You could introduce the stories in the English version and then reread them in the French versions *Mon Papa* (Browne, 2002) and *Ma Maman* (Browne, 2005b) when they have understood the basis of the story. The similes used provide a warm and vivid picture of a child's view of a parent which pupils might want to expand in their own work. This could be the start of work for a birthday or special day for a parent with the words *Maman est* or *Papa est* at the head of the page. Use the book examples to discuss the extravagance of the similes and the superheroes created in a very young child's mind. This might encourage a similar ambition in the class when they look for comparisons of their own.
- They might use extraordinary creatures such as *un mammouth* (a mammoth), *une licorne* (a unicorn) or royal characters such as *un roi* (a king), *une reine* (a queen), *une princesse* or *un prince*.

MAMAN

Maman est forte comme un ours polaire.

Maman est jolie comme une princesse.

Maman est grande comme un géant.

Maman est aimante comme un chaton.

Maman est énergique comme un chiot.

You could stop at this point and compile several different collections of similes such as:

- a poem for a birthday or special day – for example, Mothers' Day or Fathers' Day, with the words *Maman est* or *Papa est* at the centre of the page;
- a book of classroom friendship similes with a page for each child and everyone adding a simile about them (making it clear that positive images are important!). Set this out with the prompt *Nicolas est* or *Maddie est* at the centre;
- each child makes a page for their best friend or a teacher at school with as many comparisons as possible;
- assuming children have learned the days of the week, they describe their own mood on each day of the week, for example, *lundi je suis timide comme un hamster, samedi je suis fatigué comme un hérisson* and illustrate the diary.

Next Steps

Many students will have reached their limit at this stage, but there are further extensions to the similes which you might try if you have a curious and imaginative class. You may choose to stop after Step One or continue with ever-decreasing numbers of children to Step Six. It is better for each child to succeed at his or her own level rather than be daunted by too many extras.

We encourage students to extend their sentences in literacy lessons by adding connectives, adverbs or descriptive details. Have a go in the new language too.

Step One

Add a place at the end of the simile: for example, *dans la mer, dans la piscine, dans une boîte, dans une poubelle*. So you would write: *je suis timide comme un hamster dans la forêt*.

Step Two

Teach the pronoun *qui*, meaning who or which. Demonstrate the format: *je suis timide comme un hamster dans la forêt qui* …

Step Three

Collect verbs which describe an action by an animal: for example, a sound or a movement. Put all the verbs in the 3rd person singular (to agree with *il* or *elle*). So you would collect: *dort, mange, boit, court, nage, mange*, etc.

Step Four

Add the verb to the sentence, so that it now reads: *je suis timide comme un hamster dans la forêt qui dort*.

Step Five

Add an adverb after the verb to add more depth. Create an adverb bank on the board to help, for example, *lentement, vite, heureusement, malheureusement, doucement* (students will soon recognise the suffix *-ment* as the equivalent of the English *-ly* to denote a suffix). Finally add the adverb to the sentence: *je suis timide comme un hamster dans la forêt qui dort heureusement*.

Step Six

Those students who have followed to the end could add their descriptions to a zig-zag book of their different animals and illustrate them or create a display for the classroom or a classbook to be read at story time. They certainly deserve a reward sticker!

Check it out

Remember that in these later steps, your adjective always agrees with the PERSON who is described and not the animal, for example, if you are female you would write *Je suis PETITE comme un hamster*. If you are male, you would write *Je suis PETIT comme un hamster*.

Project 2   Telling stories with a parachute

Project outline

Requirements: large space (for example, a hall), parachute at least six metres in diameter. Props – for example, animal headbands – for a full performance
Event time: half an hour to practise a story; ten minutes to perform
Language used: French and Spanish

Introduction

Telling a story with a parachute adds a completely new dimension and can make a captivating central feature in an assembly or other performance. It could also simply be used to add some drama to a story-telling session with a class. Because it is a colourful spectacle, a parachute lends itself to storylines which need movement and action, so experiment a little to see what you can match up. Simple stories such as *La Tempête* (see Project 1 in Part I *Fun with parachutes*) work well and are easy to organise with few props. Stories with animals as characters are effective, showing how a range of animals move in different ways. The following drama is based on zoo animals and could follow work inspired by any animal book or photographs. The text is available in Spanish on the accompanying DVD.

Organisation

First, investigate the different ways that you can move the canopy with a whole class holding the edge. Possible ways might be:

■   move it up and down as high and low as possible;
■   move in to the middle and out again;
■   wave it from side to side vigorously;
■   gentle, hardly perceptible movements up and down;
■   hold it high with one hand and move round in a circle bobbing it up and down;
■   hold it tight and smooth and make it ripple.

The example in this section portrays zoo animals behaving badly in a zoo at night whilst a zoo-keeper tries to control them. It could take the shape of an informal story-telling with a class or be practised and used as part of an assembly, with students making headbands or masks of the animal group they belong to. It could be a stand-alone activity or part of an animal project inspired by reading *Cher Zoo* by Rod Campbell (Campbell 2004).

Possible animal movements with the parachute

Les singes (monkeys) could wave the parachute up and down at waist height vigorously.

Les serpents (snakes) could move the parachute from side to side like a slithering sensation.

Les oiseaux (birds) could move it up high in the air and down to the ground.

Les éléphants could make big waving movements in the air like using their trunks.

Les girafes (giraffes) could have a stately movement, bobbing up and down, with one hand very high in the parachute.

Les lions could rush in to the centre and out again as if they were attacking.

Performing the story: Le Zoo à Minuit

Choose a narrator. This could be the teacher, as there are many small speeches, or a confident volunteer or group to take turns. This person needs to have a strong voice to be heard over the parachute excitement!

- Students decide which animal group they would like to join from *les singes*, *les serpents*, *les éléphants*, *les oiseaux*, *les lions*, *les girafes.* Try to keep the numbers roughly even.
- Choose someone to be *le gardien* (the zoo-keeper). This person needs to be able to shout warnings in French to stop the trouble. He could wear a cap with *Le gardien* written on it and a jacket with *Le Zoo de Paris* (or your town name) on the pocket.
- Animals could make their own simple headbands with a picture of the animal stuck in the centre, or animal masks if there is time.
- Arrange the class around the parachute, holding the edge of the canopy. It works best if the animals are spread around the parachute so that there is a monkey, then a lion, then a giraffe etc., rather than have a clump of monkeys in one corner. The idea is that each set of animals called out in turn take hold of the parachute and move it in their special way and then return it the original place so that everyone holds it again. At the beginning and the end, all the animals move and make a noise in unison. Only the narrator and the *gardien* stand to the side, but the *gardien* moves around during the story, remonstrating with the animals.

Le Zoo à Minuit

Narrator:	*Il est minuit au Zoo. Tous les animaux dorment.* (All raise and lower the parachute slightly, as if sleeping, snoring softly)
Narrator:	*Soudain il y a un grand bruit!* (Something noisy for example, loud alarm clock, big drum banging, crashing cymbals, etc.)
Narrator:	*Les singes grimpent dans les arbres!* (Only monkeys wave the parachute up and down in their way)

Gardien: *Arrêtez tout de suite!*
        (Shakes his fist at the monkeys etc.)

Narrator: *Les serpents glissent!*
        (Only snakes move parachute from side to side in their way)

Gardien: *Arrêtez tout de suite!*
        (Shakes his fist at the snakes etc.)

Narrator: *Les éléphants sont furieux!*
        (Only elephants wave parachute high in the air in their way)

Gardien: *Arrêtez tout de suite!*
        (Shakes his fist at the elephants etc.)

Narrator: *Les oiseaux volent!*
        (Only birds bring the parachute up and down to the ground in their way)

Gardien: *Arrêtez tout de suite!*
        (Shakes his fist at the birds etc.)

Narrator: *Les lions attaquent!*
        (Only lions rush into the middle and out again)

Gardien: *Arrêtez tout de suite!*
        (Shakes his fist at the lions etc.)

Narrator: *Les girafes marchent!*
        (Only giraffes move with right hand held high, bobbing up and down)

Gardien: *Arrêtez tout de suite!*
        (Shakes his fist at the giraffes etc.)

Gardien: *Il est minuit! C'est la nuit! Dormez doucement!*

Narrator: *Et bientôt les singes dorment, les serpents dorment, les éléphants dorment, les oiseaux dorment, les lions dorment, les girafes dorment. … Et finalement le gardien dort.*
        (All of the animals are still restless then gradually, as each group is mentioned, they quieten down

and go back to sleep, put their heads on the parachute and start to snore softly. The parachute moves gently up and down.)

Telling stories with a parachute: additional DVD materials

1.   Spanish text for story

Project 3   The fairy tale

Project outline

Requirements: preparation time to enlarge and laminate the artwork; flip chart.
Event time: one 40-minute lesson
Language targeted: German

Introduction

Many primary students are familiar with fairy tales in their own mother tongue. Such stories as *Hansel and Gretel, Little Red Riding Hood* and *Sleeping Beauty,* for example, need no introduction for that reason. But exploring fairy tales in the target language is frequently more of a challenge than first anticipated, as the vocabulary used is often unusual or uncommon and there seems to be quite a lot needed! Using pictures to explain key items in the story is an effective way to bring the tale to life and appreciated by the students who are, after all, usually familiar with the basic outline of the story itself. This project presents the famous German fairy tale *Rumpelstilzchen* using pictures and a bit of fresh air to enliven the story and encourage students to participate actively with it. Most fairy tales fit the model presented, however, and the project is easily transferable to other languages too.

Preparation

You need to choose a fairy tale to start with – perhaps one that you liked yourself as a child or one that you like reading aloud. It helps if the title of the tale is quite long in the target language. Thus *Schneewitchen, Aschenputtel* and *Rotkäppchen* would all serve the purpose equally well. The fairy tale which forms the heart of this project is *Rumpelstilzchen* written by Jacob and Wilhelm Grimm in the nineteenth century.

Step One

Extract the key elements of the story. The number of key elements should match the number of letters in the title of the fairy tale. Thus, *Rumpelstilzchen* has 15 letters in it, so you need to break the story down into 15 elements. *Aschenputtel* has 12 letters, so 12 elements and 12 pictures would need to be found. The key elements form the basis of the pictures you need. Here is the pictorial representation of *Rumpelstilzchen* and the role each picture plays in the tale.

1. *Der Müller* – the miller, who has a beautiful daughter (who, he promises, can spin gold from straw).

2. *Das Schloß* – the castle where the king lives.

3. *Die Müllerstochter* – the miller's daughter, who cannot spin gold from straw and who engages Rumpelstilzchen to help her. She eventually becomes queen.

4. *Der König* – the king who threatens the cut the miller's daughter's head off if she does not spin gold from straw. He eventually marries her.

5. *Eine Axt* – an axe with which the king will cut off the miller's daughter's head if she fails to spin gold from straw.

6. *Ein Raum voller Stroh* – a room full of straw which needs to be spun into gold by the following morning.

7. *Das Spinnrad* – a spinning wheel which the miller's daughter should use to spin the gold.

8. *Ein kleiner Mann* – Rumpelstilzchen (or Rumpelstiltskin), the central character in the tale.

9. *Der Goldhaufen* – the pile of gold which is spun by Rumpelstilzchen.

10. *Das Geschenk* – the present which Rumpelstilzchen asks from the miller's daughter if he is to help her spin the gold.

11. *Die Halskette* – the necklace which the miller's daughter gives to Rumpelstilzchen on the first occasion he asks her for a present.

12. *Die Königin* – the queen, who is also the miller's daughter.

13. *Das Baby* – the baby, the first-born child of the royal couple.

14. *Das Lied* – the song which Rumpelstilzchen sings, and in which he gives away his name.

15. *Das Fenster* – the window through which Rumpelstilzchen jumps at the end of the story, never to be heard of again!

Here are the fifteen pictures. They are also displayed electronically on the accompanying DVD to this project.

Der Müller

Das Schloß

Die Müllerstochter

Der König

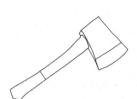

Eine Axt

Ein Raum voller Stroh

Das Spinnrad   Ein kleiner Mann   Der Goldhaufen

Das Geschenk   Die Halskette   Die Königin

Das Baby   Das Lied   Das Fenster

Step Two

Enlarge each picture to A4 size. Underneath each picture write the word in German but not the English translation, as the picture itself serves as the translation.

Step Three

On the back of each picture write one letter chosen at random from the title word – in this case one letter from the 15-letter word *Rumpelstilzchen*.

Step Four

Laminate each picture, now complete with its letter on the back and vocabulary item underneath.

Organisation

1. Hide the laminated pictures around the playground, assembly hall or other large area (preferably not the students' own classroom, as a change of scene is often refreshing). Students know lots of good hiding places in and around their school, so after they have done the whole activity, they could set it up themselves for another class. If you do this, don't forget to ask the students to tell you where the hiding places are!

2. In pairs (assuming 30 students), students have to find one picture and bring it back to a central table in the classroom.

3. Students write the letter on the back of the picture they have found onto a flip chart or equivalent. Tell them that the 15 jumbled letters make up the title of the story you are going to read them in German. They need to try to unscramble the letters before you reach the part of the story where Rumpelstilzchen says his real name. Students may be able to guess if they know the story, but the German spelling is slightly different.

4. When the whole class has returned with their pictures and all the letters are assembled on the flip chart (still jumbled), go through the vocabulary items in German by asking: *Wer hat … der Müller*? And so on. The pair with the correct picture in each case should hold it up for the rest of the class to see.

5. Now it is time for the story. Read it slowly the first time and ask students to hold up their picture when they hear it spoken. Allow time for the students to recognise the word and then display their picture.

6. Read the story again, this time slightly faster and ask the students to again hold up their pictures.

Rumpelstilzchen

(**Note:** the words in bold are represented by pictures – they are only in bold once only, but your students will need to show their pictures more than once.)

> Hier ist **der Müller**. Er hat eine schöne **Tochter**. Eines Tages geht der Müller zum **Schloß**. Er sagt dem **König**: "Ich habe eine Tochter. Sie kann aus **Stroh Gold** machen."
> "Wunderbar!" sagt der König. "Sie kann vor morgen dieses Stroh zu Gold machen. Hier ist das **Spinnrad**. Und wenn sie das nicht macht, dann schneide ich ihr den Kopf ab mit meiner **Axt**."
> Die arme Tochter kann natürlich nicht das Stroh zu Gold machen. Sie sitzt und weint.
>
> Plötzlich kommt **ein kleiner Mann** in den Raum. Er hat eine lange Nase, kurze Beine und einen roten Bart.
> "Ich kann das Stroh zu Gold machen," sagt der kleine Mann, "wenn du mir ein **Geschenk** gibst".
>
> "Du kannst meine **Halskette** haben, wenn du für mich Gold machst," sagte die schöne Müllerstochter. Und am nächsten Morgen ist der Raum voller Gold. Und der König ist sehr glücklich. Aber er will noch mehr Gold haben. Du musst noch mehr

Gold spinnen!" sagt der König der Müllerstochter. "Wenn du das machst, bist du meine **Königin**. Wenn du das nicht machst, schneide ich dir den Kopf ab mit meiner Axt!"

In dieser Nacht kommt der kleine Mann wieder. Die Müllerstochter sitzt und weint. Der kleine Mann sagt, "Ich mache aus dem Stroh Gold, wenn du mir ein Geschenk gibst."

Aber die Müllerstochter hat kein Geschenk. "Ich habe nichts!" sagt sie traurig.
    "Dann nehme ich dein **Baby** wenn du Königin bist," sagt der kleine Mann.
    Die Müllerstochter ist sehr traurig aber sie muss 'ja' sagen.
    Dann ist der Raum voller Gold. Der König ist ganz glücklich. Die Müllerstochter ist Königin.
    Ein Jahr später ist das erste Baby geboren – ein Mädchen. Plötzlich ist der kleine Mann in dem Raum.
    "Das ist jetzt mein Baby," sagt er und stampft hart auf den Boden.
    Die Königin weint und sagt: "Nein! Nein! Nein! Ich liebe mein Baby! Du kannst es nicht haben!"

Der kleine Mann sieht, daß die Königin das Baby sehr liebt.
    "Du kannst dein Baby haben," sagt er "wenn du raten kannst, wie ich heiße. Du hast drei Chancen."

    Die Königin fragt, "Heißt du Heinrich?"
    "Nein," antwortet der kleine Mann.
    "Heißt du Baltasar?" fragt die Königin.
    "Nein," antwortet der kleine Mann.

    Er ist so glücklich, daß er ein **Lied** singt:

> *Ach, wie gut dass niemand weiß, dass ich Rumpelstilzchen heiß!*
> *Ach, wie gut dass niemand weiß, dass ich Rumpelstilzchen heiß!*

"Du mußt Rumpelstilzchen heißen!" sagt die Königin laut vor Freude. Der kleine Mann, oder Rumpelstilzchen, ist jetzt sehr böse. Er stampft auf den Boden, er hüpft in die Luft und plötzlich springt er aus dem **Fenster** des Schlosses. Er ist nie wieder zu sehen. Und wenn sie nich gestorben sind, dann leben die Königin, das König und das Baby noch heute!

Extension

1. This activity, if rehearsed properly, would be a good one to demonstrate in assembly, as the pictures will help other staff and students understand the main events (see also the first project *Being creative in assembly* in Part V). The story of *Rumpelstilzchen* is presented as a charming play on the voyage-kids website (see the list of useful websites on the accompanying DVD for this project).

2. Students can either colour in the pictures provided, or draw their own imaginary fairy-tale character, which they colour, name and describe in German. These can be displayed in your classroom along with their titles in German.

The fairy tale: additional DVD materials

1.   The fifteen pictures for the key elements of the story
2.   Useful websites

Project 4   Story-writing (*Le château*)

Project outline

Requirements: prior learning of rooms of a house, family members, activities
Event time: half hour sections of a weekly language lesson over a month. One hour to make the book
Language used: French

Introduction

Most language work in primary schools is of necessity based on oracy and it is only in the later years that children have built up sufficient expertise and accuracy to think of much independent writing. With help in the form of careful scaffolding, children in Years Five or Six (ages ten and eleven) should be able to write a short story and set it inside the shape of an interesting format, just as they might display their work in Literacy on occasions. This project involves making an A4-sized book *Le Château* and writing a story about a journey through the castle rooms. The book cover includes a character cut-out on a string and a pocket for additional characters and features to make the Château setting more authentic looking. Photographs of the finished book are included in the additional DVD materials which accompany this project.

Organisation

There are two parts to this book: writing the text of the adventure in the castle, and making the book and its extra pieces, which turn the story from a short tale to a magical booklet.

Theme of the story

There are several choices to be considered for the central story set in the castle. The need to keep within the bounds of the students' linguistic knowledge obviously limits the scope of the plot and the tense used in the story (it can only be written in the present tense). Students like to add a touch of humour or suspense to their work, so some possibilities are:

■   A haunted-house story, with the main character being scared in several rooms, perhaps meeting a ghost and running away (see Project 2 in Part V *La Maison Hantée* for vocabulary and further ideas);

■   The main character is feeling hungry, goes into the castle, eats different combinations of food in each room, ends up feeling ill. This could be a cumulative story, for example, with one croissant being eaten in the first room, two snails in the second, three frogs' legs in the third, etc. (*un grand croissant, deux petits escargots, trois cuisses de grenouilles. J'ai une faim de loup* – I'm starving; *J'ai mal à l'estomac* – I've got a tummy ache).

- Main character goes into castle, meets teachers from the students' school in different rooms, has a brief conversation with each one (this could simply be *Comment tu t'appelles? Quel âge as-tu? Comment ça va?*, etc) and they answer with the wrong name, etc. (*Je m'appelle Père Noël; J'ai cent ans; Ça va très mal*).

- Main character's dog has run into castle. He goes from room to room looking under objects, behind doors, etc. Dog could be in the cellar eating ice cream, etc. This is a good opportunity for learning prepositions (*sous* – under; *sur* – on; *derrière* – behind; *devant* – in front of; *dans* – in; *mon chien méchant* – my naughty dog; *il mange une glace au chocolat* – he's eating a chocolate ice cream).

- Main character goes into the castle and finds a member of his family in each room doing an unusual activity (for example, playing tennis in the bathroom). This is the story explained in the next section.

Writing the story

1. The students will need groups of vocabulary to select from to make their own individual sentences. You could introduce this vocabulary as you go along and make a collection for the children to see and select. You will probably have taught most of this vocabulary already and may just need to jog their memories. However, a printed list in the form of a column on the whiteboard is a handy and easily followed resource for each group of vocabulary. The story is cumbersome to construct at first, as you have to explain each step, but follows a pattern and speeds up.

2. Use a language dictionary, so that students can find words independently or teach the names of rooms in a house or château if they have not covered this topic. Students will not need to use all the rooms, so they can choose five or six favourites which will add most to the story.

    > *Le salon* – sitting room; *la salle à manger* – dining room; *la cuisine* – kitchen; *le couloir* – corridor; *la cave* – cellar; *la chambre* – bedroom; *la douche* – shower; *la toilette* – toilet; *la salle de bain* – bathroom; *le grenier* – attic; *la bibliothèque* – library.

3. Teach students some basic verbs in the first person: *je vais* – I go; *j'entre dans* – I go into; *je vois* – I see. Your dictionary might have a verb section where they can see how verbs are conjugated. Also teach a repeated question which you use on each page: *que fais-tu?* – what are you doing?

4. Start the story with a time of day to set the scene, just as you might in a literacy lesson. Elicit from the students the parts of the day in French and write them in a vertical column on the board: *un matin, un après-midi, un soir, une nuit*. Help them to find in the dictionary the words for seasons. Show them how to put the two words together. For example, *un matin d'été; un après-midi d'hiver; un soir de printemps; une nuit d'automne.*

Encourage students to swap the beginnings and endings to find the maximum number of permutations. For example, *un matin d'automne*. They choose one time and season to start their story.

5. Add the rest of the opening sentence to get the character into the castle. Use the first person as it is the most familiar to them.

   Un matin d'automne je vais au château.

6. Choose the room to start from the preferred list: for example, *le salon*. Add the required verb, *j'entre dans*, and decide which family member they will find and name the person (possible members are: *mon père; ma mère; mon frère; ma soeur; mon oncle; ma tante; mon cousin; ma cousine; mon grand-père; ma grand-mère*).

   Un matin d'automne je vais au château. J'entre dans le salon et je vois mon cousin (insert name).

7. Assuming that you have taught some hobbies/activities, use your collection of phrases for the students to select from.

   Possible sports are *je joue au tennis /foot/volley/rugby/cricket*.

   Possible activities might be *je joue aux cartes* (play cards); *je joue avec mon ordinateur* (play on the computer); *je joue du piano* (play piano); *je joue de la* guitare (play guitar).

   More passive ideas might be *je regarde un film* (watch a film); *je lis un magazine* (read a magazine); *j'écoute de la musique* (listen to music).

   Lively activities might be *je fais du ski* (go skiing); *je fais du vélo* (cycle); *je fais du patinage* (skate); *je fais de la gymnastique* (do gym); *je fais de la* natation (swim); *je fais de la voile* (sailing).

8. Add the repeated question which the main character is going to ask and an unlikely answer in reply from the relative.

   Un matin d'automne je vais au château. J'entre dans le salon et je vois mon cousin Robert.

   Que fais-tu?

   Je fais de la natation.

9. Go into the next room in the same way and choose from the same options:

   Un matin d'automne je vais au château. J'entre dans le salon et je vois mon cousin Robert.

   Que fais-tu?

   Je fais de la natation.

   J'entre dans la cuisine et je vois ma grand-mère.

   Que fais-tu?

   Je joue avec mon ordinateur.

10.   Continue for as many rooms as you like. Finish on the main character going into a room and doing something unexpected, for example:

Et moi? J'entre dans la douche et je joue de la guitare.

Making the book

Shopping list

A2 sugar paper of a neutral colour

red and brown wax crayons

1 piece of A4 card

small piece of Velcro

piece of ribbon

A4 piece of white paper with story written on

optional photo of your head, approx. 5cm × 4cm

separate picture of a door

Instructions

1.   Take a piece of A2 sugar paper in a neutral colour. Find some wax crayons in earthy colours, for example, brown and dark red. Using scrap paper, experiment with different surfaces around the school to make a wax rubbing to suggest a stone surface. When you have found the right one, press the A2 card against it and make a suitable wax rubbing on one side only with the crayons.

2.   Fold down the middle to make two equal parts approx. 30cm × 40cm. Press the edges flat. Make sure the waxed surface is facing outwards towards you.

3.   Keep the fold at the top of the paper and mark lightly in pencil where the midway point is on the fold line.

4.   Fold the paper in on the right hand side to the middle mark so that you have an opening door. Repeat with the left hand side. You should have two doors which meet in the middle.

5.   Fix the doors closed temporarily with a paper clip at the bottom and measure out 4 evenly spaced battlements approx. 3 cm wide and 3 cms tall with three empty spaces in between. The end ones will look like doubles when you open the book up. Cut carefully through the layers to create the battlement shapes.

6.   Open up the book and staple a piece of spare waxed paper to make a pocket in the inside left hand corner. *Make sure* you only staple through the inner layer of the book. This is a pocket to keep your characters in.

7.   Make arrow slits to stick under the battlements. They should be 10cm long × 2cm wide with a tapered point. You need four for the outer doors, and another four to put on the inside of the doors. You could colour the outer door slits in black crayon and the inner ones in multicolours to resemble stained glass windows. Glue in place.

8.   Arrange your story into several sections like rooms on white paper and glue or staple them on to the inside empty back wall.

9. Make a large picture approx 22 cm tall × 9cm of yourself (the main character) standing full length, colour it brightly, stick it onto card and laminate to keep it strong. You could always add a photo of the head to a drawn body if you prefer. Attach a piece of string or ribbon approx. 18cm long to the back of the figure with sellotape and attach the other end of the ribbon between the 2 layers of the book behind the battlements. The figure will then be able to move around the book.

10. You need a suitable door to bridge across the two opening doors. Look on the internet to find one you like or draw one with a suitable surround. Or you could use the template below – or draw your own. It needs to be about 12cm wide × 15cm high.

11. Colour it, cut it out and stick it down with *only the left half attached, just to the left of the opening door. Leave the right hand part unstuck.* Stick a 2cm piece of Velcro to the back of the right-hand door part and the matching Velcro to the place on the right-hand wall where it fits. In this way you can open and fasten the door.

12. Draw onto card the other characters in the story approx. 10cm tall, colour and laminate them and cut them out. Place them in the inner pocket to take part in the story.

13. Have fun reading your story and letting your characters move around the scenery. You may find that new stories develop. Choose a different book each day to read their story aloud to the class.

Story writing (Le château): additional DVD materials

1. Picture gallery

Project 5   Der Elf

Project outline

Requirements: prior learning of days of the week
Event time: one 40-minute lesson
Language used: German

Introduction

This project builds on the work presented at the start of this chapter about incorporating poetry into your language lessons and using poetic devices. It is a short project which builds on a simple but nevertheless effective poem called *Der Elf*. It provides good revision of the days of the week in German and introduces a specific grammatical point. This language work can be further extended, and students are encouraged to make their own little drawstring bags into which they can place various objects for a specific purpose. Magic!

Organisation

Revise the days of the week with your class in German.

Montag:	Monday
Dienstag:	Tuesday
Mittwoch:	Wednesday
Donnerstag:	Thursday
Freitag:	Friday
Samstag:	Saturday
Sonntag:	Sunday

Remind your class that if they want say '**on** Monday' for example, they must use the word '*am*' in German as in *Am Montag ...*

Here is the poem. Read it aloud to your class, first very slowly, and see if they can understand the things that the elf puts in his bag (*die Tasche*) and possibly why.

Der Elf

By Clare Forder

Hier ist ein Elf. Er hat eine Tasche.

Am Montag hat er in seiner Tasche ...
Eine Nadel um Sachen zu nähen
Und die Schuhe um schneller zu gehen.

Am Dienstag hat er in seiner Tasche …
Einen Apfel um ihn zu essen
Und ein Lineal um gerade zu messen.

Am Mittwoch hat er in seiner Tasche …
Ein Witzblatt um ein bißchen zu lachen
Und seine Hausaufgaben um sie fleißig zu machen.

Am Donnerstag hat er in seiner Tasche …
Einen Stuhl um darauf zu sitzen
Und einen Stift um ihn zu spitzen.

Am Freitag hat er in seiner Tasche …
Ein Bild um zu malen
Und eine Rechnung um sie zu bezahlen.

Am Samstag hat er in seiner Tasche …
Das neue Essen um es zu probieren
Und ein Handy um mit Freunden zu telefonieren.

Am Sonntag hat er in seiner Tasche …
NICHTS! Weil er zu Hause ist um sich auszuruhen!

An English translation of the poem can be found on the accompanying DVD.

Vocabulary

Nouns

die Tasche:	bag
die Nadel:	needle
die Schuhe:	shoes
der Apfel:	apple
das Lineal:	ruler
das Witzblatt:	joke book
die Hausaufgaben:	homework
der Stuhl:	chair
der Stift:	pencil
das Bild:	picture
die Rechnung:	bill
das Essen:	food
das Handy:	mobile phone

Verbs

sich ausruhen:	to rest
nähen:	to sew
gehen:	to go
essen:	to eat
messen:	to measure
lachen:	to laugh
machen:	to do/make
sitzen:	to sit
spitzen:	to sharpen
malen:	to paint
bezahlen:	to pay
probieren:	to try
telefonieren:	to telephone

Grammatical Point

'In order to (do something)' is expressed in German as *'um (etwas) zu (machen)'*. Keeping your sentences very simple, demonstrate with your own bag containing various items inside it. Here some examples (all are direct objects, so the case has changed).

In meiner Tasche habe ich...

...a ruler: *ein Lineal*   ...a drink: *ein Getränk*

...a pencil: *einen Bleistift*   ...a book: *ein Buch*

Then repeat the procedure but, this time, add the reason why (*um ... zu ...*).

In meiner Tasche habe ich ein Lineal, **um** *meinen Tisch* **zu** *messen.*

In meiner Tasche habe ich ein Getränk **um** *es* **zu** *trinken.*

In meiner Tasche habe ich ein Buch, **um** *es* **zu** *lesen.*

In meiner Tasche habe ich einen Bleistift **um** *Notizen* **zu** *schreiben.*

Tip

This is a good opportunity to introduce/revise some everyday items around the classroom. Sticky labels on the things themselves, labelled in German with the correct gender, are a great way to encourage students to notice what is going on around them and learn the vocabulary items in the natural classroom setting.

Making a drawstring bag

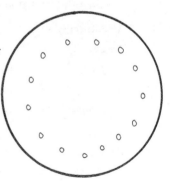

Little bags are fun to make and here is a simple pattern for making a drawstring bag.

1. Draw a large circle on a piece of felt.
2. Make a series of holes around the edge with a hole punch.
3. Weave a ribbon or some string through each alternate hole.
4. Pull tightly together and tie off the ends in a bow.

There are some finished drawstring bags in the picture gallery for this project on the accompanying DVD. The students can make one each and then put some classroom objects inside. You could place some items (for which you know the students know the names in German) on a central table for the students to use.

Der Elf: accompanying DVD materials

1. English translation of the poem
2. Picture gallery
3. Useful websites

Project 6   Using animals as an inspiration for writing

Project outline

Requirements: prior learning of animal names, habitats.

Event time: one lesson for each project, or a series of half-hour lessons over a half term

Language targeted: French but some aspects of lessons could be multilingual

Introduction

This collection of projects can be taken as a series or as individual themes and builds onto skills developed in literacy in Key Stage Two. It should follow some preliminary work on animals and their habitats. Its aim is to look at some imaginative and creative ways of describing animals and to use some instructional language. The additional materials accompanying this section provide examples of class work on these themes.

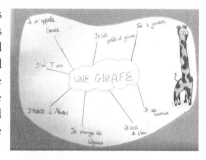

Organisation

One tried and tested way into the topic of animals is via the popular book *Cher Zoo* by Rod Campbell, translated from his childhood favourite *Dear Zoo* (1969). This well-loved book is greeted warmly even by older primary classes because of its flaps, its comical yet sweet story and its gentle familiarity. It can be used to build up background knowledge of animal names, some description and a background of a zoo. Alternatively, flash cards, whiteboard materials and many other sources can be used.

Syllable animals

- Make a collection of animal names, using bilingual dictionaries and make a list on the board.
- Break the names into syllables and sound them out as separate parts of the word, for example,

    li-on, cham-eau, poi-sson.

- Take the first syllables from one animal and add them to the final syllables of another, for example,

    li-sson, cham-on

Note: It is advisable to have a consonant between the sections, as too many vowels can make the new name difficult to pronounce.

- Students practise pronouncing the new animal words by saying them quietly under their breath, then with a friend, and then sharing with the class. Everyone guesses which animals were combined.

- On sheets of A4 paper, they draw the new animal with features from both its original parents and label the parts of its body in French, for example, *la tête, les bras, les jambes, les oreilles, les yeux, le nez, la queue* (tail), etc. Rather than searching for animal body names, keep to parts of the human body – they are more useful in the long run.

- Start to collect some information about the animal, either around the page or on one side as a series of bullet points, like a non-fiction book. Write the new animal name and decide on its habitat. Collect possible habitats: for example, *dans la mer, dans l'air, dans un nid, à la ferme, dans le désert, au zoo*, etc. Write in the first person: for example, *le lisson, j'habite dans la mer*.

- Think of all the basic information your class can say about themselves – for example, their age, their name – and ask them to write these phrases for the animal: for example, *je m'appelle Lenny, j'ai huit ans*.

- Collect words to describe your animal using colours; for example, younger children could write *je suis vert et rouge*, while more experienced children could write in a more detailed way, for example, *ma tête est verte, mon nez est bleu* (making adjectives agree with the gender of the noun).

- Give the animal a speech bubble to say *Bonjour* or *Comment ça va?*

- Students take their animals around the classroom to visit other animals. Their animals talk to each other in French and ask questions, for example, *Où habites-tu? Comment tu t'appelles? Comment ça va?*

Further steps

- Make little plays where the newly-named animals meet each other.

- Hot-seat a brave student with their animal. A volunteer sits on a chair at the front of the class and pretends to be their new animal, e.g. *un lisson*. Pupils in the class ask questions about the animal which the volunteer answers as if they were the animal – for example, *Comment tu t'appelles? Je m'appelle Louis Lisson*.

- Choose an animal a day as a star and talk about their features.

- Make a class book – for example, *Les animaux de Classe Six* – for everyone to read in their free time (see also the Project 1 in Part II *Creating imaginative, simple books* for other ideas).

Postcards from the zoo

Instructions

Make a list of the zoo animals which students know well. If necessary, use a bilingual dictionary to supplement the list. You only need ten or so to have a variety.

You will be writing the correspondence between the zoo keeper and the recipient of the animal to tell the *Cher Zoo* story. If possible read the French story again. If not give a recap of the basic story.

Fold a piece of A4 card in two to make a postcard effect. Students will write the first request on the left-hand side, with the address at the side and the complaint or thanks on the right-hand side of the card with a picture. Or make the card a vertical one, with an upper and lower part.

Everyone decides which animal they are requesting and what kind of character he should have, for example, *aimable, tranquille, content, féroce* (friendly, quiet, happy, fierce).

Teach how to start a formal letter with *Monsieur*. Write the address as *Le gardien, Le zoo de…*, then choose a French town, look on the internet to find the Department and code it might have on its address.

Teach the instruction *Envoyez-moi* (send me) and remind them of the phrase *s'il vous plaît* (please). They then construct a request: for example,

Monsieur, envoyez-moi un singe s'il vous plaît.

Remind the class of the polite verb phrase *Je voudrais* (I would like) and help them to make a sentence using their adjective, such as *Je voudrais un singe content*.

Add *Merci beaucoup* and their name to end the first part of the card.

On the reverse, start again with *monsieur*, and give an opinion about the animal, using the vocabulary from the book, for example, *le singe est parfait; le singe est trop féroce*. If they are unhappy about the animal, they repeat *Envoyez-moi* with a different animal, maybe a more ferocious one for a joke. Add another *Je voudrais un lion sauvage*. If they are happy with the animal, they say *Au revoir et merci beaucoup* and sign their name.

Decorate the card with a French-looking stamp, pictures of the animal and zoo.

Animal posters

Introduction

The aim of this exercise is to find out about public notices which give information and to use those expressions in an imaginative way on the topic of animals. After all, keeping safe in a different country or environment is crucial, especially if a school trip is coming up, or summer holidays approach. Making someone welcome to your school or classroom is also a great asset.

Designing posters or labels to say Welcome

Investigate how to say *Welcome* in other languages.

Recap on literacy-based work on persuasive writing.

What makes a poster striking and effective? Possible ideas would include short, catchy slogans, use of alliteration, word-play or humour, bold design with lettering large, clear and colourful, image not too cluttered, maybe a border, etc.

Look at the French way of expressing welcome: *bienvenue*, literally meaning 'well come'. Work out ways you could use this in school for example, make up some labels for classrooms, or for the school entrance or canteen.

Play a simple communication game in the classroom where everyone goes around shaking hands or kissing cheeks and bidding each other *Bienvenue dans notre classe* (Welcome to our class).

Use part of a school assembly to teach the same phrase to the rest of the school and to introduce *Bienvenue à notre école* (Welcome to our school).

Design some posters for use in school using the French expressions. Students could draw and label school subjects, classroom equipment – for example, pencils and rulers – to make the picture lively.

Look back at the animal work and design some posters for *Bienvenue au zoo* for a display of the classwork. Students could draw the animals they recognise in French and label them.

Laminate the school posters and use them around the corridors and entrance. You could make this a whole-school competition and award simple prizes – for example, a French bookmark or pack of croissants!

Designing Posters to give Warnings

As before, investigate how to say *Danger! Watch out! It's forbidden* …in other languages.

Discuss how these sayings would be useful in a school setting, for example, near stairs, outside the caretaker's room, next to PE equipment. etc.

How could you use these phrases for animals, for example, in a zoo? Look for ways to use French expressions such as

Danger de mort – Danger of death

Attention aux animaux sauvages – Watch out for wild animals

Défense d'entrer dans la cage – It's forbidden to go into the cage

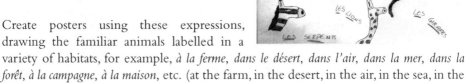

Create posters using these expressions, drawing the familiar animals labelled in a variety of habitats, for example, *à la ferme, dans le désert, dans l'air, dans la mer, dans la forêt, à la campagne, à la maison*, etc. (at the farm, in the desert, in the air, in the sea, in the forest, in the country, in the house).

Grammatical Points

Keep to the same part of speech as the examples given, for example:

- *Danger* can be used on its own or followed by *de mort*.
- *Attention* can be used on its own or followed by *au, à la, à l'* or *aux* plus a noun, for example, *Attention au lion* (1 lion) *Attention à la souris* (1 mouse) *Attention à l'ours* (1 bear) or *Attention aux lions, aux souris, aux ours* (all plural).
- *Défense de* should be followed by a verb in the infinitive, for example, *Défense de parler, Défense de grimper, Défense de manger, Défense de toucher* (It's forbidden to speak, to climb, to eat, to touch).

Using animals as an inspiration for writing: additional DVD materials

1. Picture gallery

Project 7   Writing poetry – making a little language go a long way

Project outline

Requirements: a class set of bilingual dictionaries .
Event time: half-an-hour sessions to dip into over a school year
Language used: French

Introduction

Over the last few years students in primary schools have been exposed to exciting literacy developments to encourage poetry writing in English and to be more creative and free in their choice of language. Some of these ideas can be adapted for a second language, so that students can experiment within a prescribed framework. Even secondary school students are not accustomed to conjuring up their own descriptive phrases, but it is possible for young learners to write simple poems based on their own imagination. Although the outcomes will not necessarily look like some conventional poetry (i.e., there will be no rhyme), they will have the appealing freshness of early poetry writing.

Organisation

Keep the writing in the present tense to make it easier.

Dans le miroir magique – In the magic mirror.

This title invites the writer to suggest mismatching images, unusual juxtapositions of nouns and verbs. It might be a whimsical and rather frivolous theme to get the class started on the idea of writing in another language on a theme not directly related to a cross-curricular topic. A key teaching element will be to introduce the word *qui* (who) to connect the two parts of speech.

Decide on your category of nouns. They could be family members, professions (such as a doctor), animals, or even a type of creature: for example, a bird poem about different kinds of bird. Once the category is decided, students will need a bilingual dictionary to make their own glossary of about a dozen possible nouns and meanings.

The next step is to collect in the same way a selection of interesting verbs which will contrast with the nouns. They could be verbs describing movement, sound, etc., or even the daily routine verbs which everyone might have encountered describing how they get up in the morning.

Grammatical point

Keep all the verbs in the 3rd person singular, to agree with *il* or *elle*. If you are not confident about this, look for verbs in the dictionary which have the infinitive ending in *er*. Most of these verbs will end in *e* in the 3rd person singular: for example, *manger*, *il* or *elle mange* – *he or she eats*. Reflexive verbs such as *se lever* need to keep the pronoun *se*: for example, *il se lève* – he gets up.

> Watch out however for some common irregular verbs. Normally a dictionary has a section for irregular verbs, so check first

Favourite nouns might be:

un hibou – an owl; *un aigle* – an eagle; *un colombe* – a dove.

Verbs might be:

marche – walks; *se lave* – washes; *se brosse les dents* – cleans teeth; *se couche* – goes to bed; *joue* – plays.

A student might write:

un aigle qui se lave – an eagle who is washing; *un hibou qui mange* – an owl who is eating.

Introduce the versatile verb phrase *il y a* – there is or there are. Start the sentence with this phrase, as in:

il y a un aigle qui se lave; il y a un hibou qui mange.

Further parts to these lines could be nouns: something unexpected for the owl to eat perhaps:

il y a un hibou qui mange un croissant.

Alternatively students could add adverbs to describe the way the bird is acting:

doucement – quietly; *vite* – quickly; *avec soin* – carefully.

Il y a un aigle qui se lave avec soin.

Some of the class might add both and still want to add more detail, as in the following examples.

Il y a un aigle qui se lave les mains avec soin – there is an eagle washing his hands carefully.

Il y a un hibou qui mange vite un croissant – there is an owl eating a croissant quickly.

Put together a group of these sentences like a verse, and you have a little poem with the title *Dans le miroir magique* ….

Ma famille

If you opt for the family members instead, try to create a wistful combination of phrases, suggesting what they might each be doing if they were completely alone. This time it would probably be more appropriate to use the verb *je vois* – I see

Family members can easily be researched in a dictionary to achieve sentences such as these:

Dans le miroir magique je vois mon frère qui pleure doucement – I see my brother crying softly.

Dans le miroir magique je vois ma tante qui danse lentement – I see my aunt dancing slowly.

Dans le miroir magique je vois mon père qui rit follement – I see my father laughing madly.

Dans le jardin enchanté (In the enchanted garden)

Another similar idea could have the form and title of *Dans le jardin enchanté*. Use *il y a* again to introduce a description, but use the dictionary to choose some flower, tree or garden words – for example:

> *un pommier* – an apple tree; *un rosier* – a rose bush; *un tournesol* – a sunflower; *une bêche* – a spade.

The sentence you have created reads thus: *dans le jardin enchanté il y a un tournesol.*

Add colour words after the noun or words to denote size, for example:

> *gigantesque* – gigantic; *miniature* – tiny.

Look for interesting colours and shades of colour:

> *bleu foncé* – dark blue; *bleu clair* – light blue; *bleu marine* – navy blue.

Bolder colours might be:

> *d'argent* – silver; *d'or* – golden.
>
> *Dans le jardin enchanté il y a un tournesol d'argent* – a silver sunflower.
>
> *Dans le jardin enchanté il y a un pommier d'or* – a golden apple tree.
>
> *Dans le jardin enchanté il y a une bêche gigantesque* – a gigantic spade.

As before, make a collection of several lines and illustrate them with the given title.

Dans le trésor (In the treasure chest)

Another exotic place which lends itself to a list of entrancing objects is a treasure chest. Make a list of precious objects – such as coins, jewels, crowns – and add colours as before. Turn some pirate's booty into treasure too: for example, a parrot; a map; a compass.

> *Dans le trésor il y a un collier d'argent* – a silver necklace.
>
> *Dans le trésor il y une couronne d'or* – a golden crown.

Moi-même (Myself)

A poem about a person's changing moods and character could be written using a similar structure, but starting from a different standpoint.

Teach the verb *Je suis* – I am. Students could select a different living creature for each line (for example, an animal, a bird) and add a suitable verb to describe what they might be doing. These descriptions might fit certain parts of their character which change from time to time.

> *Je suis un serpent qui dort* – I am a sleeping snake.
>
> *Je suis un hibou qui chasse* – I am an owl hunting.
>
> *Je suis un chat qui sourit* – I am a cat who smiles.

This could turn into a *Guess who?* Poem, where clues are given in the form of the animal links and a question put at the end for readers to work out the identity of the writer. The title could be *C'est qui?* – Who is it?

Le Nouvel An (The New Year)

Introduce the class to the theme of the Chinese New Year, where each year has a different animal as its symbol. Encourage students to think up a new collection of animals with a brief description to cover a year.

First search in a bilingual dictionary for animal names, perhaps with a theme – for example, from polar regions, rainforest creatures, poisonous and dangerous animals. Add a brief description of, say, colour, character or size.

> *L'année de l'ours polaire timide* – the year of the shy polar bear.

> *L'année du serpent rusé* – the year of the crafty snake.

> *L'année de l'araignée lumineuse* – the year of the luminous spider.

A year-long list of unusual symbolic animals illustrated in vibrant colours would make a striking poem.

Dans le bois sombre (In the dark wood)

In this poem a series of prepositions can be used to develop a description of a place. Each line will focus in more and more closely until the final line reveals the most precious heart of the place.

Build up a collection of prepositions which might include:

> *sur* – on; *sous* – under; *en face de* – opposite; *à côté de* – next to; *près de* – near to; *loin de* – far from; *dans* – in.

Choose some country or woodland words from the dictionary: trees, flowers, etc. Add a simple adjective and start by using *dans le bois sombre* – in the dark wood.

> *Dans le bois sombre il y a un grand chêne* – In the dark wood there is a big oak tree.

Choose a different preposition, woodland word and adjective. Start the next line with the last words of the preceding one.

> *En face du grand chêne il y a un petit pommier* – opposite the tall oak tree there is a small apple tree.

As before, change the preposition, word and adjective and add to the final words.

> *Sous le petit pommier il y a un rosier vert* – Under the little apple tree there is a green rosebush.

Continue in the same way over several lines until you reach the secret centre of the picture. Decide what precious thing might be lying or hiding or buried there.

> *Sur le rosier vert il y a un papillon d'or* – on the green rose bush there is a golden

Project 8   Writing a mini pocket book

Project outline

Requirements: A4 card, glue, scissors, short piece of string or wool
Event time: half an hour to write and another half hour to make the book
Languages used: Spanish, French

Introduction

Students enjoy making little books to fit a short piece of writing. There are a variety of different kinds which are simple for small hands to execute. One example is a fold up mini-book with a pocket for a character to be placed in and taken on a journey.

The accompanying DVD materials for this project include further language activities in French for a Year Two or Year Three class to celebrate a simple story, such as the Katie Morag books (Hedderwick 1985) or any text involving a family.

Organisation

This format suits the story of a character on a journey, who could be travelling from one country to another, or moving from place to place around a local area or around a building.

The example given is loosely based on cross-curricular work on the familiar geography topic of Katie Morag and her home in the Scottish Islands (Hedderwick 1985). A little story could describe the places where she might travel around her island or any character might go on an imaginary island.

Alternative themes could be:

- a trip around a zoo to see a variety of animals;
- a walk to different locations in your school;
- a shopping trip along the high street, going into several shops;
- a visit to the seaside, looking at a range of attractions;
- a round trip to European capitals, looking at their main tourist sites.

First, using a bilingual dictionary, make a list of places which might be visited. For an island story there might be:

	French	*Spanish*
the beach	*la plage*	*la playa*
the post office	*le bureau de poste*	*la oficina de correos*
the farm	*la ferme*	*la granja*
the hill	*la colline*	*la colina*
the loch	*le lac*	*el lago*
the school	*l'école*	*la escuela*
the house	*la maison*	*la casa*

Begin with the title *Où est Katie?* – Where is Katie? *Où est Matthew?*, etc. (in Spanish: *¿Donde está Katie/Matthew?*). Then in French, start the story *Katie va* (Katie goes) and add the destinations using *au, à la, à l'* according to the gender of the place named (in Spanish, start with *Katie va* and add destinations with *a la* or *al* according to their gender).

In French this text would read: *Katie va à la colline, elle va à la ferme, elle va à l'école, elle va à la maison, elle va à la plage, elle va au bureau de poste, elle va au lac.*

In Spanish the text would be: *Katie va a la colina, va a la granja, va al escuela, va a la casa, va a la playa, va a la oficina de correos, va al lago.*

Making the book

To make the book, take a piece of A4 paper or card. Fold in half lengthways, and keep the fold at the top. Fold in half across the width of the page, and place the new fold to the left like the spine of a book. Take the further edge of the front page (on your right) and fold it back to join the left hand spine and press down the new fold half way along the width of the book. Turn the book over onto the back and do the same: fold the furthest edge over to join the left hand spine and make a new fold.

To finish, make sure that your lengthways fold is at the top of your book and adjust your folding book so that it flows from front to back. You now have the possibility of eight pages or seven plus the title page. If this is too many, keep it to a four-page book just on the front pages of your book. Write your text on each page and illustrate appropriately.

As a final flourish, make a small square card to stick or staple to the title page to make a little pocket. Decorate it with a picture of a flower or tree, or something in keeping with your journey. Draw onto a separate piece of card a picture of your main character dressed in suitable clothes, colour in brightly, laminate and cut out. Attach a piece of wool or string to the back of the figure with sellotape and stick the other end inside the little pocket, out of sight.

Now take your character out for a walk to all the places in your story. Each person can make up their own story, visiting places in any order, or the teacher could recount the story in French or Spanish while the class take their characters for a walk to the places mentioned in the correct order.

Writing a mini pocket book: additional DVD materials

1. Activities to fit an island family story (such as Katie Morag or an imaginary family)

7

Languages beyond the classroom

Introduction

This exciting chapter takes your languages lessons outside the classroom – whether virtually, as in the eTwinning project, or actually, as in the Spanish nature trail, for example. The chapter encourages you to make the best use of the spaces around you – spaces which are often very familiar to your students but which tend to be overlooked by adults. The seven projects encompass drawing competitions (*The foreign languages draw*), eating healthy lunches and sharing them with friends (*Healthy lunches*), planting in your school garden (*Making use of outdoor spaces*) and making books to take home and share with your family (*Home reading scheme*) and much more besides!

Project 1   Fly the world from your own school airport!

Project outline

Requirements: large hall with space to fit tables around the edge and plane in the centre. Data projector and screen above centre space.

Event time: each flight takes about 30 to 40 minutes to organize, assuming that two classes go together. A school of 400 students would probably need a day and a half or two days to take everyone on one flight.

Languages targeted: Mainly the language taught in Key Stage Two, but airport announcements can be made in any language

Introduction

Now and then you have an unforgettable experience which draws a whole school together and is talked about for years afterwards. Creating an airport in your own school hall to take every one of the students and adults on a flight abroad is exactly that. It is a flexible

model which can be used as the starting point for a week of languages or international events, or as the culmination of a week of activities. It is suitable for all age groups, involves all members of the school community and is a golden opportunity to develop and enhance team work. Moreover, it is a great model to give a purpose to language learning and to inject a sense of fun and excitement into school life. It highlights the role of students with English as an additional language, as they become stars for the week, interpreting or explaining cultural aspects. Students who have experienced this activity have developed an appetite for learning more languages and a sense of the global community, while many adults have declared the event one of the best days of their lives!

You will need a team of creative and imaginative colleagues to think through the logistics of how to use your own school site and how to create different areas in the 'Airport Terminal', but it will be worth the effort! This event creates unforgettable experiences for pupils and adults alike. Look around the school to see how you can adapt equipment from role play areas and store cupboards and ask your caretaker and local shopkeepers for materials to recycle. The additional DVD materials that accompany this section include many additional resources, such as templates for departure sheets; tickets; luggage labels; resources for teachers, including ideas for airport-week activities; airport arrangements check list; sample first-class menus; class-made Japanese newspapers; in-flight magazine.

Organisation

First of all, decide how you might use your airport and where you might fly to. If you are about to celebrate an International Week, each class could fly to a country of their choice and then return to their classroom, which will become their destination country for the day or week and where you can explore a whole range of cultural and linguistic activities. Alternatively, you may be studying Spanish all through your school and decide that all flights will go to Spanish airports, and each classroom destination will become a Spanish region or city for the week or day.

- Start planning this event well ahead. Look at your school hall, or other large space, and see how the journey to be taken around the hall can be achieved with minimal disruption to the school week. You may have to move the airport desks and plane to one side for lunchtime, assembly, etc., so make your plans flexible.
- The layout of the hall needs to incorporate the check-in desk, a baggage drop, passport control, security gate, departure lounge, exit gate to the plane, and the plane itself. It is best to have the plane in the centre and the tables, etc., for the other activities around the edge of the room to form a journey.
- On the day, students will have a great surprise when entering the familiar hall with their class to see a transformed space and proceed through each desk or section until their plane is announced. They will board to a numbered seat, see and hear the flight take off, have a light refreshment and then leave for their new classroom destination.

How to make your airport look authentic

Check in desk/ Baggage drop

You may need to double up these desks, unless you have a very large hall at your disposal. Look for old phones, keyboards, clipboards, class lists to tick names off. Place bathroom scales on the floor to weigh each bag, seek out genuine airport materials or make your own (for example, *fragile* or *heavy* stickers for bags, leaflets, posters about liquids).

Passport desk

You need an old phone, clipboard, stamp and inkpad to stamp each passport. Stick a taped line on the floor in front of the table so that each passenger must wait for a confidential interview with the passport officer. You could also use a keyboard here, as well as leaflets about customs allowances.

Security Gate

You need: cardboard tubes, sprayed or covered to look silver, to make a frame to walk under (a carpet shop is a good place to ask, as they often have empty carpet tubes); a simple doormat on the ground to create a different texture; a cardboard box covered in black crêpe paper with classroom tray inside to pull out and place valuables inside; high-visibility jackets for adults; hand-held zapper to frisk each passenger (use a cable detector for this – maybe your caretaker has one in his cupboard).

Departure lounge

You need: benches for children to sit on when they have gone past check in, passport control and security while they wait for everyone to be ready to board the plane; newspapers (made in class) on benches to keep them occupied; a flip chart with details of flight numbers, destinations and comments, for example, delayed for two hours.

Walls

You need: bunting; large international flags; signs; posters of international scenes and children from around the world.

Aeroplane

The aeroplane should comprise rows of numbered chairs facing the front with a central aisle. On the back of each seat there could be a plastic wallet with a travel brochure inside. Front row passengers may have a first-class menu on their seats (made in class). Place stripy car-park-type tape along the sides of the plane, so that the only entrance is via the departure gate. The captain's chair needs to be labeled at the very front of the room. A screen at the front of the hall visible to everyone will show announcements, pictures, etc. A sound system can broadcast the sounds of take-off, etc.

Airport announcements

You need: a desk with a microphone system or tannoy system for the announcer; two chime bars to strike the two-tone airport calling sound; simple, prepared announcements in suitable languages about security, boarding, etc.

Refreshment trolley

You need: a lunchbox trolley (check that it will fit down the centre aisle of the plane); basic packs of biscuits (nut-free) for refreshments – enough for each passenger; silver foil dish to present the biscuits more attractively (drinks are just too fiddly and time-consuming to provide).

Baggage collection

You need borrowed supermarket trolleys (one for each class on a flight). They will be needed to load the bags brought by each class when they check in for their flight. If trolleys are not available, look for another way to move the bags out of the airport space during the flight, so that they can be collected upon arrival at the flight destination. The best solution is to have them moved into a corridor outside the airport room after check-in and baggage weigh-in, so that disembarking passengers do not disturb any other flights taking off.

Before the Airport Day

1. Write to parents to explain what is happening and to ask for any airport contacts or links, any expertise, help on the day or resources, including old uniforms, posters, etc. It's surprising what turns up!

2. In class, decide which country you will visit or the region/city, and brainstorm what is known and what pupils would like to find out. Look at an atlas to plan the flight route. Look on the internet for the weather forecast and decide what you will do in the country: for example, go to the beach, ski in the mountains, etc.

3. In class, fill in a departure sheet (a template is included in the additional DVD materials) detailing flight number and time, destination, expected weather. Inside a suitcase-shaped picture on the departure sheet, draw and label five or so items of clothing or luggage suitable for the country and intended activities – such as sunscreen, wellies, brolly, teddy bear.

4. Students take home the completed departure sheet to show their family. Ask parents to help their child to pack a small suitcase or bag with the items they have drawn on the sheet and to bring the bag on the day.

5. In class, each class makes up a couple of newspapers from the chosen country or region. Students could choose a suitable title, for example, for a Japanese paper *The Sumo Sun* or *The Tokyo Times* and in pairs write articles and newsworthy items about the country: for example, in a Japanese newspaper, Mount Fuji erupting. They could make up advertisements for

products from that country, such as Kimono adverts or new Honda cars, and cartoons or illustrations. Either print out the papers or stick and paste in the traditional way; laminate several copies and have them ready to distribute along the benches in the departure lounge.

6. Make up first-class menus for the plane (see examples in the additional DVD materials), draw ing pictures of food for different courses; place them on the first couple of rows of seats of the plane for the first-class passengers.

Handy hints

The first 'flight' takes longer to carry out while all the airport staff at the desks get used to their jobs. Make sure that your timetable allows for a slow start to the day. Have some runners (Year Six?) to summon the next classes when the first passengers have disembarked.

You don't want students to be bored in a long queue at check-in, so have two or three check-in desks, and direct the first six students to the furthest desk to queue, the next six to the middle desk, and the next six to the nearest desk, etc. In that way, your queues should be more manageable and will move along easily.

Encourage adults to join in the fun and have proper airport conversations for example: Did you pack your bag yourself? Are you travelling for business or pleasure? Have you any liquids in your bag? They could summon airport security to detain troublesome passengers!

You may find that having two classes flying together makes the event run more smoothly. It works well to have classes from different year groups (and destinations which would be normally in totally different directions) travelling together. Your plane could touch down at the nearest place, one class disembarks, and the other class continues on the plane to their country.

If you have Reception students (aged five) taking part, pair them up with a Year Six class (aged ten and eleven) to help them around the circuit and encourage them if they find the experience daunting or noisy. It's a great opportunity for Personal, Social, Health and Economic education work across the age groups.

The Aircraft sound turned up very loud and pictures on the big screen make all the difference to the event. Choose someone to be the captain who can improvise about the flight and make announcements – for example, 'Cabin crew, prepare for take-off'; 'Dim the lights,' etc. – and even comment on the flight: 'We're cruising at 20,000 feet; 'If you look over on your left you will see the English Channel'; 'We're passing the Himalayas,' etc.).

You don't need to fly the passengers home again after their journey to their new country but you could do so after a few days if it's been a success. Students quite naturally accept that they are in a new country and talk at playtime about their arrival in Japan or India and their plans for the day!

As an alternative to the tourist leaflets on the back of the plane seats, your class could make their own Duty Free magazines. Cut out pictures of products from shop catalogues, stick them on card, look on the internet for prices (these could be expressed in Euros or any foreign currency) and label the items, perhaps in another language. You could make the leaflet seem more authentic by adding suitable phrases, such as, For Sale, Special

Offer, Reduced Price, etc., from Internet sites (examples are provided in the accompanying DVD materials for this project).

Preparation by Adults

Allocate roles at desks, security, announcement desk, captain, etc.

Decide on an airline name and logo. Make up simple badges with the logo and name attached by safety pin for every adult to wear.

Decide on a corporate image for the day. Think about airline uniforms and decide on an easy colour and image, such as black T-shirts and a cheap red scarf. Red lipstick adds to the glossy image! Maybe make headband-type hats from long strips of card with the badge attached.

Add logo to tickets, boarding cards, passports (templates for tickets are in the additional DVD materials) and print out one of each of them for each student.

Collect travel leaflets or magazines, place them in plastic wallets and stick on the back of each seat with tape. Prepare number cards to put on the front of each seat.

Prepare ICT slots for the airport screen in the hall as follow.

1. Flight announcement screen with flight numbers, destinations and status.
2. Sequence of photos of pilot in cockpit, cabin, runway, aerial view from plane, mountains during flight, etc., to run during the flight.
3. From the internet, capture aircraft take-off noise and amplify to loud noise.

    Collect props: for example, phones, keyboards, leaflets.

Invite all the adults connected with the school to fly on the plane – teaching assistants, governors, secretarial staff, mid-day supervisors, cleaners.

Plan activities to happen in the classroom. Look for cross curricular links, for example:

Languages
Learn useful expressions and use them in class for the week. Make posters of words, faces with speech bubbles, find out about a festival from the country and celebrate it, count to ten in the language, play Bingo with the numbers …

Geography
Map work, physical features of the country, climate, settlements.

Music
What instruments are played? Listen to typical music.

Dance/PE
Move to music, learn popular dance movements, play local or international games.

Literacy
Write postcards home or diary entries about events.

Maths
Look at money and prices of items sold. Convert local currency to English pounds and pence. Have a shop in the play area.

Science
Look at food from country, make recipes and taste. What is manufactured? Any famous inventions?

History
Famous events, people, clothing, customs. What sort of government operates? Are there any conflicts?

Personal, Social, Health and Economic education
Picture a student of the same age from that country. After research, on A4 sheet folded in half across, make up a two-part piece – for example, *My Spanish friend Yolanda and I* – with on one side a drawing of the imaginary friend and details of her life: e.g. family members, where she lives, hobbies, pets, etc. and on the other side, the same details about the English student.

Art
Look at famous artists from the country. Study their style and recreate a mini postcard version effect.

Checklist for the night before take off

- Set up the Airport, stick numbers on seats and first-class menus on the front row
- Get the ICT loaded and tested for the big screen
- Set up the announcement system with microphone and chime bars
- Put out a labelled seat at the very front of the plane rows for the captain
- Put out the trolley and biscuits, supermarket trolleys for bags in the hall
- Have uniforms, badges, lipstick, headbands ready
- Stick plastic wallets with leaflets on back of seats
- Put scales, keyboards, phones on check-in desks and passport desk
- Set up security gate with zapper from caretaker and valuables tray
- Put out benches and class newspapers in the departure area for children waiting to board
- Hang bunting, flags, signs on walls: e.g. departure lounge
- Have tickets, passports printed and ready in each classroom; boarding cards (numbered to match the seat numbers) on the check-in desks
- Seal the hall off with tape from children so that it looks enticing
- Have an exciting introductory activity ready in the classroom for when you land

- Get your camera ready to take photos of the day
- Call in the local paper to make a splash

The student's journey on the Airport Day

- Arrive at school with bag packed with five or so items and departure sheet.
- In class fill in passport details, draw pictures of self.
- Fill in ticket with details of flight destination, number of flight, airport destination.
- When summoned, take bag, passport and ticket to hall. Another class goes at the same time to check-in desk as directed.
- Exchange ticket for a numbered boarding pass.
- Hand over bag to be weighed. Questioned about flight, bag, etc. Bag put in supermarket trolley with the rest of the bags from that class.
- Go to passport control and wait for private talk. Passport stamped and photo checked.
- Go through security gate, hand over passport and boarding pass into crepe paper tray. Zapped by security officer.
- Go to departure lounge to sit on bench and wait for boarding. Read newspapers, listen to announcements.

- When everyone has got to the departure lounge, shown to numbered seat on plane matching boarding card. Safety announcements on plane: e.g. oxygen masks.
- Lights dim, plane noise, take off. In mid-air, trolleys brought round and biscuit served.
- Pictures and noise of the plane landing.
- Leave plane at destination, go out of hall, collect bag from trolley outside hall, go to classroom destination ... in a new country!

Fly the world from your own school airport!: additional DVD materials

1. Resources documents

Project 2   Home Reading Scheme

Project outline

Requirements: blank audio CDs, laminator, camera, basic sound-recording programme on computer
Event time: could be delivered over a term or could be attached to a particular project
Languages targeted: current language being taught in Key Stage Two classes

Introduction

In primary school it is expected that each pupil takes home a school reading book and reads aloud with an adult regularly. Why not extend this idea to books in the foreign language being taught in the school? Although it is possible to buy bilingual books (see Mantra Books on the additional DVD materials to this project), the cost of equipping a class series would probably be beyond the budget of many schools. You may also be concerned about the text level being unsuitable for your beginners or that students may not be able to read aloud correctly or confidently.

This project gives you the chance to provide a personal and meaningful alternative quite cheaply, with simple materials and standard IT skills, by making your own books based on the current topic you are covering in Primary Languages lessons.

In addition, this is an excellent opportunity to involve the whole family in the language learning going on at school and to encourage them to read, listen and join in with their child from the comfort of their own sofa.

The additional materials in the DVD that accompany this project include: two sample books of pages with photos and text based on favourite class animals; text for both books in French, Spanish and German; sample letter to parents asking for feedback; list of useful websites.

Organisation

Choose an area of your current topic that lends itself to a simple narrative, maybe with a sense of fun or humour, for example, your class-favourite puppets go on an adventure; a teddy gets dressed in the wrong clothes.

Take photos either in your classroom setting or take familiar classroom toys or objects to a new location. Make the pictures bold, colourful and eye catching. Make up a simple story using the vocabulary you have practised on many occasions with the class and add the simple text to each page. Limit yourself to about one sentence per page. Laminate the pages of the book and attach them together with treasury tags or any other cheap method.

So far, this will seem like a familiar, tried and tested method used in many classroom activities. However, a home reading book in another language has an extra dimension: how will the student or family be able to read the text aloud correctly and pronounce unfamiliar words? Record yourself on CD reading the text in the new language slowly enough for someone to follow the story on their own. Read the book to the class and demonstrate how the CD and book work together. Make four or five copies of the book and CD to lend out in rotation to the class to take home.

> **Tips**
>
> Place the book and CD in a brightly coloured plastic wallet which can't be lost at home.
>   Attach a class list to the front of the wallet and tick off the name of each pupil as they borrow it.

The books are versatile enough to be used in different ways: the CD just listened to and the text followed with a finger; the student joining in with the reading aloud; repeating after the CD; finally reading aloud without the prompt of the CD.

You need to bear in mind that the text should be manageable for a student to read unaided at home, maybe with an adult with no knowledge of the foreign language. Ideally you also want the reader to have a good role model on the CD to pronounce words correctly, so if you aren't confident about speaking, try to find a colleague who might help you.

You might like to get some feedback from both parents and students about their experience of using the home-reading scheme: for example, how/where they used the book, what drawbacks and advantages they found, what improvements and future steps they would like to implement. Recent feedback from parents using this scheme has been very enthusiastic. Families have listened to the book on car journeys, at bed time, with babies and toddlers and have been keen to explore more books. They have all emphasised the need for quite a slow pace on the CD, so that there is time to repeat the phrases.

Further Steps

This has proved to be a very successful scheme for spreading the word about language learning and including the whole family. You might want to explore further possibilities. They could include:

- As a class, work out the next adventure and write it together;
- If your class is older, ask them to work in a group and write different adventures for the same characters, illustrating them for homework;
- Take photos of the students in the class and incorporate them in the stories. You could then record the text on a CD in the same way as before, or use a bilingual student in school to help;
- Invite Year Six students with more experience of the language to write a simple story for Year Three students. They could take the photos in locations around the school, incorporate the text themselves and read it with the student.

Home reading scheme additional DVD Materials

1. Sample letter to parents
2. Animal text and photos for home reading book
3. Alternative reading book: *Bonjour les animaux!*
4. Spanish text for first photo story
5. Spanish text for second photo story
6. Useful websites

Project 3   Making use of outdoor spaces

Project outline

Requirements: any space outside, for example, a garden area or playground
Event time: could be as little as ten minutes of playtime or an hour of a lesson
Language used: French

Introduction

In your school you may be lucky enough to have large playgrounds and a delightful garden area where flowers and vegetables can be grown, or just a tarmac space where all students play and have Physical Education. No matter how much or how little space you have out of doors, languages can be incorporated into this space and can flourish in the open air. In this section there will be ideas about playground games for short playtimes and longer lunch hours, gardening themes, sensory signs, weekly game schedule. Additional resources on the accompanying DVD for this project include a stunning display of photos of school gardens, sensory garden labels, seed-saving and class-made seed packets.

Organisation

Clapping games for short playtimes

Playgrounds are full of students playing familiar rhymes in clapping games, either in pairs or groups. With a little effort it is possible to have a whole year group or more clapping rhymes in another language and teaching each other new ones. Why not spend a little lesson time one week putting together rhymes in French which can be used outside at playtime? It is easy to try, costs nothing and catches on quickly. The main requirements are that the language should be:

- simple to understand;
- easy to remember;
- repetitive but not rhyming;
- catchy, to fit a clapping rhythm.

If you want this to start with Year Three students (age eight), familiar vocabulary – such as numbers, colours, greetings – will work well. Older students have used compass directions, weather expressions, seasons, family members, body parts, animals and their habitats to construct their own rhymes. A typical early rhyme would be:

Un, deux, trois,

Rouge, bleu, jaune

Un, deux, trois,

Blanc, vert, noir.

AU REVOIR!!

These words can fit into the 'cross hands and spin around' concept of many games.
Year Four or Five (ages nine and ten) might work on the basis of:

Au nord il y a du soleil

Au sud il y a du vent

A l'est il y a un orage

A l'ouest il neige, il pleut!

Cinq, quatre, trois, deux, un, ZERO!

This can fit in with the topics worked on in lessons but end with a turn, triumphant star jump, or any other funny flourish.
A Year Six pair (aged eleven) produced :

Je voudrais une framboise

Je voudrais deux framboises, un, deux

Je voudrais trois framboises, un, deux, trois

Je voudrais quatre framboises, un, deux, trois, quatre,

Je voudrais cinq framboises,

UN, DEUX, TROIS, QUATRE, CINQ!

Further Steps

- Everyone writes up their rhyme to make a class book.
- One class pairs up with a different class and teaches them their rhymes.
- Post up a new rhyme each day in the playground for everyone to practice.
- Have a long chain of people clapping out rhymes on each other's backs.
- Perform one in assembly for the whole school to learn.

Playground games for lunchtime

Lunchtimes are difficult for many students and you may have pro-active 'buddy' students or mid-day adult supervisors who can sweep students of all ages up into circle games. One popular game on a familiar theme is:

Poissons dans la mer (Fish in the sea)

Students stand in a circle linking arms or hands with three or four chosen to be fish (*les poissons*) who stand away from the circle. The circle group – the net (*le filet*) – whisper to choose a secret number between one and ten. The net circle raise and lower their linked arms to simulate a fishing net in the sea. The fish children run in and out of the circle as the net chants *poissons dans la mer, poissons dans la mer, un, deux, trois*, etc., until they reach their special number and lower arms to catch any fish. Any caught fish swap with new children for a new game.

Le facteur arrive (The postman's coming)

Students sit in a circle with one child chosen to be the postman (*le facteur*) holding a letter. He/she runs around the outside of the circle while everyone else chants briskly and slaps their knees, saying *le facteur arrive. Quelle heure est-il?* They then chant the hours of the clock (*une heure, deux heures* …). When *midi* is reached, the postman drops his letter behind the student nearest to him. That person chases the postman around the outside of the circle before he gets back to the spare place. The loser then becomes the next postman, picks up the dropped letter and the game continues.

You can vary the speed at which they run by calling out *première classe* or *deuxième classe*, so that the game can be played fast or in slow motion.

L'échelle (Ladder game)

Students sit in pairs on the floor with feet stretched out to meet in ladder formation. Give each pair a number/ animal/month/food to remember. When you call out their number, etc., they must run up the middle to the top of the ladder, back down the outside and back up to their place. With older students, make up a story so that they have to listen hard. You may need to make two separate ladders, so that two lots of pairs have the same word – more running and more fun.

Dessinez-moi (Draw me)

This is a quieter game which can be played sitting on a bench in pairs with paper and pencil or mini whiteboards and pens. Students group themselves in pairs or threes (any smallish number, so that no one is left out) with a whiteboard/pen or paper/pencil for each group. One person from each group approaches the adult in charge who shows a flashcard of an animal /fruit /family member, etc., which all the children know in the language. The student draws a picture of this object on the board, and the others in the group have to say the French word. Then swap who draws next time.

Tips for success

- Write up the rules for a new game each week in the playground or in each classroom.
- Teach Year Six students (aged eleven) how to play and ask them to help with the foreign language, if your adult helpers are not confident.
- Demonstrate the new weekly game in assembly at the beginning of the week.
- If you have a weekly home letter for parents, include the game details in this, so that the family can have some fun too, or at least can explain the rules.

Improving the environment with sensory signs

We all try to make our outdoor spaces attractive and inviting for students by providing colours, shapes to relieve the monotony of tarmac and brick. Involve a group of artistic or keen students in creating some sensory signs to put up in the playground or hang from a tree or fence. They could design the pictures to fit the words you provide about five senses:

touchez – touch

regardez – look

écoutez – listen

sentez – smell

goûtez – taste

Discuss what natural things you might touch, see, etc., in your playground and write signs to describe them. You might come up with:

Touchez les feuilles – touch the leaves

Regardez les oiseaux – look at the birds

Sentez les fleurs – smell the flowers

Écoutez les abeilles - listen to the bees

Goûtez les fruits – taste the fruit

Make up posters with the words/pictures, laminate them and hang or fix them in prominent places. Introduce them in assembly so that students know what they mean and respect other people's work.

In the school garden or mini veg patch

Put up signs in each bed to show what vegetables are being grown. Students can look up vegetable names in a dictionary and draw pictures, or have their photos taken as they garden.

Dans le potager nous cultivons beaucoup de légumes.	In the vegetable garden we're growing lots of vegetables.
Cherchez les haricots verts!	Look for the beans!
Cherchez les tomates! Cherchez les radis!	Look for the tomatoes and radishes!
Cherchez les oignons!	Look for the onions
Cherchez le maïs!	Look for the sweetcorn
Comptez les citrouilles!	Count the pumpkins!
Cueillez les herbes!	Pick the herbs!

If you have a shed to store garden tools, make a list of tools in French as a check list:

Dans l'abri de jardin il y a des outils de jardinage (In the garden shed there are some gardening tools):

cinq bêches (spades)

deux râteaux (rakes)

cinq arrosoirs (watering cans)

Une brouette (wheel barrow)

six paires de gants de jardinage (pairs of gardening gloves)

dix paquets de graines de tournesol (packets of sunflower seeds)

Semons les graines (Let's sow some seeds)

Take photos of students gathering seeds from plants ready to use for next year. Label and display them.

Make seed packets with colourful designs to display your saved seeds. You could set up a stall to sell them for a small price at a school fundraising event, or exchange them with a gardening group at another school.

Keep a log of the quantity of vegetables grown over a season and work out some easy recipes in French for salads and soups, for example:

Une salade aux tomates	**Tomato salad**
Un demi-kilo de tomates	Half a kilo of tomatoes
Deux petits oignons	Two small onions
Du sel, du poivre, de l'huile	Salt, pepper, oil
Des feuilles de basilic	Basil leaves
Coupez en tranches les tomates et les oignons.	Cut the tomatoes and onions into slices.
Mettez les oignons sur les tomates.	Put the onions on top of the tomatoes.
Ajoutez du sel, du poivre, de l'huile et des feuilles	Add salt, pepper, oil and some basil leaves.
de basilic. Bon appétit!	Enjoy your salad!

Making use of Outdoor Spaces:additional DVD materials

1.   Picture gallery

Project 4　　The foreign languages draw

> ### Project outline
>
> **Requirements:** topic-based vocabulary; a long wall in a central venue (for example, a school foyer, a corridor, an assembly hall, etc.)
> **Event time:** one day for the main event when the pictures are put on display
> **Languages targeted:** any

Introduction

The Foreign Languages Draw was inspired by the National Drawing Campaign in 2011 (see list of useful websites on the accompanying DVD). It was first delivered by Routes South on a small scale at a German Christmas event in 2011 and then again on a larger scale in 2012 to celebrate the London Olympic and Paralympic Games. This project was awarded a Springboard Grant from the University of Brighton in 2012, which enabled a formal final awards ceremony to be held for the winners of the categories from schools across West and East Sussex. However, the event can be organized on a simpler scale, involving just one class or year group in your school.

The basic shape of The Foreign Languages Draw is very simple and, as long as there is a suitable, central venue available, relatively easy to organize. The main aims of this project are:

- to enable students to celebrate a topic-related theme in a foreign language;
- to learn new vocabulary items and related genders (where relevant);
- to have fun whilst using the target language and being creative.

Essentially, students are asked to draw a picture (or pictures) around a theme. The subject of the picture should be a noun or even a simple sentence, and the heading for each picture should be presented in the foreign language, with the appropriate gender where relevant. Any foreign language can be chosen. The two model invitations provided in this project are, firstly, in German to celebrate Christmas at a German-style Christmas event, with Christmas vocabulary, and, secondly, in any language to celebrate the 2012 London Olympic and Paralympic Games, with vocabulary based around the theme of sport. The additional DVD materials for this project include a picture gallery of some of the artwork presented at the German Christmas event in December 2011, which was held at The University of Brighton for a group of visiting Year Seven to Eleven students. The invitations serve as a good example of what can be done on a larger scale to stimulate and sustain an interest in foreign languages, although, as previously mentioned, the project can also be delivered on a much smaller scale.

Organisation

In order to organize the *Foreign Languages Draw*, you need to

1. **Choose a meaningful theme.** This could relate to a particular celebration, for example, the *Day of the Dead* (see also Part III, Project 2) or a special event that is taking place: for example, the 2012 Olympic and Paralympic Games in London. The theme could be a particular season (for example, summertime, spring or autumn), or the students' hobbies or favourite colour (interpreted in any way they wish), or jobs. Any area of vocabulary is appropriate if it fits in with something happening at the moment or some area of work students have already covered or are likely to meet soon.

2. **Identify a suitable location to display the pictures.** This could be for example a local church hall, a school assembly hall, a town hall, a library, a long corridor in your school or your local college/university, the walls of your school canteen etc;

3. **Identify a day** when students can come to the central venue, bringing with them their decorated picture(s) on a piece of A4 paper, or by when they need to have submitted their artwork. Enough time needs to be left for teachers to disseminate the information in the first place and for students to complete the artwork;

4. **Identify your judges.** Depending on the extent and formality of your *Foreign Languages Draw*, the artwork judge could be a local figure, someone from your school community, or else a person you know who is simply interested in drawing as a hobby. The language judge should ideally be a linguist. This person could be your Foreign Language Assistant (see Part IV), a different language teacher perhaps, or someone from the parent community. It is not advisable for the regular class/school language teacher to act in the role of judge – a more neutral outsider is probably best.

5. **Identify participants**. Invite as many students to take part as appropriate/practicable. Your *Foreign Languages Draw* can be organised as a whole-class event or across several classes. It could be an inter-school competition or organized across a region. Potentially the regional finals could feed into a national final, with the winning pictures being used for further publicity;

6. **Set up the task and prepare the invitations.** Below is a sample invitation which could be used to help celebrate a German Christmas event (see Part III, Project 1). It is based on the one used for the German Christmas event which was held at the University of Brighton in December 2011. A second model invitation follows, which advertises a larger-scale Sussex *Foreign Languages Draw* and was used to invite students to a central venue at the University of Brighton in April 2012 to celebrate the diversity of languages united by the theme of sporting activities involved in the 2012 London Olympic and Paralympic Games.

Example One: Celebrating Christmas at a German-style Christmas market with Christmas vocabulary.

𝕿𝖍𝖊 𝕱𝖔𝖗𝖊𝖎𝖌𝖓 𝕷𝖆𝖓𝖌𝖚𝖆𝖌𝖊 𝕮𝖍𝖗𝖎𝖘𝖙𝖒𝖆𝖘 𝕯𝖗𝖆𝖜

Looking for an exciting way to celebrate Christmas? Wondering how to combine German with another subject? Then look no further!

As part of our German Christmas celebrations, we are holding a *Foreign Language Christmas Draw*, which will be held at (venue) on (date) from (time). All your students have to do to enter is to complete the word ***Weihnachts-*** with a suitable noun (and its gender) which they should illustrate and decorate!

Prize

There will be three prizes awarded at (the event venue). One prize will be for the best artwork, one prize will be for the most effort made, and one prize will be for the most imaginative noun with the correct gender. Prizes will be awarded by (the foreign languages team). (Name of artwork judge) will judge the artwork, and (name of linguist to judge the foreign language) will award the language prize.

Rules

1. Pictures should be drawn on A4 paper (one per word). The correct gender of the noun should also be included as part of the heading.
2. Pictures can be sent in advance or brought along on the evening to be displayed on our wall frieze. Individuals may enter as many items as they wish.
3. Pictures must be the artist's own, original handwork (i.e. computer graphics are not acceptable).
4. Only one artist should draw and decorate each picture. The name and age of the artist should be clearly indicated on the **front** of each picture.
5. Pictures should be either sent in advance to (name) or brought in to the German Christmas event on (date) at (venue).
6. Prizes will be awarded at the end of the celebrations on (date) in three categories: best drawing; most imaginative noun with the correct gender; most effort made. The judges' decisions in all cases are final.

Here are three examples of the types of picture your students could produce and decorate.

das Weihnachtsaquarium

der Weihnachtspinguin

die Weihnachtskarte

Don't forget we are looking for the most creative drawing and the best artwork!

Example Two: celebrating the 2012 London Olympics with vocabulary based around the theme of sport. The rules are the same as for The Christmas Draw opposite.

The Sussex Foreign Languages Draw: Olympic sailing!

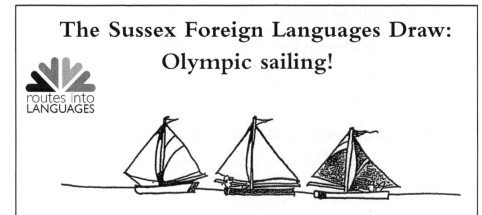

© Emma Ball

At the 2012 London Olympic and Paralympic Games, London will be host to athletes and spectators from more than 220 countries across the globe. Help us to celebrate this richness of languages and cultures by entering The Big Sussex Foreign Languages Draw. All you have to do is to choose a sport, draw a picture of it, decorate your picture, label it in any language other than English (including the correct gender where appropriate). One entry per student is allowed, and the picture must be your own original handwork (not computer drawn/coloured).

Prizes will be awarded in three categories: there will be one prize for the best artwork; one prize for the most imaginative (and correct!) use of language; one prize for the most effort made. Local artist (name) will judge the artwork, whilst (name) will be the foreign language judge. Their decision in each category is final.

 All entries must be received by (date and time). Please send your entries to (contact name). One entry per student will be accepted which must be drawn on one sheet of A4 paper. Please put your name, the language you have chosen and your age on the front of your drawing. Winners will be notified by (date) and invited to a final presentation at (venue). *Good luck! Viel Glück! Bonne Chance! ¡Que tengas suerte!*

Organizer's shopping list

- Sheets of display paper onto which the submitted pictures are pinned
- Some means of sticking up the pictures: e.g. glue, pins, staple gun or sticky tack, etc.
- Prizes for the various categories
- Tokens of appreciation for the judge(s)
- Card if formal invitations are to be posted

Reflections

The Foreign Languages Draw held as part of the German Christmas event held at the University of Brighton on Thursday December 8th 2011 was a great success with some lovely artwork on display (see picture gallery on the accompanying DVD).

It was a good idea to invite a local artist from outside the university to join in the evening and judge the artwork. Her presence avoided any conflict of interest, as she was a stranger to the schools and staff present. Students need to write their details clearly on the *front* of the pictures (not the back) to assist the prize-giving.

The Foreign Languages Draw: Additional DVD materials

1.   Picture gallery of the artwork displayed on December 8th 2011
2.   List of useful websites

Project 5   Healthy lunches

Project outline

Requirements: laminated pictures of healthy and unhealthy foods; paper and pens or pencils for posters; paper plates; paper napkins or hand wipes; plastic cutlery; food for making lunch (brought in by students)
Event time: two 30–40 minute sessions
Languages targeted: French, German and Spanish

Introduction

This section looks at language learning in the context of healthy eating. Healthy eating is just one of the aspects of the Healthy Schools approach, a government initiative established in 1999 and supported by the Department of Health and the then Department for Children, Schools and Families. It is now backed by the Departments for Health and Education in a bid to help schools support children's health and well-being (see list of useful websites on the DVD of accompanying materials). If schools can demonstrate that they have fulfilled the criteria relating to all aspects of the Healthy Schools approach then they can apply for the national Healthy Schools status award. Your Local Authority will be able to provide advice and guidance in this area. The '*Healthy lunches*' project explored here fits in very well with this scheme and can be applied to the whole school. It also complements physical activity, another area covered by the Healthy Schools approach, so you may find it useful to link this project to others in the book such as '*Playing Games*' in Part I. In addition (and discussed in more detail below) the project could serve as an excellent basis for working with partner schools in other countries (see also the section on '*eTwinning*' in this Part).

Combining language learning with another curriculum area or whole-school activity certainly helps it to gain a footing with students, rather than being seen as a novelty or one-off exercise here and there. It provides a structure for introducing, practising and using new vocabulary and adds a further dimension to the work you are already doing. In some cases it may even spark new ideas and help to develop and enhance your existing projects in ways you had not previously thought of!

The main aim of this activity is to encourage students to think about and understand healthy food options, and then to use this knowledge to prepare a nutritious and balanced lunchtime meal in class. It is based on a project originally developed by staff at St John's Church of England Primary School in Grove Green, Kent. Ideas for carrying out these objectives are presented below, along with associated vocabulary in French, German and Spanish.

Lesson One

What is healthy eating?

A good way to introduce this topic is to start a quick class discussion about healthy eating. Do students know what this is? What types of foods are considered healthy or unhealthy? How many portions of fruit and vegetables should you try to eat every day? Once you have established some collective ideas about healthy eating, you can bring in some target language vocabulary. A suggested list is below, but you may wish to add more depending on the results of your class discussion or words your students might already know:

English	French	German	Spanish
food	*la nourriture*	*das Essen*	*la comida*
fruit	*le fruit*	*das Obst*	*la fruta*
vegetables	*les légumes*	*das Gemüse*	*las verduras*
apple	*la pomme*	*der Apfel*	*la manzana*
orange	*l'orange*	*die Orange*	*la naranja*
banana	*la banane*	*die Banane*	*el plátano*
grapes	*les raisins*	*die Weinbeeren*	*las uvas*
kiwi fruit	*le kiwi*	*die Kiwi*	*el kiwi*
pear	*la poire*	*die Birne*	*la pera*
cherries	*les cerises*	*die Kirschen*	*las cerezas*
peach	*la pêche*	*der Pfirsich*	*el melocotón*
cabbage	*le chou*	*der Kohl*	*el repollo*
carrot	*la carotte*	*die Karotte*	*la zanahoria*

English	French	German	Spanish
swede	le chou-navet	die Kohlrübe	el nabo sueco
spinach	les épinards	der Spinat	la espinaca
broccoli	les brocolis	die Brokkoli	el brócoli
beans	les haricots	die Bohnen	el frijol
cauliflower	le chou-fleur	der Blumenkohl	la coliflor
courgette	la courgette	die Zucchini	el calabacín
mushroom	le champignon	der Pilz	el champiñón
onion	l'oignon	die Zwiebel	la cebolla
lettuce	la laitue	der Kopfsalat	la lechuga
cucumber	le concombre	die Gurke	el pepino
tomato	la tomate	die Tomate	el tomate
healthy	sain	gesund	sano
unhealthy	mauvais/e pour la santé	ungesund	malo para la salud
burger	le hamburger	der Hamburger	la hamburguesa
chips	les frites	die Pommes	las patatas fritas
cake	le gateau	der Kuchen	el pastel
biscuit	le biscuit	der Keks	la galleta
crisps	les chips	die Kartoffelchips	las patatas fritas de bolsa
chocolate	le chocolat	die Schokolade	el chocolate
sweets	les bonbons	die Süssigkeiten	los dulces

To help reinforce the vocabulary above and to inject some fun into the lesson you could print out and laminate some pictures of the foods listed above. Using them like flashcards you could hold the pictures up in turn and ask the class to call out what they are. To extend this game further you could also ask them to call out if the food is healthy or unhealthy.

Now that you have set the scene for healthy eating, you may wish to move on to discuss what happens if you eat healthily, and what happens if you choose unhealthy options. You can add some target language work to this by introducing (or repeating if you have already done so) the useful conjunction 'because'. Some sample sentences are: I eat fruit because it is good for me.

Je mange le fruit parce qu'il est bon pour la santé.

Ich esse Obst, weil es gut für mich ist.

Como fruta porque es buena para la salud.

I do not eat chips because they are unhealthy.

Je ne mange pas de frites parce qu'elles sont mauvaises pour la santé.

Ich esse Pommes nicht, weil sie ungesund sind.

No como patatas fritas porque no son buenas para la salud.

To end this session you could ask students to make posters (either on their own or working in pairs or tables) displaying healthy and unhealthy foods which are labelled in the target language.

Lesson Two

Healthy lifestyle survey and making healthy lunches

First part

This lesson is split into two parts. The first part (approximately ten minutes) is a healthy lifestyle survey, which you can ask students to fill in to help them voice what they think is a healthy lifestyle. If you are doing wider work on the Healthy School theme this will also help you to pinpoint where further steps might need to be taken to provide information about eating well and keeping fit. This survey can be completed in English or perhaps in the target language, or a combination of English and the target language, depending on the group's ability. The survey presented below is in English and French. Remind students that this is not a test, and that it will not be marked. Explain that you would just like to collect some information about their views of healthy lifestyles.

Healthy Lifestyle Survey/*Sondage de la vie saine*

We all know a healthy lifestyle is important. We would like you to help us by telling us what you think a healthy lifestyle is and whether (insert school name) could help you to be healthier.

This is not a test, and your teacher will not mark it. You don't even need to put your name on it!

Thank you for your help!

Questions

1.   Do you have school lunches? Please circle your answer: YES   NO

     Mangez-vous à la cantine? Entourez votre réponse: *OUI   NON*

     If yes, how many times per week do you have them?
     Please circle your answer:

     Si oui, vous les mangez combien de fois dans la semaine?

     1   2   3   4   5

     If no, why not? _____

     Si non, pourquoi? _____

2.   What things on the menu may make you want to have school meals more often?

     Quels plats vous encouragent à prendre les déjeuners de la cantine?

227

3. What sort of foods do you think make a healthy packed lunch?

   Un panier-repas sain se compose de quels types de nourriture?

4. Why do you think it is important to have a healthy lifestyle?

   Pourquoi est-il important de mener une vie saine?

5. What sort of exercise do you enjoy doing?

   Quel exercice préférez-vous?

6. Roughly how many hours do you exercise in a week?
   Please circle your answer:

   En gros, combien d'heures par semaines faites-vous de l'exercice?
   Entourez votre réponse:

   1   2   3   5   6   7   8   more/*plus*

7. Do you think you could do more exercise?
   Please circle your answer: YES   NO

   Pensez-vous que vous pourriez faire plus d'exercice?
   Entourez votre réponse: OUI   NON

8. Where you would like to do more exercise? Please tick your answer(s):

   ☐ At home   ☐ At school   ☐ At a sports club or leisure centre

   Où voudriez-vous faire plus d'exercice? Cochez votre/vos réponse/s:

   ☐ *Chez vous*   ☐ *A l'école*   ☐ *Dans un club sportif ou centre de loisirs*

9. What other sports or exercise would you like to try at school?

   Quels sont les autres sports ou exercices que vous voulez essayer à l'école?

10. How much exercise do you think is healthy per week?
    Please tick your answer:

    ☐ One hour   ☐ Two hours   ☐ Three hours   ☐ Four hours

    ☐ Five hours   Other amount (please add your answer):_____

    Il est bon de faire combien d'heures d'exercices par semaine?
    Cochez votre réponse:

    ☐ *Une heure*   ☐ *Deux heures*   ☐ *Trois heures*   ☐ *Quatre heures*

    ☐ *Cinq heures*   *Autre (ajoutez votre réponse):_____*

11. Apart from a diet and exercise, what other things do you think are important
    in having a healthy life?

    *A part un régime sain et de l'exercice, quelles sont les autres choses importantes pour
    mener une vie saine?*

    END/*FIN*

Collect the completed questionnaires and use them for further developing your school's work towards achieving Healthy School status.

Second part

The second part of the lesson is great fun! Here students will be asked to make their own version of a healthy lunch. Allow 20–30 minutes for this activity to ensure everyone has a chance to make something. It might be useful to plan this lesson for just before lunch time, so that things can be eaten straight away. Depending on your school rules for lunch breaks, students could be allowed to remain in the classroom to eat their lunch on this occasion. As this is likely to be a somewhat messy activity it may be useful to have some adult supervisors on hand to help. They can also watch over the use of knives or scissors if you intend to bring these in.

Organise the classroom so that everyone has space to make their lunch. Have two tables near the front where supplies are displayed. (You can ask each student to bring something in, for example, one could bring bread, another some butter and so on. Remember to include items that correspond to students' dietary requirements, so that nobody is left out). The different items could be labeled in the target language. You may wish to include some 'trick' unhealthy items so that students are encouraged to think about the choices they make for their lunch. These items could include crisps, chocolate spread, cakes and other typically unhealthy fare. Provide a few paper plates for students to collect their items on as well make their food. Each table should have a supply of plastic cutlery, and it may also be

a good idea to provide some paper napkins or hand-wipes. Before the group starts, ensure that everyone has washed their hands and that they are wearing something to protect their school clothes (an apron or old shirt, for example).

For some basic French vocabulary relating to food preparation, please see Part II, Project 3 *In the kitchen*, and for an extended list in French as well as German and Spanish versions, please see the additional materials on the DVD. You may wish to display some of these words on the white/blackboard or on cards throughout the room.

Once everyone has made their lunch, but before it is eaten, go around the class and ask students what they have made. They could also give it a 'healthy score' out of ten, and the rest of the class could say whether or not they agree with it. Students could give descriptions of their lunch and their 'healthy score' in the target language:

I have a salad with lettuce, tomato and cucumber. My healthy score is nine out of ten.

J'ai une salade de laitue, tomate et concombre. Mon score sain est neuf sur dix.

Ich habe einen Salat mit Kopfsalat, Tomaten und Gurken. Meine Gesundnote ist neun aus zehn.

Tomo una ensalada de lechuga, tomate y pepino. Mi puntuación de salud es nueve sobre diez.

Extension ideas

A fantastic way of extending this activity is to link up with primary schools in other countries. Students could present their ideas of healthy eating and what they have for lunch to others, and they could compare, taking note of similarities and differences. This could be done via video conferencing if you have the facilities, or via other means of sharing video files. You could also send and receive information to and from your partner school, which is a source of excitement for students in itself. If you are looking at developing target language competence, then it would be useful to try to pair up with a school from a country where that language is spoken. However, if you are looking at the broader theme of healthy lifestyles, then you can find partners from any country (or countries) of your choice. This project could form a strong basis for an eTwinning partnership (see Project 6 below), and you may find when looking online that others have had similar ideas.

A further extension activity could include taking students on a tour of the school kitchen (subject to health and safety permissions), where they can see healthy foods being prepared and talk to the school cook. If this is not possible then perhaps a short visit to a local market or supermarket could help students in learning about healthy foods. Such a visit could also include target language practice in numbers, counting and money. You may already have the necessary parental consent forms for taking students out of school but, if not, a sample form can be found in Appendix Two. If going out of school is not possible, a mock supermarket or market could be set up in the school hall.

Reflections

A healthy eating project is a great vehicle for introducing new language to students whilst fulfilling wider school objectives. It helps to cement learning in both areas and provides a fun in-class activity that encourages students to really think about healthy lifestyles. Students are keen to find out about healthy food choices, and making lunch in class is an exciting way of setting discussion points in a tangible context. There are two other projects in this book which revolve around cooking and which may give you additional ideas for recipes in the foreign language, etc. They are *In the kitchen* (Project 3 in Part II) and *Vive la cuisine* (Project 9 in Part III).

Project 6   eTwinning

Project outline

Requirements: computer and internet access in the first instance; further requirements depend on your chosen project
Event time: any – depends on your project (see below) although allow 20–30 minutes to set up an online profile.
Language targeted: any

Introduction

One way of situating foreign language learning in your school is to link it with international work that may already be in progress. It is now very common for primary schools to have some degree of international work within their curriculum, so it is worth investigating if this is the case in your school. If not, it can be introduced in a variety of different ways and can be accredited officially through the International School Award (see below and the list of useful websites on the accompanying DVD) at foundation, intermediate or full International School Award level. Developing international links offers wide-ranging benefits for students, such as helping them become responsible global citizens, fostering creativity within the curriculum, giving them opportunities to gain first-hand knowledge about other countries and cultures, and giving them a better sense of the multicultural nature of our country and the world around us. International work can also provide teachers with great opportunities for professional development, as many courses in this area are offered by the British Council or CILT, the National Centre for Languages and now part of CfBT Education Trust (see useful web addresses in the accompanying DVD materials).

Travel is another potential bonus, as funding for trips abroad is often available through the British Council (see useful web addresses in the accompanying DVD materials). Certain initiatives, such as Comenius and Connecting Classrooms (discussed below), insist on partner schools visiting each other and provide funds to ensure this takes place. International work also allows you to develop a real global perspective in your teaching, which in turn is passed on to your students as you help them make connections between their learning and the global community in which we live today.

Whether you are familiar with this aspect or are about to take your first steps towards adding an international dimension to your work, the following section about eTwinning should provide some valuable information. ETwinning is explored in detail, followed by a sample case study. We offer some useful pointers and also look at other ways of developing international links. Finally we look at the International School Award in more detail. A photo gallery to accompany the case study as well as a list of useful websites can be found on the accompanying DVD.

What is eTwinning?

Part of the European Union's Comenius programme for schools, eTwinning is an initiative whereby educational practitioners and teachers from schools across Europe (32 countries in total) can come together to work collaboratively on a range of different projects. It is designed to promote creative and inspirational practice and provides a platform from which schools can easily progress on to other activities, such as funded Comenius projects. The eTwinning portal (www.etwinning.net) provides schools with the tools to find, collaborate and celebrate learning with partners. It is free of charge and acts not only as a gateway to meeting teachers in other countries but also as a successful tool for professional development – a large number of online workshops are easily and freely accessible. This enables teachers to enhance existing skills and learn new ones to complement fast-paced developments in the technological environment. This can be done in school or at home without the need for room bookings, staying late after school, and so on.

How does eTwinning work?

Getting started with eTwinning could not be easier! You will need to set up an online profile on the eTwinning website. This is done by clicking on the registration button and filling in the requested information. You will be asked to create a user name and password and will need to remember these for future access to the site. Once you have set up your profile and logged in, you will have access to the eTwinning desktop. It is from here that you can update your profile as well as search for eTwinning partners. There are several ways in which you can search for a partner (or partners), but one of the easiest is to visit the eTwinning forum for the age group you are interested in and then search for a specific project, or just browse those that are already listed. Alternatively, if you have an idea for a project you can create your own request for partners by creating a message which is then listed in the forum. The website offers a secure way of managing your projects, and once you sign up for a specific one (following approval) you will be given access to your own 'Twinspace', where you can share work (including videos and documents) and communicate with other teachers and their students safely. If you are stuck for inspiration, or simply wish to see what's out there, browsing the forum is a great way to find new ideas. As there is no set path or route to take when working with eTwinning, all projects are unique and can be created and developed however you want. The new challenges and opportunities that this creates can lead to raised standards within your school.

(**Note:** Depending on the filters installed on your school's network, you may find that you are unable to access the eTwinning portal at school. If this is the case, you may wish to speak to your ICT technician to find out if there is a way round this, or you may need to access the website from home or a public library.)

What kind of projects could we do in school?

Put simply, the list is endless! As already mentioned, eTwinning projects are intended to foster creative working, and there are no set ways of carrying them out. This means that, providing your idea is feasible and that you have the necessary permissions under the regulations set out by your school, you can start working on a project of your choice. New requests for partners are listed on a daily basis, so it is not hard to find one you might be interested in. There is a huge range of projects on offer, from making friends in European countries to nature and eco-projects (see also Project 7 below), healthy living (see also Project 5 above) and pen pals, to name only a few. Some are projects involving students, while others look at different aspects of pedagogy, such as developing teaching materials. Projects can last for a few days, a few weeks or months, or even an academic year. Some may be thematic – for example, focusing on the Olympics or Christmas, Easter and other festivities – and others may take a wider approach involving many curriculum areas. Projects can also tie in with work you are already doing or have planned to do. You may choose to be the project leader at your school or you may wish to invite colleagues to become part of a project team. Your eTwinning project can also involve the wider school community, ensuring that parents, governors and others become part of the process. Once you have decided on an idea, found a partner school and discussed how you want to work together you can apply to set up a project. The UK eTwinning team will check the project details (such as making sure all schools listed actually exist!) and then approve them where appropriate. Once you have been given approval your 'Twinspace' will be allocated. Only schools registered to your project can view your 'Twinspace'.

How do students benefit from eTwinning?

The benefits of eTwinning are many and varied. In the first instance, getting involved in a project with students from another country or countries is very exciting for young learners. Receiving letters and/or parcels from partners, talking to them online or through video conferencing and sharing work with them are all fantastic ways of engaging even the most reluctant of students. Working on projects where thought must be given to how people in other countries view you and what you do encourages creativity and innovation, as well as helping to develop problem-solving skills. Gaining first-hand experience of other countries and cultures is extremely valuable in terms of promoting citizenship, tolerance and understanding. In particular, eTwinning encourages students and teachers alike to extend and maintain their ICT skills, as working on different projects requires use of the internet and other programmes. Lastly, and perhaps most importantly, eTwinning projects provide a 'real' audience for students' work. Gone are the days when fictitious pen pals from other countries where used as incentives in the classroom (remember the days of 'imagine you have a French friend called Pierre …'!); now students can quickly and easily link up with other students from all over Europe as they work together on projects they might not have encountered otherwise.

Case study: Let's give breath to earth (Southwater Infant Academy)

Staff and students at Southwater Infant Academy near Horsham, West Sussex, participated in an environmental eTwinning project in partnership with the 7th Nursery School of Glyfada in Athens, Greece, and the 48th kindergarten with integration groups in Zabrze, Poland. This project does not have a specific foreign-language focus (although learning new words in Greek and Polish was an additional benefit), but it is easy to see the wealth of possibilities where target language learning could be introduced.

The 'Let's Give Breath to Earth' project began with each school choosing an endangered animal from their country. The students sent a toy version of the animal to each of the partner schools. England chose a dormouse, Greece chose a sea turtle, and Poland chose a stork. Students then began to research why each animal was in danger.

In England, students began looking at the sea turtle and sea pollution. One of the tasks was to make healthy and unhealthy sea aquariums from old shoeboxes and pictures of happy and unhappy seas. Following this, students looked at air pollution for the stork. They decorated breathing masks and made kites on which they wrote messages about taking care of the air. The group also carried out an experiment to look at the effects of acid rain. One plant was watered with normal water and one with 'acid rain' to see what would happen.

For land pollution students looked at deforestation and the loss of rainforests. Each country compared what could be recycled, and everyone made recycling bins. Students drew posters and made an international video about taking care of the forests.

To finish the project, the students made an environmental board game for their partners to play, and everyone took part in writing and recording a song in all three languages. The groups also wrote a play starring the toy animals, which was videoed.

The project mentioned in this case study ran for one academic year and tied in with work already planned in this area. It is an example of the depth in which collaborative working can be explored and shows how students from three different countries can be brought together and be engaged in a shared objective.

Some useful pointers

Despite the relative simplicity of joining the eTwinning network, actually engaging in a project may seem somewhat daunting to those new to this type of work. Below are a few useful hints and tips to consider before planning a shared project:

- Try to fit international work into your existing curriculum to make it as manageable as possible;
- Take it slowly – start small and build up gradually;
- Persevere! It could take a long time and some measure of trial and error to find the right partners and/or project(s);
- Set manageable goals. A small project lasting for a term will be achievable and gives you a chance to see how your partnership works;
- Have fun! This is one area of teaching where you are not constrained by the curriculum, and there are no limits!

Other international linking sites

There are other initiatives you can get involved in if you decide eTwinning is not for you, or if you would like to extend and complement the work you do through eTwinning. A first port of call could be the British Council's Schools Online website (see list of useful websites on the accompanying DVD) where you can search for partners from all over the world. Here you can also find information about other initiatives, such as Global School Partnerships and Connecting Classrooms, as well as the International School Award. Connecting Classrooms is a British-Council-funded project that creates a two- or three-year partnership between a cluster of schools in the UK and a cluster of schools in another region of the world. In a similar fashion to eTwinning, www.elanguages.org offers a free facility to search for partners across the world.

The International School Award

If you are doing even the slightest degree of international work in your school it is well worth thinking about applying for the International School Award (ISA). This is an excellent way of recognising your school's international dimension, and in recent years the application process has been simplified to make applications more straightforward. Applying for the award encourages you to keep track of all the things you are doing within the international framework and can help you to develop an international policy, offer staff training and CPD (Continuing Professional Development) opportunities, establish partnerships with other schools, enhance the curriculum and involve the wider community. There are three different levels of award. The first is the Foundation level, which is easy to achieve, providing you have support from your senior leadership team. All that is required is a statement of intent (i.e. a statement outlining how international work will be implemented in school), which should be signed by the head teacher and the chair of governors. You can download the statement of intent from the British Council Schools Online website (see list of useful websites on the accompanying DVD). Essentially, the statement proves that you are seeking to start, increase and/or develop international work in your school. Once you have registered for the award online you can then use the online framework to record your existing and/or planned international activities (this is not necessary to achieve the Foundation level, but it will help for progressing to Intermediate level). The British Council ISA team will then send feedback to help you move on to the Intermediate level and will also assist in finding a partner school for you. You can apply at any time for the Foundation level. If your application is successful, you will receive a certificate of achievement and will also be able to use the ISA Foundation level logo on school paperwork and the school website.

The next level, Intermediate, is for schools delivering a significant amount of international work, including working with a partner school. Activities may include (but are not limited to) one or more classes working with students in a partner school (e.g. pen-pal schemes, video conferencing), trips abroad (including study visits for staff) and integrating global issues and awareness into the curriculum. To achieve the Intermediate award, three examples of international activities taking place in school must be documented; these should cover at least three curriculum areas. Schools also need to have either a draft or completed International Policy (templates available on the British Council website), the purpose of which is to ensure a whole-school approach to international work. As with the statement of intent at Foundation level, the policy must be signed by the head teacher and the chair of governors (as this helps to develop support for international activities).

Schools that have a robust international dimension evident in their curriculum and whole-school approach may apply for the Full accreditation. This international ethos must be embedded in school practice and included in such documents as the school development plan. Schools must be able to demonstrate their work with partner schools and have a significant level of curriculum-based international activity. According to the British Council's website, schools applying for this level of accreditation will likely have a history of international activity over two years preceding the application.

Applying for the award is done in two stages. First, schools submit an action plan containing at least seven proposed international activities that will take place over the academic year. These must link with a majority of curriculum subjects and a majority of pupils. Evidence of collaboration with partner schools in other countries must also be shown. Next, schools submit a self-evaluation of their international work, due in at the end of the academic year. The British Council offers help and support for schools applying for Full accreditation, including guidance for the self-evaluation process. A number of other criteria should also be fulfilled, such as engaging an international co-ordinator whose role is to help implement the school's international strategy. Full details about application criteria can be found on the British Council's Schools Online website. Those successful in their application for Full accreditation will receive an official International School Award certificate and will be able to use the Full ISA logo. They will also be recognised nationally as ambassadors for international work. The Full ISA is valid for three years.

Reflections

Conducting an eTwinning project offers opportunities for staff and students alike to engage in a wide variety of activities. At a basic level it encourages the use and development of ICT skills and the involvement of perhaps just one teacher, one class (or even small group of students) and one partner school. Beyond that the possibilities are endless! Whole-school projects can be established, and partners can be found all over Europe. With scope for wonderfully creative and imaginative projects which can link to curriculum objectives or stand alone as independent initiatives, eTwinning is easy to introduce to your school and will certainly result in new and exciting ways of working.

eTwinning: Additional DVD materials

1. Case study picture gallery
2. Useful websites

Project 7   The Spanish nature trail

Project outline

Requirements: paper and pencils or crayons for bark/leaf rubbing; art materials for making posters; A3 paper; Spanish–English dictionary (if necessary)
Event time: any – depending on the number of extension activities chosen; 20 minutes to conduct nature trail, 10–15 minutes to pre-plan nature trail.
Languages: Spanish (but can be adapted for any language)

Introduction

Taking language learning outside the classroom is a good way of showing young students how foreign languages can be used in lots of different situations. It is also an interesting way of introducing some new topics as well as new language. In this section we combine science and nature with Spanish and look at conducting an outdoor nature trail (this can be easily adapted for other languages). Most primary schools have an outside space which can be explored and, where this is not possible, suitable outdoor areas can usually be found within easy reach. Depending on your school's regulations, you may need parental permission to take students out of the classroom, especially if you intend to leave the school premises, so we have included a template for a letter home in Appendix Two at the end of this book. You may also wish to link this section to the *Life Cycles* project in Part I (Project 9).

This project can be as straightforward or detailed as you wish or have time for. You can simply map out a brief route around your school (or the area you have chosen to carry out the trail), or you can plan associated activities which students can complete as they go along. Presented below is a variety of ideas for you to choose from and which we hope will inspire you and your students!

The nature trail

Leading a nature trail is quite straightforward. Organize your class into pairs and instruct them to follow you on the route you have planned around the school grounds or other outside space. Before you go outside, however, it might be useful to go over some key vocabulary so that you can practise it as you go along. The words below are suggested to get you started, but you may wish to add others, depending on the environment you are in:

la hierba – grass	*la tierra* – soil	*el árbol* – tree
el suelo – ground	*la flor* – flower	*el sendero* – path
la planta – plant	*caminar* – to walk	*el insecto* – insect
mirar – to look at	*el pájaro* – bird	*oir* – to hear

Depending on the age and ability of your group, a short picture-matching exercise may also be useful when introducing new vocabulary. This will help students understand what to look for when they are on the trail. A sample game is given below, but you can add more pictures to make it harder if necessary. One thing you could point out to students is how similar some of the words are to their English equivalents.

Picture-matching game

These pictures and words are all jumbled up! Can you match the word to the picture?

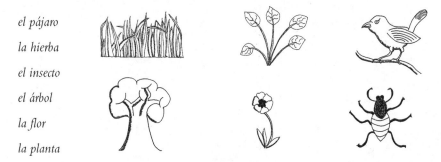

el pájaro

la hierba

el insecto

el árbol

la flor

la planta

Once you feel that students are comfortable with the new vocabulary, you can begin the trail. Remind students that they are looking out for various things and should keep their eyes open so they can find as much as possible. It may also be worthwhile preparing a few other words or perhaps taking a dictionary out with you in case students ask what the Spanish is for things you have not practised.

As you follow your route there are several different ways to include the vocabulary above. One could be to call out the names of various things as you pass them. You could ask the class to repeat the words back to you. To extend this further you could add more vocabulary, such as colours, numbers or locations (for example, *Hay 10 flores rojas en el campo*/there are 10 red flowers in the field, and so on). Another way of practising the vocabulary could be to call out the various words in Spanish and ask students to either run or point to what they think the word means.

You can extend and develop your nature trail by adding on one of the following activities if appropriate:

Bark/leaf rubbing – Calquen la corteza/las hojas

This is a fun and simple activity that does not take too much time. Give each student a piece of paper and a soft pencil or crayon. Place the paper over the bark or leaf and then rub the pencil or crayon gently over the top, so that the image of whatever is beneath the paper comes through. You can display bark rubbings by making a big tree display in the classroom and using the rubbings to make up the trunk. Alternatively, if you have made leaf rubbings, leaves can be cut out to stick on the tree. Once you have made the tree you can use its branches to 'hang' cards with the new Spanish vocabulary written on them (one word per card). This makes an attractive and eye-catching display and will help students to remember the new words. A beautiful animation made out of leaves and other natural objects can be found at this weblink: www.youtube.com/watch?v=e CnrQuwilxs. The short film, *Hedgerow Tales*, is explained in more detail in Part II Project 4: *Animation*; it is well-worth looking at.

Word search

Word searches are good ways of reinforcing target language vocabulary and also provide a calm and quiet activity to end a lesson. They are easy to create (see Part II, Project 5: *Making word games*) and take only a few minutes to complete. The search below uses the vocabulary presented previously, but you can create your own with different words if necessary:

```
P  C  F  P  F  A  B  R  E  I  H  Q
F  Y  C  C  J  O  S  Y  O  I  R  U
Á  Z  V  B  S  E  N  D  E  R  O  Q
R  Z  O  T  C  E  S  N  I  I  L  E
B  O  G  T  Y  F  P  B  U  O  F  T
O  R  Z  O  M  O  M  G  Q  N  Y  I
L  A  B  J  M  Q  N  R  O  E  A  E
Z  J  U  P  Q  M  H  Q  D  R  T  R
F  Á  Q  C  G  Q  X  P  P  R  N  R
B  P  I  Z  P  L  F  H  A  E  A  A
Q  Z  Q  M  I  R  A  R  P  T  L  L
U  R  A  N  I  M  A  C  H  E  P  D
```

árbol	*oir*	*caminar*	*pájaro*
flor	*planta*	*hierba*	*sendero*
insecto	*terreno*	*mirar*	*tierra*

Word search answers:

```
P  C  F  P  F  A  B  R  E  I  H  Q
F  Y  C  C  J  O  S  Y  O  I  R  U
Á  Z  V  B  S  E  N  D  E  R  O  Q
R  Z  O  T  C  E  S  N  I  I  L  E
B  O  G  T  Y  F  P  B  U  O  F  T
O  R  Z  O  M  O  M  G  Q  N  Y  I
L  A  B  J  M  Q  N  R  O  E  A  E
Z  J  U  P  Q  M  H  Q  D  R  T  R
F  Á  Q  C  G  Q  X  P  P  R  N  R
B  P  I  Z  P  L  F  H  A  E  A  A
Q  Z  Q  M  I  R  A  R  P  T  L  L
U  R  A  N  I  M  A  C  H  E  P  D
```

Linking to other curriculum areas

From here you can enhance the nature trail activity by linking in with numerous other curriculum areas. For example, you could link to science by looking at habitats. Ask your students if they know what a habitat is (*¿Qué es un hábitat?*) and then to think of all the different habitats that exist within the area you have been looking at. Encourage students to also think about the different insects and animals that may live in these habitats. You could perhaps write up a list of these on the board for everyone to see. You can also include different types of plants and vegetation. Once you have a list of 10–15 words, students could be asked to draw a picture of the habitat (linking to Art), including all the various insects, animals, plants and so on, leaving space for these to be labelled in Spanish. A lovely project in Part VI is all about using animals to inspire your writing (Project 6 *Using animals as an inspiration for writing*) and may give you further ideas. Further vocabulary for this exercise could include:

la araña – spider	*la cochinilla* – woodlouse
la rana – frog	*el ratón* – mouse
la ardilla – squirrel	*el caracol* – snail
la hoja – leaf	*la corteza* – (tree) bark
el barro – mud	*la piedra* – stone
el estanque – pond	*la mariposa* – butterfly
el hábitat – habitat	*el animal* - animal

To extend this activity, ask the class to think of a very different habitat to the one they have been exploring: for example, a desert or an arctic habitat. What living things might they find in these different areas? Can they be found anywhere else? Could something living in an arctic habitat live in the desert? Some useful vocabulary for this exercise includes:

el Ártico – the Arctic	*el oso polar* – polar bear
la nieve – snow	*el hielo* – ice
el caribou – caribou	*la morsa* – walrus
la tundra – tundra	*el iceberg* – iceberg
frío – cold	*mojado* – wet
el desierto – desert	*el avestruz* – ostrich
el suricato – meerkat	*la hiena* – hyena
la serpiente – snake	*el antílope* – antelope
la gacela – gazelle	*la arena* – sand
caluroso – hot	*seco* – dry

You can further develop the topic of habitats by starting a class discussion about what makes a good habitat and what makes a bad habitat. This can lead to citizenship-related areas, such as learning about behaving responsibly (for example, throwing rubbish in the bin and not on the floor; recycling; reducing carbon footprints and so on) and taking care of the planet.

Reflections

Taking students out of the classroom does not mean you have to go far! The nature trail project is a simple and easy way of setting language learning in a different context. It is beneficial, in that it easily links to other areas of the curriculum. When students are already aware of a topic this can sometimes make learning about it in a new language easier, as they feel more confident and secure in their knowledge. Building upon this confidence can mean that students begin to feel equally confident in the target language. This project is also very easy to adapt for learners of different ages and ability, and could even extend to a year-long project as you follow and observe the changes in your chosen habitat. An earlier project in this chapter (Project 3 *Making use of outdoor spaces*) also has some lovely ideas about growing seeds and making a vegetable garden – and much more!

8

Continuing Professional Development

Introduction

Inspirational Continuing Professional Development (CPD) is the key to continuous successful teaching and learning in the classroom, which is what this Part is all about. It is especially crucial in the early phase of new teaching initiatives, when most teachers need and appreciate support and direction. It continues to be essential, no matter how established the curriculum may be, in updating teachers with strategies and resources and in sharing best practice. A great training session can energise, motivate and equip teachers with the skills, strategies and materials to produce outstanding learning experiences for students. CPD should impact positively on pupils' achievement and the leadership, management and teaching which support this progress. Great CPD can help turn the mediocre into the magnificent.

Teachers of languages in primary schools come from a wide range of experience, which includes the non-specialist primary class teacher, the peripatetic specialist teacher, enthusiastic Higher Level Teaching Assistants, temporary Foreign Language Assistants (see Part IV) and supportive parents. We all have both specific and shared needs for CPD. These usually include an appetite for new practical ideas for the classroom, resources which will support our planning and the chance to network with colleagues with whom we can share successes and failures which boost our own self-esteem and knowledge. Great CPD should inspire and renew our energy, confidence and desire to improve the language-learning opportunities we provide for our students.

This Part considers the role of Continuing Professional Development (CPD) in the primary language teacher's professional practice and explores a variety of different opportunities open to you. We consider key questions to be asked regarding the role of CPD and offer ideas and resources to help you get involved in providing both small and large-scale CPD opportunities for yourself and your colleagues. All ideas are based on real experiences at and with primary schools and colleagues in and around the Brighton area. We outline how you can use or extend normal 'cascade' or training opportunities in primary schools to maximise CPD for language learning. A range of support materials are included on the accompanying DVD to support your Continuing Professional Development. These include: materials to help you plan a staff meeting based around languages; a draft plan for a Primary Languages Conference held at a primary school, with some suggestions for carousel activities; a register for a workshop; practical strategies for active language learning for non-specialist primary teachers.

Why should I get involved?

Excellent CPD will help you and your colleagues to achieve outstanding teaching and learning in the classroom. There are different reasons for CPD and you only need one to get you started. Do you want to convince colleagues that they can and should be involved in teaching languages? Do you want to support particular year group colleagues to deliver a new scheme of work? Do you have responsibility for co-ordinating languages and need to implement action points on your School Development Plan? Do you need to update and maintain support for languages in your school? Are you looking for eTwinning possibilities for your school (see also Project 6 in Part VII)? You might simply be the keenest teacher in school and want to raise the profile and context for language learning across your curriculum and wider school community.

Setting up and/or delivering CPD will also help you meet some of the current aspects of the professional Core and Post-threshold National Standards for teachers which form part of your Performance Management review annually. You will demonstrate your willingness and ability to support wider school effectiveness, develop experience in communicating and working with others, facilitate team working and collaboration and thus support your personal professional development (Training and Development Agency for Schools, 2011b).

When?

Primary timetables are jam-packed and primary teachers have little spare time; a focused CPD session can offer a welcome breathing space in busy schedules and allow colleagues to give their full attention to specific curriculum concerns or aspects of teaching and learning. A shared learning experience, delivered well, can engender a real enthusiasm and motivation in colleagues as well as showcase and share best practice. All schools encourage colleagues to share their CPD, but staff and year group or planning meetings are likely to offer only limited feedback time for this, due to necessarily tight time constraints and preplanned agendas. Timing is important, but you will probably have to work within the established parameters of your school's or institution's CPD timetable. Speak to your CPD Co-ordinator or headteacher as soon as possible to identify your opportunities: is it 45 minutes as the main item on the staff meeting agenda, or an after-school workshop in place of a planning meeting, or a full-day's conference on an In-Service Training (INSET) day? Does your school share INSET with other schools? You may be able to broaden the impact of your CPD by offering it to colleagues outside your school or institution.

Know what you need and do not be afraid to ask for what you want. Remember that you will need adequate planning and preparation time too. Try to plan a half-term ahead for an hour's workshop and at least a term ahead for a conference.

How?

A great way to begin is with an inspirational CPD session which you have already attended. If you came away feeling inspired, then it is likely your colleagues will do so too, if you can give them an equivalent experience. This will be more effective than simply telling them about good ideas second-hand. An easy way to start is to invite the speaker who inspired you to repeat the session for your colleagues. If your school or institution can afford the costs involved – likely to be at least travel expenses, but sometimes a speaker fee too – this will reduce your time and effort in preparation.

Who?

If you invite a visiting speaker, prepare a list of questions to help gather the information you will need. As the host and representative of your school and institution, you will need to be responsible for everything before, during and after their session. You will need to gather information then check and double-check arrangements. The following grid provides some sample key questions, the answers to which will help you plan:

Name of Speaker/s:	Role/job title: *eg, Primary Languages Co-ordinator at Somewhere School* **Biography supplied:** *eg, you might publish this in advance for attendees, or use it to help introduce your speaker in the session*	Contact details: *eg, email, mobile phone number, address*	Travel *eg, taking train, driving* **Estimated Travel Costs:** *eg, Train fare £ ....* *Taxi fare £ ....* *Car Mileage £ ....*
Workshop Title:	Workshop Length:	Workshop description:	Speaker Fee: *eg, £150 School or speaker to supply invoice? Check with Bursar/Finance Officer for advice*
Dietary Requirements: *eg, need to order 1 x vegetarian lunch for speaker*	Venue: *eg, Hall, my classroom*	Venue layout: *eg, table groups, semi-circle of chairs facing Interactive whiteboard, space for active games*	Fire/Health & Safety: *eg, Fire exit doors from venue, turn left to safe area in playground,* **Maximum number of attendees:**
Equipment needed: *Eg, Interactive whiteboard with sound, cables to link to Speaker's laptop, paper and coloured pens for activities, etc*	IT requirements: *eg, laptop, speakers, cables* *Play audio tracks from CD* *Play video clips embedded in PowerPoint*	Photocopying required: *eg, any handouts or workshop materials to be sent for photocopying in advance?*	Evaluation form: *eg, does speaker have own or do you need to provide for your staff anyway?*

Your speaker will probably need directions to your venue and will hope to find a convenient parking space. Your site manager may be able help reserve a parking space and to be on hand to help the speaker find it on arrival. Your speaker will appreciate being met by someone who can help with carrying workshop materials or equipment to the training space, as well as provide directions to toilets or refreshments.

Ideally, you will have prepared your venue in advance, with all equipment and furniture in place; however, if this is not possible, then plan to have enough time available to help set up ready for a prompt start at your published time. It is wise to have an IT technician or other helpful colleague waiting ready to support you and the speaker should last-minute technical problems occur.

Me?

Consider running a session yourself. Think positively about the advantages you already have. For example, you know your colleagues well, so you are in a great position to customise the CPD accordingly. You are familiar with your school building and will have some control over practical details if you use it as a venue. You may have administrative or support staff whom you can call on for support in organising and running the event.

If you are planning to copy somebody else's workshop session, then it may be courteous and politic to consult with the original presenter for permission. Most educational speakers present CPD in the hope of sharing best practice as widely as possible, so are usually pleased and flattered to know you wish to emulate them. They may be prepared to lend you their workshop materials and to give advice. However, bear in mind that some speakers generate income through presenting workshops and selling their resources. This is true for some Local Authority advisers as well as private speakers. Copyright materials should not be used without permission so it is wise to check to avoid problems.

How do I start?

Successful CPD requires careful planning as well as effective delivery. Modelling your intended CPD on a session you have previously attended will provide you with a really helpful structure.

Reflect on the CPD you attended. What was its aim, and how was that achieved? How long was the session? How was the room laid out? How did the presenter/s deliver? What activities did attendees do? What resources were used? What information or handouts were given? How was it evaluated?

Consider what worked best, then how you might adapt or improve this to suit your intended audience. The Training and Development Agency for Schools (2011a) has pointed out that CPD is only effective where it is directly relevant, practical and applicable to each participant. Tailoring CPD to meet the specific requirements of your colleagues is therefore essential to ensure that it is both valuable and successful. Be ambitious, not timid, about plans.

What do I need to do?

List some key questions to help you think through the process of setting up the CPD. Make notes about answers and add details as they occur to you. You will find it easier to enlist the support or permission of others – such as your headteacher, Key Stage co-ordinator, administrative staff or school site manager – if you have already done some clear thinking. Remember to sound confident but open to suggestion; they may have some great ideas to add to yours.

Questions to ask yourself

Key questions	Sample answers (e.g.)	Further Notes
Why is this CPD needed?	■ *To get language-teaching started in my school* ■ *To support Year 5 to implement a new Scheme of Work* ■ *To upskill colleagues in knowledge about the language* ■ *To upskill colleagues in strategies for language teaching and assessment*	■ *Does this link to my School's Development Plan?* ■ *Does this support any criteria from our previous OFSTED action points?* ■ *Does this link with our school support network or Local Authority's training plans for this year?*
Who is it for?	■ *My colleagues at school* ■ *Colleagues in Y5 & Y6* ■ *Teaching assistants* ■ *Supportive parents and governors*	*Can we share this CPD with others? e.g.,* ■ *Colleague/s from partner schools or other primary schools?* ■ *Teacher trainees from our local University?*
How will it be structured?	■ *A one-off workshop as part of an INSET day* ■ *A whole INSET day* ■ *A conference* ■ *A twilight workshop* ■ *A series of twilight workshops held over the term or year* ■ *A Staff meeting*	*Avoid being squeezed into a Staff Meeting 'slot' to follow or precede other business*
When will it happen?	■ *Next term* ■ *Later this year*	■ *Consult school calendar/diary to find potentially suitable dates and double check with others to avoid any clashes.* ■ *Try to use directed time rather than impose extra meetings on colleagues.*
Where?	■ *In my classroom* ■ *In my school – hall, staffroom, playground, variety of classrooms* ■ *At borrowed rooms in local secondary school, Sixth Form college or university/teacher training institution* ■ *At local teacher training centre*	■ *Consider factors such as access to toilets, parking and refreshment facilities.* ■ *Check regulations for fire or other Health & Safety requirements*
How much will it cost?	■ *Provide some refreshments & biscuits* ■ *Cost of building & equipment hire* ■ *Fee for visiting speaker* ■ *PR/administrative costs (printing/photocopying/phone calls)* ■ *Resources for workshop activities*	■ *Does my school or institution have a CPD fund?* ■ *Is there funding available from a languages organisation or other sponsor?*
Who will lead the CPD?	■ *Me?* ■ *Me and a colleague?* ■ *Original presenter/s*	■ *Can we afford to ask the original presenter?* ■ *Is there a Local Authority Adviser or languages organisation to help me?*

Key questions	Sample answers (e.g.)	Further Notes
How will I know if the CPD is successful?	■ *Evaluation form?* ■ *Colleagues' feedback at end of session?*	
What is the intended impact of this CPD?	■ *Teachers begin teaching language in class in regular curriculum slots* ■ *New Scheme of Work implemented* ■ *Teachers use strategies in class* ■ *Improved enthusiasm and support for language teaching in school*	■ *Ensure that CPD will facilitate this*
How will I measure the impact?	■ *Class timetables show regular weekly slots for languages* ■ *Monitoring via Classroom Climate visits or observations* ■ *Improved student progress* ■ *Regular slot in school newsletter to parents* ■ *Celebratory themed event planned for whole school community*	■ *Is there already a whole-school/ institution policy or guidelines to help me decide?*

Basic checklist

Whatever the CPD experience you choose to provide, there are some basic factors to consider to get your CPD off to a good start. Here is a brief checklist:

- CPD provision is well matched to the CPD aims and needs of attendees;
- timing and length of CPD is appropriate – not overlong and allowing for refreshment/comfort breaks if needed;
- venue is appropriate, clean and comfortable, well sign-posted for attendees, and not far from toilets for male and female adults. Toilets are signposted to help attendees unfamiliar with your venue. Extra parking is provided and signposted if needed;
- refreshments are provided, including water jug and glass for speaker/s and at least some hot and cold drinks with snacks or biscuits for attendees;
- all equipment is in good working order;
- CPD provides attendees with take-away handout/resources or emailed presentation to help them remember and use the training, as well as save them from having to write notes during the session;
- feedback/evaluation time is included within the session, not afterwards, as some people will need to leave promptly;
- allow time for some questions, or be available for questions after the end of the session or by email. Attendees need a chance to reflect and ask questions which relate to their individual needs;
- CPD starts and ends punctually.

Secrets of success

Easy access to refreshments and treats – be it a hot cup of tea or coffee, chocolates or biscuits – can really help relax and invigorate tired colleagues, particularly if your CPD has to take place at the end of the school day. If your staffroom frequently runs out of cups or milk then plan ahead, borrow or invest in the extra litre of milk, paper cups or plastic spoons to ensure that there is enough for everybody. Your audience will be more amenable once they have been revived with good-quality drink and food.

Play some calming, cheerful and relevant background music. This can help to establish a different atmosphere in your normal school or institution venue and is far more welcoming than silence. Turning the music up slightly, then down again, can help quieten down the audience ready for the start of the session, or punctuate activities, without having to raise your voice. Playing music again at the end as people exit will help maintain a convivial atmosphere.

Smile and welcome your attendees. Thank them for coming, even if it is during a directed-time CPD session which they must attend. If some of your attendees are unfamiliar, perhaps from other schools or institutions, then take the time to exchange a brief word with them as they enter and try to introduce them to other attendees, so they can begin to chat and network. Most people like to feel acknowledged rather than anonymous. If you are presenting, try to set up the session so that you allow yourself the time and space to do this, rather than find yourself rushing to get things ready as the audience enters.

If you are presenting the CPD yourself, then thank attendees again at the end. If you have another presenter, then work out in advance how to present and finish the session. Will you introduce the speaker? Will you thank them at the end, or is there a colleague you should or could ask to do this on behalf of your school or institution? All introductions and 'thank yous' should be courteous, appreciative and brief. Avoid taking up unnecessary time, as you want to avoid rushing the main business of the CPD and keeping people longer than the stated session times.

Prepare a register of attendees and have it ready to sign when people arrive. Your register could include names, roles, contact details and even space for attendees to write car registration numbers where these might be needed (see sample template on the accompanying DVD for this project). If you need to evacuate the building at any time, due to fire or safety hazards, you will know exactly how many to count, but, more optimistically, the register identifies exactly who takes part in your training and will help you to send out notes, handouts, requests for follow-up feedback or evidence etc. to the correct email addresses of both participants and absentees.

Make the training as interactive and enjoyable as possible. As teachers, we try to plan and deliver lessons which involve students in active learning experiences. We seek to reach all learners through the use of visual, auditory and kinaesthetic learning styles. We want to motivate, enthuse, challenge, support, reinforce and extend our students' knowledge and skills through well-planned, pacy lessons which match tasks to students' learning needs to maximise their depth of understanding and rate of progress. Successful CPD can help us to do this by modelling the process for us. By involving ourselves as active learners, in the same way as we hope to involve our students, we acquire improved awareness and knowledge through practical, first-hand experience.

How to structure the training session

There are different and equally valid styles of delivering CPD sessions. One commonly used involves a keynote speaker talking to the audience, supported by visual presentation materials such as a computer slide show or video clips, with short bursts of partner or group activities and feedback. While this works effectively on a receptive adult audience with good listening skills, it is less valid as a model of good classroom teaching of languages for young children. We recommend you plan your CPD sessions so that attendees are more active than passive.

When possible, for example, model good practice by being the 'teacher' and treat the audience as your 'students'. Allow the audience to practise the strategy, be it singing the song, doing the action-mimes, role-playing in silly voices, sequencing text and picture cards, writing on a partner's back, completing an 'I can ...' assessment sheet. Not only is your audience likely to have fun, but they will see, hear, feel, know and understand how these activities will impact on students' learning.

If attendees feel they enjoy and benefit from the activities, they are likely to be confident that their students will react the same way. Physically taking part in activities can help us remember them. Enjoying them can motivate us to repeat the experience and provide it for others. Practising with like-minded colleagues gives us a chance to build our confidence and abilities through rehearsal, which, in turn, helps us to use and apply in our classrooms the strategies we have learned.

Dealing with difficulties

It is better to recognise and acknowledge potential problems than to ignore them and hope they will go away. It is always worth thinking about the 'what ifs' and having a Plan B in mind should the worst occur. Ask yourself what could go wrong, then try to plan so that you avoid disasters. Potential problems are myriad, but here are some examples and suggested solutions:

Problem	Solution
Visiting speaker lets you down at the last minute	■ You already have their presentation, notes and hand-outs so can deliver yourself ■ You turn the session into a chance for colleagues to share current experiences, to identify needs & ask questions and to plan and prepare lessons or schemes of work together ■ You rearrange the session for an alternative date
The IT equipment fails	■ You have an IT technician or other colleague standing by to help ■ You have back-up equipment ready or have identified a different room into which you can move if this occurs ■ The session is planned so that it does not rely solely on the IT equipment
Attendees heckle or interrupt with questions at inconvenient times	■ Tell them when you are taking questions: for example, at the end of the session or in the feedback section ■ Have some paper or sticky notes ready to give them. Ask them to write their question or comments down.

Final thoughts

Help colleagues by showing them what to do and how to do it. Make sure they have fun doing it, encourage their attempts and praise their achievements. Well-planned and delivered professional development training will equip and empower you and your colleagues to deliver the best language-learning experiences for students. Let CPD inspire you.

Continuing Professional Development: Additional DVD materials

1. Sample register
2. Planning sheet for a staff meeting
3. Staff meeting: running order
4. Sample quiz
5. Draft plan for a primary languages conference held at a primary school
6. International Inspiration: carousel activities sample
7. Practical strategies for active language learning for non-specialist primary teachers.
8. Where to find CPD support

Parental consent form for use of images of children and young people

I/we,.. the parent(s)/guardian(s) of:

(child's full name)..

(child's full name)..

(child's full name)..

hereby give (your name) permission to use any still and/or moving images such as video footage, photographs and/or frames and/or audio footage depicting my/our children named above for any of the following uses: advertisements; marketing; leaflets; website or any other use such as for training, educational or publicity purposes. The consents will be for an indefinite period.

Signed(Parent/guardian) .... Date ....

Signed(Parent/guardian) .... Date ....

Address..

....

.... Postcode ....

Your details will not be released to third parties, or used for any purpose not related to the activity to which this consent pertains. Data held by (name) is subject to the provisions of the Data Protection Act 1998.

2

Parental consent form

Sample Parental Consent Form

Your school office may be able to provide you with the necessary parental consent forms and risk assessments for taking students out of class. If not, you may wish to use the form below.

(School address here)

Dear Parent/guardian,

Short blurb here about your activity. Include:

> *Why you are taking students out of the classroom;*
> *Where you are going;*
> *How long you will be out of school;*
> *Who is accompanying the students;*
> *What the students might need to bring with them.*

Please complete the slip below and return it to (*insert teacher's name*) by (*add date*).

Name .... Date ....
Please delete where applicable

I/we,... the parent(s)/guardian(s) of:

(*child's full name*) ....
give our consent/do not give our consent for our child or children to take part in

(*insert event*) ....

Signed ....

Signed(Parent/guardian) ....

Date ....

References

Attard, E., and Holland, R. (2005): *Ali Baba and the forty thieves*, London: Mantra Lingua.

Ahlberg, J & A. (1996) *Les Bizardos*, Paris: Gallimard Jeunesse.

Barkow, H. (2004): *Billy goats Gruff*, London: Mantra Lingua.

—— (2005) *Little Red Hen and the grains of wheat*, London: Mantra Lingua.

Brown, R. (1981): *A dark, dark tale*, GB: Anderson Press

Brown, R. (1981) *Une histoire sombre, très sombre*, Paris: Gallimard Jeunesse.

Browne, A. (2000): *My dad*, London: Random House.

—— (2002): *Mon papa*, Paris: Kaléidoscope.

—— (2005a): *My mum*, London: Random House.

—— (2005b): *Ma maman*, Paris: Kaléidoscope. Browne, E. (1994): *Handa's surprise*, London: Walker Books.

Campbell, R. (1982): *Dear zoo*, London: Abelard-Schuman.

—— (2004): *Cher zoo*, London: Mantra Lingua.

Carle, E. (1969): *The very hungry caterpillar*, London: Hamish Hamilton

Clynes, K., and Daykin, L. (2002): *Not again, Red Riding Hood!*, London: Mantra Lingua.

—— (2003): *Goldilocks and the three bears*, London: Mantra Lingua.

Coyle, D., Holmes, B., and King, L. (2009): *Towards an integrated curriculum: CLIL National statement and guidelines*, London: Languages Company. (http://www.languagescompany.com/images/stories/docs/news/clil_national_statement_and_guidelines.pdf).

Coyle, D., Hood, P., and Marsh, D. (2010): *CLIL – Content and Language Integrated Learning*. Cambridge: Cambridge University Press.

Devon County Council (2006): *Take 10 en français*, 2nd ed. Exeter: Devon Education Services.

Emberley, E. (2012) *Va-t'en, grand monstre vert*, Devon: Little Linguist.

Hedderwick, M. (1985): *Katie Morag and the two grandmothers*. London: Bodley Head.

MacGregor, H. (2004): *Singing French*. London: A. & C. Black.

Martin, Jr, B., and Carle, E. (1967): *Brown bear, brown bear, what do you see?* New York: Holt Rinehart and Winston.

—— (1991): *Polar bear, polar bear, what do you hear?* New York: Henry Holt and Co.

—— (1998): *Oso pardo, oso pardo*. New York: Henry Holt and Co.

—— (2000): *Oso polar, oso Polar*. New York: Henry Holt and Co.

McKee, D. (2002): *Bernard et le monstre*, Paris: Gallimard Jeunesse.

Rosen, M. (1989): *We're going on a bear hunt*. London: Walker Books.

Speak to the Future Campaign (2011) speaktothefuture.org/ Accessed November 2011.

TES (2011) *Primary Languages lost in translation* available from: www.tes.co.uk/article.aspx?storycode=6115602 Accessed December 2011.

Training and Development Agency for Schools (TDA) (2011a): www.tda.gov.uk under *Career prospects and development*. Accessed November 2011.

—— (2011b): See Professional standards for teachers (C6, C10, C40-41, P9-10) at www.tda.gov.uk Accessed November 2011.

Waddell, M. (1991): *Farmer duck*, London: Walker Books.

Walker, N., Williams, C. and Stewart, J. (2009): *The Rough Guide to Germany*. London: Rough Guides.

Index